TENSE BEES AND SHELL-SHOCKED CRABS

TENSE BEES AND
SHELL-SHOCKED CRABS

Are Animals Conscious?

Michael Tye

UNIVERSITY PRESS

OXFORD
UNIVERSITY PRESS

Oxford University Press is a department of the University of Oxford. It furthers
the University's objective of excellence in research, scholarship, and education
by publishing worldwide. Oxford is a registered trade mark of Oxford University
Press in the UK and certain other countries.

Published in the United States of America by Oxford University Press
198 Madison Avenue, New York, NY 10016, United States of America.

CIP data is on file at the Library of Congress
ISBN 978–0–19–027801–4

1 3 5 7 9 8 6 4 2
Printed by Sheridan Books, Inc., United States of America

For 昕

CONTENTS

CONTENTS

ACKNOWLEDGMENTS

I have given more than a few talks on various parts of this book over the last two or three years, and in several different countries. Of these talks, the one that stands out most in my memory was given in Assos, Turkey, outdoors on the edge of a cliff with the Aegean Sea glistening blue behind me and no microphone or technical equipment. Of the comments made in the different locales, I recall in particular David Papineau saying, "Oh no, not fish again!" when he heard that I was going to speak on that topic for the Sainsbury lecture in London, having sat through three previous lectures by me on whether fish have feelings. I am indebted to many people for having made helpful remarks. Those who come to mind now are Paul Boghossian, Brit Brogaard, David Chalmers, Rik Hine, Paul Horwich, Bob Kentridge, Farid Masrour, Jon Morgan, David Papineau, Katherine Piatti, Jesse Prinz, Nick Shea, Barry Smith, and Donovan Wishon.

I am especially indebted to Robert Lurz for having read the entire manuscript and for making many invaluable suggestions. Thanks as always to Mark Sainsbury for his help, especially in framing the issues in chapter 11, and to the members of my graduate seminar on animal consciousness at the University of Texas at Austin in spring 2014 for their enthusiasm and feedback.

INTRODUCTION

Do birds have feelings? What about fish? Can fish feel pain? Do insects have experiences? Can a honeybee feel anxious? Are caterpillars conscious? If trees aren't conscious but fish are, what's the objective difference that makes a difference? How do we decide which living creatures have experiences and which are zombies? Can there be a conscious robot? These are among the questions that this book addresses.

It is not uncommon for scientists (and philosophers) to throw up their hands at such questions or to prescind from them, preferring instead to occupy ground they regard as less controversial. For example, Bateson et al. (2011) say:

> Although our results do not allow us to make any claims about the presence of negative subjective feelings in honeybees, they call into question how we identify emotions in any nonhuman animal. It is logically inconsistent to claim that the presence of pessimistic cognitive biases should be taken as confirmation that dogs or rats are anxious but to deny the same conclusion in the case of honeybees. (1072)

In my view, this conservatism is unnecessary. There are answers to the questions above—answers that we cannot prove to be correct but answers it is nonetheless rational for us to prefer. Or so at least I shall argue.

One way to tackle such matters is to lay out and defend a particular theory of the nature of consciousness. That theory can then be applied to different types of creature and the results listed. I do not adopt this approach in the present book, even though I have a theory of consciousness of my own (Tye 1995, 2000, 2009). This is because theories of consciousness are uncertain beasts. There is little agreement as to which is the most promising and even whether it is within our cognitive power ever to construct an adequate theory (McGinn 1991).

How, then, should we proceed? And why are the questions with which I began seemingly so intractable? Consider, to begin with, the obvious fact that we human beings are subjects of many different mental states. Not all of them are conscious. Take beliefs. Beliefs can persist even in the absence of consciousness. For example, I currently believe that hydrogen is the first element of the periodic table. But suppose I fall into a dreamless sleep. If you were asked, "Does Michael Tye believe that hydrogen is the first element of the periodic table?" it would be bizarre for you to respond, "Of course not. He's sleeping." Beliefs aren't like that. I do not lose all my beliefs when I fall into a dreamless sleep and, miraculously, regain them when I wake. By contrast, some of my mental states are inherently conscious, namely my experiences. These states have a subjective "felt" character to them. There is something it is *like* subjectively to feel anger or fear or anxiety or to experience bright red or a loud noise or the smell of rotting meat. A person who is unconscious cannot have any experiences.

If you are a robot without the capacity to experience anything, built merely to detect unconsciously features of your environment and to act upon them, you won't have fully grasped what I've written so far no matter how much objective information you've stored in your memory banks. This is because it is not possible to provide a satisfactory definition of what an experience is in only objective language. Experiences are inherently subjective things. So there is a gap between the objective facts and the realm of experience (the *phenomenal* realm, as we might call it). This gap leaves us with a real puzzle. If the phenomenal cannot be defined in objective terms, how can we determine by objective investigation which living creatures are subject to phenomenal states?

This book begins with the objective-subjective divide and why it makes the question of animal experiences so puzzling. I've already indicated a connection between experiences and consciousness, namely that a person who is unconscious (in the sense of totally lacking any consciousness as opposed to being fast asleep but dreaming, for example) cannot have experiences. A natural question to ask now is: What exactly is the connection between consciousness and experiences? I suggest that the connection is a very simple one: a being is conscious just in case it undergoes experiences. So the problem of animal experiences is one and the same as the problem of animal consciousness.

This view, natural and simple though it is, is widely rejected. According to some well-known philosophers (most notably Ned Block (1997)), there are two different sorts of consciousness: phenomenal consciousness and access consciousness. To say that a state is phenomenally conscious is to say that there is something it is like to be in that state. To say that a state is access conscious is to say that the state is available for use in reasoning and the rational guidance of speech and action. Some think that only phenomenal consciousness is tied to experiences. I argue in chapter 2 that this view is mistaken. I also argue against the view that what makes an experience have the subjective character it does is its being accompanied by a higher-order thought to the effect that one is undergoing the relevant experience. Thought, I argue, is involved not at all in how experiences themselves feel.

The philosopher who is best known for his opposition to nonhuman experiences is Rene Descartes. Writing in the seventeenth century, Descartes held that you've got to be human to have a soul, and you've got to have a soul to be a conscious being (and to undergo experiences). This view is laid out in detail in chapter 3, as is the historical context in which it arose.

Chapter 4 takes up the classic philosophical problem of Other Minds. I know that I have mental states, but what entitles me to hold that you (and other humans) do as well? I approach this question first in the case of mental states that are not inherently conscious, states such as belief and desire. The answer I offer, namely, that supposing that other humans have beliefs and desires provides the best explanation of their behavior, extends to the case of experiences. Even though experiences are states having a subjective "feel" or phenomenology as part of their very nature, whereas beliefs and desires are not, this difference does not undercut the applicability of the appeal to explanatory power.

The trouble is that when we come to other species, the applicability of this appeal seems threatened by the neurophysiological differences we find. Some animals lack a neocortex, for example, whereas in humans experiences are generated by cortical activity. If the internal causes of behavior are different in different species, how can we justifiably claim that the common behavior we sometimes witness is reason to hold that there is common experience? Chapter 5 discusses this issue in detail. There I show that differences in the neurophysiological explanations of behavior do not, in and of themselves, undercut the ordinary psychological explanations.

Chapter 6 moves to the case of fish in particular. The scientific evidence that bears on the question of whether fish feel pain or fear or anxiety is presented. The chapter then discusses the evidence within the framework of the earlier theoretical discussion of the considerations that tell for or against the attribution of consciousness. In light of this, I conclude that fish undergo a wide range of experiences.

Chapter 7 bolsters the conclusion drawn in chapter 6 by looking at the case of birds. Like fish, birds have no neocortex. Interestingly, they have a brain region that is a homologue of the neocortex, however. This region—the dorsal ventricular ridge—supports experiences in birds, or so I maintain. And fish, it has recently been hypothesized, have a similar brain region too. The chapter also discusses the case of reptiles.

Chapter 8 moves further down the phylogenetic scale. Recent striking experiments involving honeybees and crabs are reported. The overall weight of evidence seems to count against the view that insects generally feel pain, but a good case can be made that honeybees are subjects of pain and a range of emotional experiences including anxiety. The same is true for hermit crabs.

Chapter 9 has two aims: to consider what the biological functions of various experiences are and to propose a test, the passing of which gives us good reason to believe that a living thing is a zombie (a thing without any consciousness). The test is applied to protozoa, caterpillars, and plants.

Chapter 10 extends the theoretical discussion of chapter 5 to the case of robots. Commander Data in *Star Trek: The Next Generation* is an android. With his "emotion chip" in place, he certainly functions as if he undergoes experiences, but does he? His brain is very different from ours, being made of an alloy of platinum and iridium. Does this difference make it impossible for us to say whether he genuinely undergoes experiences? What about a robot rabbit made to look and behave just like a real rabbit? The position I take is that it is rational for us to prefer the view that Commander Data is conscious. He undergoes a range of experiences. We should take a similar view of Robot Rabbit.

The final chapter, chapter 11, takes up the ethical treatment of animals and related issues, including whether we should be vegetarians, in light of the positions developed in the book.

EXPERIENCE AND ITS LIMITS

The Problem

If I ask you to define for me what a triangle is in objective terms, you can probably tell me: a triangle is a closed, three-sided figure. So this, you will immediately say, is not a triangle:

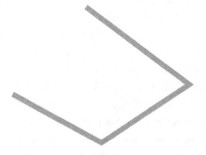

It fails to meet the condition of being closed. But this is:

Can you give me an objective definition from your armchair of what an experience is? No, alas, you cannot—and through no fault of your own. Suppose, for example, you propose that an experience is a brain state of a certain chemical sort. This isn't a good *definition*, since we can clearly conceive of creatures with brains very different from ours that nonetheless have experiences. (All we have to do is to think about the creatures or beings from other planets that figure in many sci-fi movies.) These experiences need not be subjectively like our experiences, but they are still experiences. In the triangle case, we cannot conceive of a triangle that isn't a closed, three-sided figure. The idea of such a triangle is simply not a coherent one. But the idea of an experience occurring in a creature with a different internal physical constitution is perfectly coherent. We can certainly make sense of the idea of there being sentient bugs, robots with feelings, and so on whether or not there really could be such things. Likewise, it won't do to try to define what an experience is in terms of a state's internal functioning, for example, by the way it is produced by the environment and the way it causally interacts with other internal states to generate behavior, for the idea of an experience occurring in a creature whose internal states respond to the environment differently from ours and interact with one another causally in different ways, thereby producing different behavior, is perfectly coherent. There is no *contradiction* involved in supposing that there could be a differently functioning alien who nonetheless has experiences.

What goes wrong with such *objective* a priori definitions of experience? The answer surely is that they leave out the *subjective* element that is crucial to our understanding of experience. In trying to define a priori what an experience is in objective terms—chemicals, functioning, information flow, or whatever—they leave out the essential ingredient: the subjectivity of experience.

Here is another way to make the point. However a creature is constructed, be it made of the stuff we are made of or very different stuff, we can surely conceive of it meeting the conditions proposed in the objective definition and yet not really *experiencing* anything at all.[1] If this is correct, then the objective definition must fail. Again, it is not like this

---

1. The hypothesis that there could be a being that is functionally just like you or me but who lacked experiences altogether is sometimes called "the absent qualia hypothesis."

in the case of a triangle. Once we conceive of a figure as closed and three-sided, we cannot coherently conceive of it as being anything other than a triangle.

Alternatively, suppose that you are a nonhuman, intelligent being incapable of undergoing any experiences—a *zombie*, as philosophers like to say.[2] You register things in your environment, you detect them—think here of an automatic door opener detecting someone's presence—but you don't experience them (any more than the door opener does). Unlike the door opener, you are able to reflect rationally on the information provided to you in this way, make decisions, form plans, and suchlike, but you do not experience or feel anything as you do this. By reflecting on a putative objective definition that is proposed to you of what an experience is, could you come to understand the idea of an experience? Again, surely not. The definition will fail. Of course, you might grasp that in creatures that undergo experiences, so-and-so objective state is always present. But that won't illuminate for you what you are missing. You won't know how the internal states of these creatures *feel*; you won't have any idea of what makes them *experiences*.

If we try to fix up the definition by including something subjective in it over and above whatever objective conditions we specify, we end up where we began, for now we are covertly smuggling into our definition the very notion we wanted to define—that of experience.

So how do we get someone to understand what an experience is? Assuming that the individual is herself a subject of experiences, one thing we can do is to give some examples. We might say: look, you are familiar with following—the experiences of anger, fear, anxiety; the experiences of smelling excrement, seeing a shooting star, tasting chocolate; the experiences of being dizzy, being elated, being tickled; the experiences of touching something prickly, mentally picturing a caterpillar, hearing a loud trumpet; the experiences of pain, lust, jealousy. By pointing at these mental states, we can ostensively illuminate the notion of an experience.

2. Zombies, as philosophers talk of them, are not Hollywood zombies. They do not come out at night and wander around eating people. Zombies, for the purposes of philosophical discussion, are creatures or beings that lack experiences even though they may well be (and standardly are) intelligent.

Having done this, we can add that there is something in common with these mental states, something that is shared by all experiences—they are mental states which are such that there is something it is *like* subjectively to undergo them. Take the case of pain, for example. Pain is an experience. There is something it is like to undergo it, something usually very unpleasant. What it is like to feel pain is very different from what it is like to feel a tickle, for example. Experiences thus vary in what they are like subjectively. To switch to a visual example, what it is like to experience red is more similar to what it is like to experience orange than to what it is like to experience green.

Of course, in saying these things we are not giving a definition of what an experience is in objective terms, for we are using a subjective notion, that of *what it is like*. Still, someone who is a genuine subject of experiences, by reflecting upon the examples and what they share subjectively, can gain a reflective awareness of what an experience is.

This reflective awareness can be enriched further by appreciating that the existence of experiences gives rise to what is often termed "the explanatory gap" (Levine 1983). Suppose I know just which brain states give rise to the experience of anger in normal human beings. Even having this information, I may find myself puzzled. Why do those brain states give rise to an experience with *that* subjective "feel" or phenomenology? Why don't they give rise to a different "feel," or no "feel" at all for that matter? As Thomas Huxley famously put it in 1866: "How it is that anything so remarkable as a state of consciousness comes about as a result of irritating nervous tissue, is just as unaccountable as the appearance of the Djin, when Aladdin rubbed his lamp." There seems to be a gap here in our understanding that can be appreciated by anyone who grasps what an experience is. So a further thing we can say about experiences is that they give rise to this very special explanatory gap.

It is important to realize that conceiving of experiences as states that are subjective in the above way automatically distinguishes them from many other mental states. Take the belief that the earth is ninety-three million miles from the sun. I've had that belief for a long time, since I was at school. I don't lose it when I go to sleep and regain it when I wake up, even if I sleep dreamlessly. Moreover, I didn't lose it when I was knocked unconscious by a cricket ball a number of years ago on a return visit to the United Kingdom. It has been with me throughout my adult life. This belief is not an experience. There is nothing it is subjectively like to believe that the earth is ninety-three million miles from the sun. If there were, I couldn't retain the belief when completely unconscious. Of course, if you were to ask me now, "How far is the sun from the earth?" my belief would manifest itself in my consciousness, and the conscious thought I then undergo might well count as an experience. I might have the sudden experience of thinking that the sun is ninety-three million miles away as the words flash before my mind. But the belief itself is not an experience.

Here is another example. Vision is highly complex. Most of what goes on psychologically as we see things occurs unconsciously. Seeing begins with the mental representation of the intensity of the light striking individual retinal cells and then progressively builds up representations of changes of light intensity, lines of such changes, edges and ridges in the visual field, two-dimensional surfaces, distance away of surface parts, three-dimensional surfaces, and objects. The representations that are generated before the final stage are unconscious. For example, as I type these words, I have no consciousness at all of the light intensity (or wavelength) striking my eyes. I am conscious only of the computer before me, words on the screen, and surrounding items out there in the world. The unconscious states generated at the earlier stages of visual processing are not experiences. There is nothing it is like to undergo them. Even so, they are properly classified as mental, since they are part of the subject matter of psychological theories specifying how vision works.

It is not just that we cannot objectively define what it is for a state to be an experience. We also cannot objectively define what it is for a state to be an experience of a given subjective sort—what it is for an experience to have the characteristic felt quality of pains, for example. This is shown by the fact that we can easily imagine having complete knowledge of all the relevant, objective facts and yet still not having any grasp at all of what it is like to undergo the given experience (that is, how that experience feels). One famous example of this is provided, according to some philosophers (notably Thomas Nagel (1974)), by the experiences bats undergo when they use their sense of echolocation. No matter how much we come to learn about the physical and chemical structure of bat brains, this still seems to leave us in the dark as to what it is like for the bats subjectively as they use echolocation. For we ourselves lack the relevant sense—we cannot emit high-pitched sounds and use the echoes to determine where objects are located—and so we cannot undergo those experiences. Or so it is usually supposed.

Unfortunately, this example does not hold water. Some blind people, by making clicks with their tongues and listening to the echoes as the sounds bounce off objects around them, have learned to navigate as if they were sighted. Ben Underwood, a boy blind from early childhood, so developed his ability to use echolocation that he could roller skate in an environment with many obstacles just as if he were sighted. After many years of practice, he came to know what it is like to use echolocation to navigate around the world even if humans generally do not. Of course, the pitch of the sounds he emitted is different from the pitch of the sounds the bats emit, but he was doing just what the bats are doing: using echoes to locate objects.[3]

A better example is provided by the case of kestrels and voles. The vole population in northern Europe oscillates in a four-year cycle. A crash in the vole population in a region can result in a thousand-kilometer migration of those kestrels that feed primarily on the voles. Up until fairly recently, we knew almost nothing about how the kestrels are able to track the vole population over such large areas of land. However, it is now known that when we illuminate vole scent marks, which male voles use to indicate their paths, with ultraviolet light, the marks contrast with their background. To normal human perceivers in standard conditions, these scent marks are invisible. To kestrels, however, they are not. Through extensive field experiments on wild kestrels, Viitala and colleagues (1995) showed that under normal lighting conditions, kestrels concentrated their hunting in areas containing straw that had been soaked in vole feces and urine and ignored areas containing straw that had been soaked in water.

How does vole urine *look* to the kestrels? It seems impossible for us to say. This is because kestrels and many other birds are tetrachromats, unlike humans, who are trichromats. Their eyes contain retinal cells that respond to ultraviolet light as well as to the short-, medium-, and long-wavelength light to which human retinal cells respond. We can study

---

3. Sadly, Ben died in 2009 at age sixteen from cancer.

kestrel brains as much as we like; we can work out just which channels of neurons respond to just which patterns of incoming light. But we can't know what it is like for the kestrels as they peer down from the sky at the vole trails. The vole urine reflects ultraviolet light, and some of the kestrels' retinal cells respond to that light, producing in the kestrels, as they peer down from the sky, color experiences whose subjective character is different from any color experiences we undergo.[4]

Of course, we do not need to restrict ourselves to actual examples to make the point. We can easily imagine there being alien creatures with sense organs very different from ours. If we encounter such aliens, and, as they die, we do autopsies on them, we may discover that their brains are physically and functionally very different from ours. Suppose that we develop a detailed understanding of the chemical and physical structure of their brains. That knowledge may still leave us wondering what it is like for these creatures as they use the alien sense organs.

What these examples directly show us is that no objective a priori definition is possible of what it is like to undergo any specific experience any more than an objective definition of an experience is *period*. To grasp what a particular experience *feels like*, you just have to undergo it yourself. As Louis Armstrong supposedly said, when asked what jazz is, "Man, if you gotta ask, you'll never know!" The same retort may be made to a zombie asking what an experience is. We can cite examples, but they won't help, for the zombie has no experiences. We can give him our subjective definition, but again he will remain puzzled, lacking any real grasp of the relevant subjective condition.

This is what makes the question of how widespread experience is in nature so puzzling and hard. If we could give an objective a priori definition of an experience in the way that we can for a triangle, then we could go out into the world, find out which creatures meet the objective conditions in our definition, and then announce our list of the types of creatures that have experiences. And we could do the same, using corresponding definitions, for specific types of experiences. The problem

---

4. For the purposes of this example, I am assuming that kestrels do genuinely undergo visual experiences (rather than simply functioning as if they do). This assumption may be challenged, of course, and later, in chapter 7, it will be discussed further.

situation then would be no more difficult than it would be if I were to ask you to look at the collection of figures below and put a check mark by the ones that are triangles.

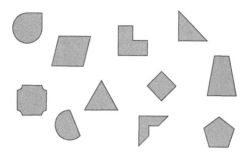

Unfortunately, there is no such definition. So how are we to decide? What are we to look for?

Suppose, for example, I become an expert on fish. Lacking an objective definition of experience, notwithstanding my knowledge of the workings of fish brains and fish sense organs, how am I to decide if fish have experiences? How am I to decide if fish feel pain or anxiety or depression? Consistent with my knowledge of the objective facts, I may take the view that fish are zombies. You may hold the opposing view. Or you may say that fish feel pain but not depression. Is the fish shown below feeling depressed?

How are we to determine who is right? Lacking any access to the subjective states of fish, it may seem that this question is unanswerable. It is precisely this apparent unbridgeability of the objective-subjective divide that makes the problem of where experience ends so perplexing and difficult.

Perhaps you will reply that we don't really need a *definition*, as understood above, to bridge the divide. After all, take the case of games (Wittgenstein 1953). We can agree that baseball is a game and that selling a car is not, but no one can provide a straightforward definition of what a game is. Games vary immensely. Think of professional football, solitaire, chess, tennis, hide-and-seek, blind man's bluff. Some of these activities are for fun, others are for money. Some of the activities involve multiple players, others do not. Some use a ball, some a racket. What do these activities all have in common that distinguishes them from activities that are not games? It is very hard to say. It seems that the best we can do is to list the central features of prototypical games and then count an activity as a game so long as it has *enough* of those features. Here is a possible list of the relevant features:

- has a playing field
- uses ball, dice, or cards
- has rules
- is recreational
- involves competition
- involves two or more players
- score is kept

These conditions are not individually *necessary* for an activity to be a game. Some games have single players (solitaire); some do not keep score (practice one-on-one basketball); some are not recreational (professional tennis). Some games arguably don't even have rules. Think of a game without clear rules that schoolchildren play as they run around the schoolyard. Still, the conditions are jointly *sufficient*. Any activity that meets all the conditions is certainly a game.

Why, then, is selling a car not a game? Obviously, it doesn't have enough of the features listed above. What about a mating contest between male walruses? Probably not, but there are rules of a sort; such a contest involves two "players," and it is highly competitive.

Concepts that are definable in the rather open-ended way described above are sometimes called "cluster concepts."[5] One suggestion, then, might be that the concept of experience is a cluster concept, where the relevant cluster consists of features belonging to prototypical experiences. If many of these features are objective and a given creature has all or nearly all of them, then the creature should be counted as undergoing experiences. If many of the features are objective and a given creature lacks most of them, then the creature should be counted as lacking experiences. This supposedly crosses the divide, since even if phenomenal subjectivity[6] is one of the features, that won't prevent us from making an evaluation of a creature as having experiences.

The trouble with this suggestion is twofold. First, the ordinary concept of experience is not a cluster concept, involving both objective features and the feature of subjectivity. Experiences do have objective features, to be sure. The feeling of pain typically causes guarding behavior, for example, and it is typically caused by bodily damage. But when it comes right down to it, what is really crucial—indeed, *all* that is really crucial—to having experiences is having internal states such that there is something it is like subjectively to undergo them. Secondly, even if there is (or were) *a* cluster concept of experience involving both phenomenal subjectivity and objective features, what puzzles us is not how a creature might satisfy that concept in virtue of having enough of the relevant objective features but rather what objective features a creature must meet in order to count as having phenomenal subjectivity, that is, having internal states such that there is something it is like subjectively to undergo them. The fact that there may be a concept of experience that can be satisfied by the creature having the salient objective features helps not at all with that. What puzzles us most is how we could ever decide whether there is something it is like subjectively to be, for example, a fish, a lobster, a bee and whether, more specifically, fish, lobsters,

5. Concepts are ideas or notions.
6. By "phenomenal subjectivity" I mean the general characteristic a state has of being such that there is something it is like subjectively to undergo it.

bees, and so on can feel the sort of thing we feel when we feel depressed, anxious, and so on.

There is one final reaction I want to consider, namely, to say that an a priori definition is not needed to cross the bridge. So long as we have an a posteriori (empirical) theory spelling out the objective nature of experience, we have all we need. Think, for example, of the case of water. There is no a priori definition of what it is for something to be a sample of water (or so at least many philosophers would say). Still, water has an objective nature that has been discovered through empirical investigation: water has as its essence H_2O. Why should the same not be true for experience? The answer is that it may be; but the trouble is that there is no agreement whatsoever about the objective nature of experience (unlike the case of water) or even whether it has an objective nature (McGinn 1991). Indeed, there is no agreement about whether we could *ever* discover a theory of this sort. Furthermore, on the face of it, appealing to such a theory is putting the cart before the horse, for a condition of adequacy on any theory of the nature of experience is that it cover all and only creatures that have experiences. But if we don't already agree on which creatures these are, how are we to construct the theory in the first place?

The solution to the quandary we find ourselves in is to realize that what is needed to cross the bridge is not a metaphysical principle spelling out what experience is in objective terms (either via an a priori definition or an a posteriori theory) but an evidential principle on the basis of which we can justifiably make attributions of consciousness to animals. Even if consciousness itself has a nature that is unknowable to us, so long as we can justifiably make attributions of consciousness to others, we can solve the problem of animal consciousness. I shall develop this epistemic view fully later. First, however, I want to take up the question of the relationship of consciousness to experience, for sometimes the divide is presented as being between *consciousness* and the objective facts; thus, it behooves us to be clear right from the start whether there is only one sort of consciousness and whether there can be consciousness without experience or experience without consciousness.

[2]

EXPERIENCE AND CONSCIOUSNESS

What is consciousness? As with experience, the easiest way to proceed is by example. There is a scene in an old movie, *Marathon Man*, in which Laurence Olivier, who plays the part of Dr. Szell, an evil Nazi dentist, drills holes in the teeth of a marathon-running history student, played by Dustin Hoffman, without any anesthetic as he attempts to find out the information he thinks the student has. Hoffman's character feels intense pain, and in so doing he is the subject of a deeply unpleasant conscious mental state (as are we, the cringing viewers, to a lesser degree)—a state that briefly disappears from consciousness as Szell applies oil of cloves to the teeth he has been drilling.

Take next the case of visual consciousness. That's something we have at every moment at which our eyes are open.[1] When we shut our eyes, it vanishes. Generalizing from these cases, we may say that consciousness is something we have whenever we are awake and sometimes when we sleep, as when we dream. We lose it when we fall into a dreamless sleep or we are completely anaesthetized (Papineau and Selima 2000).

One simple way to draw a connection between consciousness and experience is this: a creature is conscious at time *t* if and only if it is undergoing one or more experiences at *t*. Further and relatedly, a mental state is conscious if and only if it is an experience.[2] Assuming that an experience is a mental state such that there is something it is like to undergo it, it follows that a mental state is conscious if and only if there is something it is like for the subject of the state to undergo it.

1. I leave aside certain highly abnormal cases. I'll return to these later.
2. This needs one qualification, which for the moment I shall ignore. See here pp. 14–15.

I hold that the Simple View, as we might call it, is the right one. I take the Simple View to trace back to Nagel's famous paper "What Is It Like to Be a Bat?" Nagel says, without any restriction to what has come to be called "phenomenal consciousness" (on which more later), the following:

> Conscious experience is a widespread phenomenon. . . . Fundamentally an organism has conscious mental states if and only if there is something it is like to *be* that organism—something it is like *for* the organism. (Nagel 1974)

I take it, then, that the divide presented in chapter 1 is really just the divide between consciousness and the objective facts.

Let us begin this chapter by discussing some objections to the Simple View.

2.1 PROBLEM CASES?

One objection to this proposal is that it ignores conscious thoughts, memories, and desires. These aren't experiences, but they are conscious states.

Not so, I reply. Consider my suddenly remembering that I have a dental appointment in half an hour. That sudden memory is an experience. I have the *experience* of suddenly remembering the appointment. We all know what it is like to have such a sudden memory. But if there is something it is like, then there is an experience.

What is not so obvious is in what this experience consists. Is it a matter of undergoing, along with the propositional memory, a visual image of the dental office or the dental chair or the look on the dentist's face as he realizes that I haven't shown up on time? Or is it a matter of my saying to myself under my breath, as it were, "Oh God! I'm going to be late for my dental appointment!" or some such thing? In this case, I can "hear" myself saying the words—I have an auditory experience as of my uttering the sentence in my usual pattern of stress and intonation. Or is it some combination of these? Or is the experience of suddenly remembering something sui generis—a state that may be accompanied by perceptual or quasi-perceptual images of one sort or another but is not reducible to these?

On this matter, I have views (Tye and Wright 2011). But they need not play a role here. What is important is simply that it be conceded that there is an experience of suddenly remembering so-and-so. And it is hard to see how this could be denied, for surely we must agree that there is something it is like to suddenly remember.

Similar points apply to other cases. If I have a standing desire for a vacation on the Galapagos Islands, this desire may well become conscious from time to time. As it does so, I have the experience of desiring a vacation in the Galapagos Islands. Visual images of the island or of Darwin may float before my mind. I may say to myself, "How I would like to go there!" And as I do this, I can hear myself saying these words. But whether or not there are these states, if my desire is conscious, I have the experience of desiring to go to the Galapagos. This is because if my desire is conscious, when it is, there is something it is like for me to have it. Just as desires can be conscious, so too can beliefs. They manifest themselves in consciousness in conscious thoughts, and these themselves are experiences. Consider, for example, my belief that beryllium is the fourth element of the periodic table. When that belief becomes conscious, as for example if you ask me, "What is the fourth element of the periodic table?," I have the experience of thinking that beryllium is.

A second objection is that the Simple View is inconsistent. Some experiences are unconscious. Take, for example, the visual experiences of the distracted driver as she drives her car down the road. She is concentrating hard on other matters (the phone call she is answering about the overdue rent, the coffee in her right hand, etc.), so her visual experiences are unconscious. But her experiences exist alright. How else does she keep the car on the road? An unconscious experience is impossible, however, on the Simple View, for such an experience is an experience that is not an experience!

This calls for a minimal revision in the Simple View. Sometimes when we say that a mental state is conscious, we mean that it is, in itself, inherently a conscious state. At other times, when we say that a mental state is conscious, we have in mind the subject's attitude toward the state. We mean then that the subject of the mental state is conscious *of* it or conscious *that* it is occurring. The latter consciousness is a species of what is sometimes called "creature consciousness." The Simple View has it that, in the first sense, a mental state is conscious (conscious₁) if and only if it is an experience. In the latter sense, a mental state is conscious (conscious₂) if and only if another conscious₁ state, for example, a conscious thought, is directed upon it. The Simple View holds that this higher-order conscious state (in being a conscious₁ state) is itself an experience, for example, the experience of thinking of the first-order state or thinking that the first-order state is occurring.

The visual experiences of the distracted driver are unconscious in that she is not conscious *of* them. Nor is she conscious *that* they are occurring. So she lacks creature consciousness with respect to certain mental states that are themselves conscious₁. Being distracted, she is not conscious of what those experiences are like. There is no inconsistency here. The objection conflates high-order consciousness with first-order consciousness. Experiences are first-order conscious states on which second-order conscious states may or may not be directed.

This brings us to a third objection that might be raised to the Simple View, namely, that it cannot adequately account for the phenomenon of higher-order consciousness. Each of us is subject to a wide range of mental states, and we can often know what mental state we are undergoing by introspection. When we do so, we are conscious of the mental state we introspect, but there is no experience involved in this conscious act, or at least there need not be. So consciousness can occur without experience, and the Simple View is mistaken.

One reply to this objection is that introspection is itself quasi-perceptual in nature. When we introspect, we "perceive" what is going on in our minds. If this is so, then introspection is experiential in character just as perception is. Just as when we see, we undergo visual experiences, and when we hear, we undergo auditory experiences, so when we introspect, we undergo introspective experiences. These experiences are directed inward upon our own mental states (unlike our perceptual experiences) and form the basis for our knowledge.

Unfortunately, this position seems very implausible. If introspection were a quasi-perceptual faculty, then we would expect it to possess a special phenomenology of its own just as visual perception or hearing do. But when I introspect a pain, for example, and I become aware that I am feeling pain, no extra, special quasi-perceptual phenomenology is to be found. There is the phenomenology attaching to the pain and there is also some phenomenology that attaches to any occurrent thought I may form about my pain, but the act of introspecting does not itself "feel" any way. It is transparent or diaphanous.

Here is another way to make this point. Suppose that I am having a visual experience of a red ball and that I introspect my experience. In undergoing the experience, the ball looks some way to me. Does my experience itself also look some way to me as I introspect? Is it an additional perceptual object of which I am perceptually aware in the way that the ball is? Can I switch my perceptual attention from the ball to the experience and back again? The obvious answer to these questions is no. In introspecting, I am aware that I am having a visual experience of a red ball, but I do not see or "quasi-see" the experience. Nor do I monitor the experience in any other sensory way.

Still, even though introspection is not quasi-perceptual, it does often have an associated phenomenology, albeit one that is not special or proprietary. This is because when we introspect and we thereby are conscious of which mental state we are in, we form a higher-order thought about the first-order mental state, a thought to the effect that we are undergoing the first-order state. And this thought has a phenomenology. We undergo the experience of thinking that we are in pain, or that we want an ice cream or that we are feeling anxious. This experience, as noted earlier, may or may not be reducible to the auditory phenomenology of saying appropriate words in foro interno, for example, "Ouch; that hurts!" But there is definitely an experience of thinking that we are in a certain mental state, if we are conscious of the latter mental state by introspection. The thought we experience is directed on the mental state, and the presence of the experience is what makes it true that we are conscious of the mental state introspectively. So the Simple View is safe.

Perhaps it will be objected that introspection can occur without a conscious thought. One can simply *believe* that one is in a certain mental state without the higher-order belief manifesting itself in any conscious thought.

In this case, one is conscious of the lower-level mental state, but there is no experience of thinking, and so the Simple View is still in trouble.

My response is that in such a case, while one knows on the basis of introspection what one's first-level mental state is, one is not *conscious of* that mental state. Whether or not the Simple View is correct, intuitively to be conscious of a mental state M is to undergo a conscious state that is about M. After all, if the higher-order state were about M but were itself unconscious, how could it make one conscious of M simply by one's undergoing it? However, in the case at hand, the higher-order belief is not conscious. So one is not conscious of M.

In a case of this sort, introspection is functioning as a knowledge-generating faculty, but not as a source of consciousness of one's own mental life. Arguably, via introspection in such a case one forms the belief that M is present, where that belief is true and the product of a reliable process. So one knows that one is undergoing M, but one is not conscious of M.

A further objection is that the Simple View makes the mistake of supposing that a mental state can be conscious without one being conscious of the state. For it takes it that a state is conscious (in the most basic sense) just in case it is an experience, and experiences can occur without one being conscious of them, as, for example, in the earlier case of the distracted driver. This objection brings us face to face with what is usually known as the higher-order theory of phenomenal consciousness. The issues that arise here will occupy us in the next section.

2.2 THE HIGHER-ORDER THEORY OF CONSCIOUSNESS

One standard view in the philosophical literature has it that experiences may be either conscious or unconscious. The visual experiences of the distracted driver are unconscious (*period*), as is the toothache I feel at times at which I am engrossed in conversation and briefly do not notice it. On this approach, the Simple View is straightforwardly mistaken. When an experience is conscious, this is wholly a matter of our being conscious of it.[3] This, in turn, on the higher-order approach, is a matter of our undergoing another mental state about the experience, a monitoring state which itself may be a higher-order thought or a perception. The main problem with the perceptual version of this view is that introspection itself has no phenomenology, as it should if it is a special kind of perceptual experience. If, for example, I introspect an experience of red, the only subjective, felt character is that which attaches to the experience of red. For this reason, the most popular version of the higher-order approach is the higher-order-thought view. The version of that view I shall focus on in this section has it that the monitoring state is a higher-order thought to the effect that the subject is undergoing the experience (the HOT theory). The higher-order thought is arrived at non-inferentially—not by inferring its presence from one's own behavior or a scan of the brain. The phenomenology of the experience—what it is like to undergo it—derives from the higher-order thought that accompanies the experience when it is introspected (at least according to the version of the higher-order theory I shall be considering). Where an experience is unconscious, there is nothing it is like to undergo it, no phenomenology. Phenomenal consciousness, as it is usually called, is not something intrinsic to experiences but rather something that is contributed via the accompanying higher-order thought (Rosenthal 1986).[4]

This has consequences for how we treat animals, for, on the HOT view, pains that lack an accompanying higher-order thought are not conscious, and thus their possessors, in having them, do not suffer. Animals that lack a theory of mind lack the concepts to undergo the

3. This view is held by some scientists as well as some philosophers. For example, Brian Key (2015) says: "To feel pain requires that you are aware or conscious of your own mental state." He adds that consciousness of a stimulus or state requires attention to it. In my view, both these claims are mistaken. We can feel pain without being conscious that we are feeling pain, and we can be conscious of a stimulus S without attending to S. For more on attention and consciousness, see Tye 2010.
4. Carruthers (2000) holds a dispositionalist version of the higher-order-thought theory. On this view, what makes a state phenomenally conscious is its availability to cause (non-inferentially) higher-order thoughts about itself. In earlier work, Carruthers holds the HOT theory, as presented in the text. See Carruthers 1989.

relevant higher-order thoughts.[5] So such animals do not suffer, and how we treat them is of no immediate concern.[6]

Were the higher-order view to restrict itself to offering an account of what makes an experience go from being unconscious at one moment to conscious at another, it would have some plausibility. But it goes further than this in its usual form. It purports to tell us what it is for an experience to *feel* the way it does. It purports to tell us what the subjective aspect of an experience consists in. More generally, it offers us an account of what it is for an experience to "feel" any way at all. On the higher-order theory, an experience's "feel" is a matter of its being accompanied by a certain higher-order thought (arrived at non-inferentially). Different "feels," different thoughts. Further, what it is to undergo an experience that "feels" any way at all is for it to be accompanied by some higher-order thought or other (again arrived at non-inferentially).[7]

This view faces at least three objections, all of which are decisive. First, if an experience can exist without our being conscious of it, as the HOT theory allows, what makes it an experience? If there is no phenomenology, nothing it is like to undergo it, as is entailed by the HOT theory, surely it isn't an experience as such at all. Secondly, either the higher-order thought is conscious or it isn't. If it isn't, then how can its presence make us conscious of the experience? For, as already noted, consciousness of a thing requires a conscious state about that thing. Relatedly, if the thought is unconscious, and the experience, in and of itself, is also unconscious, it is a mystery how putting together two unconscious mental states can generate a mental state that is conscious, namely, a conscious experience. On the other hand, if the higher-order thought *is* conscious, what makes it conscious? Presumably, on the higher-order-thought theory, the higher-order thought, to be conscious, must be accompanied by a third-order thought. But now we can ask the

---

5. Gennaro argues that more animals than we might suppose have the relevant concepts. See Gennaro 2004.
6. See here Carruthers 1989. Later Carruthers amends his view. See Carruthers 1999.
7. On Carruthers's later version of the HOT theory (see Carruthers 2000), the crucial link is availability, not accompaniment. Below, I focus on the actualist version, though the objections presented apply, mutatis mutandis, to Carruthers's theory too.

same question again, and an infinite regress beckons. Thirdly, patients with Anton-Babinski syndrome adamantly insist (and so think) that they can see when in reality they are blind. Imagine now a person with a syndrome something like Anton-Babinski's except that in reality she sees the world in black and white, yet insists that she is seeing it in color (notwithstanding plentiful evidence to the contrary). This person at time t is experiencing a certain shade of gray, but she thinks that she is experiencing red. On the higher-order theory, the phenomenology of this person's visual experience is red, as it were. Her experience has a red "feel." But by hypothesis she is experiencing a certain shade of gray. So even though she *classifies* her experience as phenomenally red, *in reality* it is phenomenally gray. Her situation is not unlike that of Marianna, the woman who has spent her life in a black and white room and who is then released into another room in which there is a green patch of paint on a white wall. Above the patch is the word "red." Marianna thinks that she is seeing red ("Now I know what it is like to experience red," she mistakenly concludes), but in reality she is experiencing green. Of course, Marianna here is using supplementary evidence, namely, the presence of the word "red." But we all draw on associated concepts when we classify our visual experiences via introspection, and the process of association can go wrong, as it does for Marianna and the word "red." Again, the HOT theory ends up with the incorrect result.

In my view, the HOT theory gets things backwards. It assumes that all consciousness is consciousness-of or monitoring consciousness. It then tries to account for the conscious, subjective features of experiences in terms of such consciousness. Neither view is at all plausible. Better to start with the basic notion of an experience, understood via examples, and the use of "what it is like" terminology. Then both state consciousness and creature consciousness can be explicated via the notion of an experience. This is what the Simple View does.

Still, even though the higher-order-thought theory is an implausible theory of the nature of the subjective character of experience, it is worth stressing that it may nonetheless be the case that investigating higher-order thoughts (metacognition) in animals is an empirically profitable method for investigating first-order consciousness in animals (Shea and Heyes 2010). Here is why. Suppose that we have behavioral evidence that a given animal solves a problem by think-ing about or forming some other cognitive state about how an object *looks* to it (rather than about how the object really is). Since the way an object looks to a subject is the way that subject experiences the object as being, it follows that the animal undergoes conscious$_1$ mental states. Nothing that I have said is intended to undermine or diminish the importance of studying consciousness in animals in this way. Where we should demur, it seems to me, is with the further claim that if there are no higher-order thoughts in a given kind of animal, then that is strong evidence that there are no conscious$_1$ mental states in animals of that kind. To see why this is a mistake, consider the case of two-year-old human children. At that age, children have no psychological concepts. So they are incapable of thinking to them-selves that they are feeling pain or that they are visually experiencing the color red. That comes later, around the ages of three or four. But surely no one wants to claim that two-year-old children cannot feel pain or experience red!

I shall return to the higher-order-thought program in animal cogni-tion research later (in chapter 5). It will be shown there that this pro-gram may be viewed as providing a specific, partial implementation of the general methodology I advocate for determining the presence of first-order consciousness in animals.

2.3 PHENOMENAL CONSCIOUSNESS VERSUS ACCESS CONSCIOUSNESS

In this section, I want to look at another very different kind of objection to the Simple View, namely, that it conflates two kinds of consciousness that must be kept distinct: phenomenal consciousness and access con-sciousness. This needs some explanation.

On one fairly standard view (see Block 2002a, b), the ordinary concept *consciousness* is a mongrel or hybrid concept, subsuming two very different kinds of consciousness that must be differentiated if confusion is to be avoided. On the one hand, there is phenomenal con-sciousness, where phenomenal consciousness is just experience, so that phenomenally conscious states are just experiences, and phenomenally conscious properties are experiential properties, that is, properties the totality of which is what it is like to undergo the experience. Phenomenal consciousness is to be understood by example, and also by appeal to the famous absent qualia hypothesis and the explanatory gap.[8]

On the other hand, there is access consciousness. This is a functional notion that, according to Block (2002a, b), plays a "deep role in our ordinary 'consciousness' thought and talk." It can be defined objectively and presumably can also be explained to beings without experiences. A state is access conscious if and only if (a) it is available for the rational control of speech (in creatures capable of speech); (b) it is available for the rational control of action; and (c) it is inferentially promiscuous, that is, it is available as a premise in a range of cases of reasoning.[9] Take, for example, my belief that the capital of Sweden is Stockholm. If you ask me to name the capital of Sweden, I'll say "Stockholm." So condition (a) is met. If you show me a map with all the major cities marked and you ask me to point to the capital of Sweden, I'll point to the dot with the name "Stockholm" by it. So condition (b) is met. If you tell me that if a person lives in the capital of Sweden, on average, he or she will live longer than a person who lives in the capital of the United States, I'll infer that on average people who live in Stockholm live longer than people who live in Washington, DC. And in inferring this, I'll be drawing on my belief that the capital of Sweden is Stockholm. Since this is far from an isolated case, condition (c) is met. So my belief is access conscious.

8. See chapter 1, pp. 3–4.
9. This minimally oversimplifies. Here is what Block actually says:

> A state is access-conscious (A-conscious) if, in virtue of one's having the state, a representation of its content is (1) inferentially promiscuous (Stich, 1978), i.e. poised to be used as a premise in reasoning, and (2) poised for [rational] control of action and (3) poised for rational control of speech. (I will speak of both states and their contents as A-conscious.) These three conditions are together sufficient, but not all necessary. I regard (3) as not necessary (and not independent of the others), since I want to allow non-linguistic animals, e.g. chimps, to have A-conscious (access-conscious) states. I see A-consciousness as a cluster concept, in which (3)—roughly, reportability—is the element of the cluster with the smallest weight, though (3) is often the best practical guide to A-consciousness. (p. 231)

According to Block, to whom we owe this distinction, access consciousness and phenomenal consciousness can come apart: states can be access conscious without being phenomenally conscious, and vice versa. Furthermore, in actual fact phenomenally conscious and access conscious states do come apart in this way. The result is that theories of the realization of access consciousness are not directly theories of the realization of phenomenal consciousness at all, and philosophers and/ or scientists who think otherwise are badly confused.

Block's distinction has been widely influential. But it now seems to me entirely wrongheaded. The ordinary concept *consciousness* is not a mongrel concept. There is no such thing as access consciousness. Consider again my belief that Stockholm is the capital of Sweden. That's a belief I have at times at which it does not manifest itself in a conscious thought or speech. At such times, it is unconscious. Yet it meets all the conditions for access consciousness, as noted above. The simple fact is that Block's notion of access consciousness is a technical notion. It has *nothing* to do with the ordinary concept *consciousness*. What is true is that my belief is rationally *accessible*, but it hardly follows from this that my belief is a certain sort of conscious state (or for that matter that I am conscious of it).

If there is no such thing as access consciousness, then there is no need to talk of phenomenal consciousness. There is just consciousness simpliciter. This is what the Simple View says. Block has introduced a certain sort of cognitive accessibility and claimed without foundation that it is a sort of consciousness. The concept *consciousness* is not analyzable in terms of Block's accessibility, nor does his accessibility provide an a priori sufficient condition for consciousness. This is shown by the fact that there is no incoherence in supposing that a being might undergo all Block's conditions for having "access conscious" states and yet not be conscious at all. On this point, I am in agreement with Block. An imaginary example of such a being is provided by Block's super blindsight subject (1997), to which I now turn.

Blindsight is a condition in which (at least according to the usual view) there is no visual phenomenal consciousness with respect to a portion of the visual field as a result of brain damage. Blindsight subjects, if forced to guess whether certain stimuli are present in the blind field, for example, whether there is an X or an O, tend to guess correctly, however. Here are some comments made by the blindsight subject GY (as reported to me by Bob Kentridge):

> I'd be none the wiser if you were not putting any stimuli up just to fool me. . . . I just listen for the beep and press a button. . . . There's no point going on with this, I can't do it.

At the time at which GY made these remarks, he was performing a visual discrimination task at near 100 percent accuracy.

Block asks us to imagine someone who comes to believe his guesses and so is functionally like a normal subject even though he has no experiences with respect to the relevant region of the field of view (call it R). Block claims that this subject's state with respect to R is access conscious but not phenomenally conscious. I agree with Block that her state is not (phenomenally) conscious (since by hypothesis there is no experience with respect to R). I also agree that her state is nonetheless rationally accessible in the way Block requires. So here we have a conceptually possible case in which Block's conditions for accessibility are met but there is no (phenomenal) consciousness.[10]

What about the other way around? Is it conceivable that a state is conscious (phenomenally conscious in Block's terms) and yet not accessible in the way Block specifies? Block thinks so, and he gives examples to support his claim. Let us look next at these examples.

First, an imaginary case with some minor modifications (1997). I was tortured in a red room in my youth. I have deeply repressed visual images of this room. (They cause me to react violently at the sight of red dining rooms, red walls, etc.) These images are phenomenally conscious, according to Block. But they are not access conscious.

---

10. Of course, were we to meet such a super blindsighter, we might come to the conclusion that she is experiencing various stimuli in R on the basis of her functioning in visual tests. But we would be wrong. Still, not knowing that the individual has blindsight, would her behavior provide us with *good grounds* for supposing that she has visual experiences with respect to R? I think it would. A variant on this epistemological question will occupy us in chapter 4, namely, whether my discovering that you function much like me in visual tests is good grounds for supposing that you undergo visual experiences as I do.

We can agree with Block that these images are not access conscious, for there is no such thing as access consciousness. Nor are they rationally accessible. But then equally they are not conscious simpliciter. After all, if the images of the red room were still conscious, then both intuitively and according to the Simple View, I would continue to have experiences of the red room. But I don't now have experiences of the red room, not even repressed ones. If you doubt this, suppose that I have an experience of a loud noise. There is something it is like to have such an experience. What it is like is the same as what it is like to experience a loud noise. This patently is not a coincidence. Why do these things necessarily go together? Because having an experience of a loud noise just is experiencing a loud noise. But necessarily if one is experiencing a loud noise, one is conscious of a loud noise. So having an experience of a loud noise entails being conscious of a loud noise. Generalizing, it follows that one cannot have an experience of an F unless one is conscious of an F. Since I am not now conscious of a red room, or so we ordinarily would think and say about this case, I do not now have an experience of a red room.

It is important to stress that nothing I have said here counts against the existence of a deeply repressed *representation* of a red room. My claim is simply that such a representation is not conscious. At least as we usually employ the term "image," it is not an *image* of mine at all.

Here is another example of Block's. My refrigerator makes a humming noise. I am used to it, and most of the time I do not notice it. Suddenly the noise stops. I notice this, and I then realize that I have been hearing the humming for some time in the background, even though I did not notice the noise earlier on. Since I was hearing the humming noise, I was undergoing auditory experiences caused by it, but, in one sense, I was not conscious of the noise. There was phenomenal consciousness of the noise but no access consciousness of it (Block 1997).

Whether I really did hear the noise earlier on, given that I heard the noise stop, can be disputed. I was certainly aware at a particular moment *that* the noise had stopped. But it does not follow from this that I was conscious of the noise at earlier times. It is a well-known fact that changes can be experienced within the specious present.[11] So I need not have been conscious of the noise in the past in order to experience the noise stopping. Still, assuming I did indeed hear the noise, it is true that there was phenomenal consciousness of the noise. After all, if I heard the noise, it must have sounded some way to me. How could it have sounded any way to me if I was not conscious of it? For it to have sounded some way, I must have experienced it. So I must have been phenomenally conscious of it. At the times at which I was so conscious, I was engrossed in conversation, and so I never consciously thought to myself, "Damned noise!" or "I wish that noise would stop" or anything like that. Such a thought, had it occurred, would have involved the *experience* of thinking it. And there was no experience of that sort. So there was one episode of phenomenal consciousness (the experience of the noise), or, as I would say, consciousness simpliciter, but not another such episode (at the level of thought).

Was my experience of the noise rationally accessible to me? Obviously, it wasn't rationally accessed. And perhaps, given how Block has spelled out rational accessibility, he is right to say that the experience was not even rationally accessible. Still, it is worth asking whether there is any sort of cognitive accessibility here. For example, given that I was engrossed in conversation, *could* I, on the basis of my conscious state, have thought, "That's the fridge," with respect to the humming noise?[12] I did not in fact think this, of course. But *could* I have done so without shifting the central focus of my attention from our conversation? If this minimal condition is not met, then my own view is that I did not genuinely *experience* the noise at all. I was not conscious *of* it. So

---

11. For example, I can experience a finger moving now. This experience isn't just a succession of different experiences of the finger in different positions. At any given moment, it is an experience of the *movement* of the finger. That cannot occur unless there is an experienced present relative to which movement is itself experienced. Just how long the specious present is in objective time is a matter of some dispute. There is evidence that it lasts at least 30 ms. See here Tye 2003, p. 87.

12. A further example of Block's in Block 2007 involves a subject, G. K., who, according to Block, is having an experience of a face even though it is impossible for him to know anything of this experience. The evidence that an experience is present is supposedly provided by recurrent processing in the fusiform face area of G. K.'s cortex, processing

this is not clearly a case of consciousness without *any* sort of cognitive accessibility.

I shall return to the topic of access and consciousness in chapter 9.

2.4 SELF-CONSCIOUSNESS

In defending the Simple View above, I am not presupposing that consciousness does not come in different types. In this section, I shall take up very briefly the interesting topic of self-consciousness.

Self-consciousness has been much discussed in both philosophy and psychology. As so discussed, self-consciousness is not the feeling of self-consciousness that one gets when one is overly concerned about how one is being perceived by others but rather awareness of the self. Self-consciousness is consciousness *of* the self. This occurs when, for example, seeing a trail of sugar on the floor in the supermarket, I follow it wondering who is leaving sugar there, until as I go round the aisle one more time it suddenly dawns on me that the sugar is coming out of a bag in my cart and thus that *I* am the one trailing sugar (Perry 1979).

This is also the sort of consciousness the mirror test developed by Gordon Gallup Jr. in 1970 is intended to measure. In this test, animals are presented with their own mirror image. They are surreptitiously marked with dye having no odor, and then their behavior is observed. If they behave by turning in various ways so as to get a better look at the marking on their bodies, or if they poke at the marking with a finger while looking in the mirror as they do, this is taken to be an indication that the animals are aware that their own bodies are marked with dye. In being so aware, they are aware of themselves. They are conscious that *they* have a dye mark on *them*.

---

of a sort that goes on in subjects that we all agree are having a face experience. A full discussion of this example would take us too far afield. My own view is that a conceptually necessary condition on a representation's counting as a visual experience of a thing X is that it be suitably poised for some cognitive response or other with respect to X, even if only momentarily, and thus that none of the representations in the fusiform face area of G. K.'s cortex should count as a face experience.

Human children do not pass this test until 1.5 to 2 years of age or older. Dogs typically simply ignore the mirror. Chimpanzees, orangutans, dolphins, and elephants are among the animals to have passed the test. It is unclear whether failing the test really shows a failure of self-consciousness or whether it merely shows something about the animal's reaction to mirrors. Consider, for example, the case of a small dog that sits whining at the base of its master's bed. The dog wants to lie on the bed, but it is aware that *it* is too small to jump up, so it tries to attract the attention of its master. The dog here apparently has self-awareness, for it is aware that *it* can't jump up on its own, even though it fails the mirror test.

The case of self-consciousness does not undermine the Simple View. Self-consciousness, in the sense of the feeling one gets of being overly concerned how others are assessing one is just that, a feeling, that is, an experience of a certain sort. Similarly, self-consciousness of the sort measured by the mirror test is conscious awareness that the dye mark is on one's own body, where this awareness is a kind of experience. The animal consciously thinks to itself, "What is that doing on my body?" (or something similar), or it consciously wonders this or is consciously puzzled by this. These mental acts are experiences. The animal has the experience of thinking, wondering, or puzzling about the dye mark and its location. As noted earlier, it is a substantive and difficult question as to in what exactly such an experience consists. Is it that there is an occurrent thought that has, in addition to its propositional content, some phenomenal or "what it is like feature," or is it that there is an occurrent thought accompanied by a further phenomenal state so that the experience of thinking, wondering, and so on is really a hybrid state? I shall not try to answer this question here. The point I want to emphasize is simply that there is no problem here for the Simple View.

Self-consciousness, then, is one kind or species of consciousness simpliciter. There are others, for example, introspective awareness and perceptual consciousness. Even so, there is just one *concept* of consciousness: that of experience. If you are in a state for which there is nothing it is like for you to be in that state, then you are not in a conscious state, nor are you conscious of anything. Or so the Simple View holds.

2.5 THE UPSHOT FOR ANIMAL CONSCIOUSNESS

Animal consciousness, at its most basic level, is just animal experience. The problem of animal consciousness is the problem of bridging the divide between subjective experience, on the one hand, and the objective, physical facts and behavior, on the other. Once we have established that a given kind of animal undergoes experiences, we can go on to ask whether the animal is capable of higher-order consciousness, whether, that is, it is capable of undergoing the experience of thinking that such-and-such an experience is present and, relatedly, whether it is capable of self-consciousness. The latter consciousness is arguably involved in higher-order consciousness, for thinking that an experience is present may be taken to demand that one think that *one* is undergoing the relevant experience. But self-consciousness does not require higher-order consciousness. It suffices that one have thoughts about oneself. No mental concepts need figure in the thoughts for self-consciousness to be present.

In what follows, my interest is in the fundamental question of animal experiences. The other questions are interesting and worthwhile, but they will not form the focus of this book.

[3]

IT'S GOT TO BE HUMAN!

Charles Darwin took it to be beyond any reasonable doubt that animals other than humans undergo experiences, including emotional experiences. In *The Descent of Man in Relation to Sex* (1871), he wrote:

> The lower animals, like man, manifestly, feel pleasure and pain, happiness and misery.

And:

> The fact that the lower animals are excited by the same emotions as ourselves is so well established that it will not be necessary to weary the reader by many details. (p. 511)

What was obvious to Darwin was not obvious to Rene Descartes, the famous French philosopher, writing two centuries earlier. Indeed, Descartes' view (or at least his official view)[1] was diametrically opposed to Darwin's. For Descartes, as for Malebranche (one of his followers),

> [Animals] eat without pleasure, cry without pain, grow without knowing it; they desire nothing, fear nothing, know nothing. (Quoted in Jolley 2000, p. 42)

In this chapter, we will look at Descartes' view and what motivated it.

---

1. For more, see 3.1 below.

3.1 DESCARTES AND THE ANIMALS

Rene Descartes was born in 1596 and published his most famous book, *Meditations on First Philosophy: In Opposition to Skeptics and Atheists*, in 1641. Descartes was unquestionably a brilliant man. He was not only a philosopher but also a mathematician. He essentially invented geometry (that is, modern analytic geometry), and he was much struck by the certainty that was given him by mathematical proofs. This certainty played a role in the development of Descartes' method of systematic doubt in philosophy, and it was at the foundation of his most famous argument, the argument from systematic doubt, about which I shall say a few words shortly.

Descartes was writing at a time of great scientific change. The Polish scientist Nicolaus Copernicus (1473–1543) had put forward the view that the best explanation of certain astronomical observations[2] was that the earth rotated around the sun, in opposition to the long-established view of the ancient astronomer Ptolemy, and the German Johannes Kepler (1571–1630) was maintaining, again on scientific grounds, that the planets moved in elliptical orbits. These scientific claims were inconsistent with the Bible on a literal reading. The earth was no longer the center of creation, and the planets did not move around it in perfect circles. What was to become of Holy Scripture?

Descartes, who was a devout Roman Catholic, was deeply concerned that in the face of these scientific claims, the church would lose much of its popular support, as indeed the church itself was. The reaction of the latter was to issue a decree declaring the doctrine that the sun stood still and the earth moved to be false and to suspend Copernicus's *De Revolutionibus* until corrected. The church also summoned the most famous Italian scientist of the time, Galileo Galilei (1564–1642), to Rome and ordered him to abandon Copernicus's ideas. This he did not do with sufficient alacrity or clarity, with the result that later in 1632 he was summoned before the Inquisition, found guilty of heresy, and sentenced to house arrest for the rest of his life.

---

2. This in *De Revolutionibus*, which was published in Nuremburg in 1543 just before Kepler's death.

Descartes' own reaction was more moderate. He wrote *Meditations*, and in it he set out to *prove* that two fundamental tenets of Catholicism were true: that human beings have souls and that God exists. And by "proof" here, Descartes had in mind a piece of reasoning yielding the sort of certainty that mathematical proofs have. Such a proof needed an indubitable starting point, of course, so Descartes in the first chapter of *Meditations* began his philosophical reflections by trying to doubt everything he conceivably could so as to find a firm foundation, if any existed, upon which such a proof might be erected.

He believed that he had discovered such a foundation in the famous proposition "Cogito, ergo sum" (I think, therefore I am). Descartes' point was that, whatever else you might doubt, you surely cannot doubt that you yourself exist, for such an act of doubting involves a thought, and if you are thinking, you (and your mind) must exist. By contrast, Descartes held that he could conceivably doubt that his body existed—indeed, that any material thing existed (including his brain), for it was conceivable that his life was one long dream, so that he was really dreaming that he had a body and that he had a brain.[3]

Putting these two claims together, Descartes drew the conclusion that he/his mind could not be one and the same as any material thing. After all, he could doubt that the latter existed but not the former. So how could they be literally just one thing?

This led Descartes to hold that mind and body are two radically different substances. The body is a physical substance made of matter. Its essence is that of spatial extension, and it is governed by physical laws. The body is a public thing. By contrast, the mind is an immaterial substance. Its essence is that of thought (understood broadly to include thought-like states including judgments, acts of willing, etc.); the mind is not governed by physical laws, and it is not in space. The mind and its workings are private.

---

3. Have you ever seen your brain? If not, isn't it conceivable that you lack one, that you have little men inside your head or even just a big hole? And even if you have seen your brain, isn't it at least conceivable that your senses were misleading you at the time (as when you are subject to illusions elsewhere)?

Descartes' argument for his dualism of mind and body is prob-lematic, for other structurally similar arguments clearly fail. Suppose, for example, that I am an amnesiac and I am kept locked in a room in which there are many books and computers. Eventually I start reading about one Michael Tye, but also, having been reading skeptical philoso-phers, I wonder whether what I am reading is accurate and even whether Michael Tye exists in reality at all. Evidently, it would be a mistake for me to reason:

(1) I cannot doubt that I exist
(2) I can doubt that Michael Tye exists,

Therefore,

(3) I am not Michael Tye.

What follows from (1) and (2) is something much weaker, namely,

(4) I can doubt that I am Michael Tye.

Correspondingly, all that Descartes' argument from systematic doubt really establishes is that it is possible to *doubt* that the mind is one and the same as any material thing, not that in actuality the mind is not one and the same as a material thing. That, however, is not strong enough for Descartes' purposes. After all, a dyed-in-the-wool materialist can grant that it is possible to doubt the truth of materialism, just as it is possible to doubt the truth of the atomic theory of matter, say, or the principles of thermodynamics.

Having proven to his satisfaction that humans have immaterial souls, Descartes seems to have moved very quickly to the view of the church that these souls belong to humans alone. But the move was not without supporting argument. Descartes notes that animals are unable to talk, and this, he took it, is a good reason for holding that they are incapable of thought and rationality.

Animals, he asserts, "have not indicated by voice or other signs anything referring to thought alone, rather than to movement of mere nature" (letter to Henry More, 1648). What is puzzling here is the inference from this to the conclusion that they lack minds (souls). After all, is there not consciousness apart from thought? The answer, it seems, is that Descartes took consciousness and thought to be inextricably mixed. For Descartes, an animal only really feels pain if it is conscious of pain, and this consciousness for him involves a thought-like propositional awareness. The animal must think or judge for itself that it is in pain in order to genuinely feel pain, or at least the animal must bring to bear some concept classifying its state as having a negative affect if it is to experience anything like pain. Descartes, thus, was a conceptualist about experience. Experiences for him fall within the "space of reasons" (to use a term of John McDowell's), and since animals cannot reason, they are not genuine subjects of experiences.

Descartes' line of reasoning, in a nutshell, is this: minds are souls (established by the argument from systematic doubt); the essence of the soul is thought (established by the cogito and the further reflection that in the absence of thought, one would have no reason to believe one existed); animals cannot talk and therefore cannot think; so animals lack souls. If it is objected that consciousness itself is distinct from thought and so it cannot be of the essence of the soul to think, Descartes' response is to deny the premise. On his view, consciousness involves thought or a mental activity or state that is thought-like.

This left Descartes with a problem, of course. Animals have sense organs and nerves similar in nature to ours. Human sense organs and nerves generate perceptual and bodily experiences. Why don't the sense organs and nerves of animals do the same? Furthermore, animals behave as if they have experiences, including the experience of pain. Is this not good evidence that animals have experiences, after all?

Descartes' response is to note that we can build machines lacking minds that are capable of all sorts of complex motions. Given that we can build such machines, or automata, as he calls them, it's perfectly sensible to suppose that Mother Nature can do this too. Indeed, it is perfectly sensible to suppose that Mother Nature can build machines far superior to the ones we can construct. He comments in a letter to More in 1649:

> It seems reasonable since art copies nature, and men can make various automata which move without thought that nature should produce its own automata much more splendid than the artificial ones. These natural automata are the animals.

These natural automata or organic machines would be able do some impressive things, including engaging in behavior similar to the behavior we engage in as we undergo various experiences. And since we do these things in part via the use of sense organs, it would hardly be surprising if Mother Nature employed similar devices for gathering information in animals.

For Descartes, then, animals are really biological robots lacking any minds. Descartes takes it that we are not in the same boat, since we are capable of thought and reasoning, and so we must have minds (indeed, for reasons given above, immaterial minds).

I should add that it is sometimes disputed whether Descartes really held that animals altogether lack experiences. And in one letter (to Newcastle), he certainly says things diametrically opposed to the view usually attributed to him:

> If you teach a magpie to say good-day to its mistress when it sees her coming, all you can possibly have done is to make the emitting of this word the expression of one of its feelings. . . . Similarly, all the things which dogs, horses, and monkeys are made to do are merely expressions of their fear, their hope or their joy.

Yet it is also clear that Descartes engaged in or at least happily witnessed vivisection and that he was not disturbed at all by treatment of animals that we would regard as extremely cruel and inflicting pain (as shown in the figure overleaf).

FIGURÆ EXPLICATIO.

A. *Crus canis dextrum.*   B. *Crus canis sinistrum.*
C. D. *Ligatura subiecta arteriæ & venæ, qua femur firmiter con-*
stringitur, expressa in dextro crure, ne litterarum linearumque con-
fusio in sinistro crure spectatorem posset turbare.
E. *Arteria cruralis.*   F. *Vena cruralis.*
G. *Filum quo constricta est vena & est elevata.*
H. *Acus, cui filum est traiectum.*
I. *Venæ pars superior & detumescens.*
K. *Venæ pars inferior à ligatura intumescens.*
L. *Guttæ sanguinis, quæ ésuperiori parte venæ vulnerata, sensim*
distillant.
M. *Rivulus sanguinis, qui, inferiori venæ parte vulnerata, continuò*
exilit.
                                                              F 2   vero

J. Walaeus, *Epistola Prima de Motu Chyli et Sanguinis* (1647)

For example, in *OD*, vol. 1 (*OD* refers to the twelve-volume *Oeuvres de Descartes* edited by Adam and Tannery), Descartes tells us that if you whip a dog while a violin is played, it will whimper and whine in time to the music. Later, in volume 11 of *OD*, he comments:

> If you cut off the end of the heart of a living dog and insert your finger through the incision into one of the concavities, you will clearly feel that every time the heart shortens, it presses your finger, and stops pressing it every time it lengthens.

And in a letter to Plempius of February 15, 1638 (pp. 79–85) he says:

> For this is disproved by an utterly decisive experiment, which I was interested to observe several times before, and which I performed today in the course of writing this letter. First, I opened

the chest of a live rabbit and removed the ribs to expose the heart and the trunk of the aorta. I then tied the aorta with a thread a good distance from the heart. (Descartes 1991, p. 81)

It seems impossible to reconcile all of these passages. Perhaps Descartes was ultimately of two minds about whether animals undergo experiences. More likely, the letter to Newcastle simply misrepresented his considered view, since his concern there is to argue that animals don't really use language even if they can produce sounds that we would regard as meaningful if produced by other humans.

That Descartes could have viewed animals in the ways indicated in the passages from AT is not only disturbing but also remarkable for one so manifestly intelligent. Descartes was, it seems, a brute to the brutes.[4] That certainly was the position of Voltaire, who, writing after Descartes' death, had this to say about the sort of position Descartes held:

Hold then the same view of the dog which has lost his master, which has sought him in all the thoroughfares with cries of sorrow, which comes into the house troubled and restless, goes downstairs, goes upstairs; goes from room to room, finds at last in his study the master he loves, and betokens his gladness by soft whimpers, frisks, and caresses.

There are barbarians who seize this dog, who so greatly surpasses man in fidelity and friendship, and nail him down to a table and dissect him alive, to show you the mesaraic veins! You discover in him all the same organs of feeling as in yourself. Answer me mechanist, has Nature arranged all the springs of feeling in this animal to the end that he might not feel? (1764)

3.2 DESCARTES AND TURING

Recall that the objective/subjective divide, as discussed in chapter 1, is the divide between the objective and the phenomenally subjective.

---

4. John Cottingham (1978) has contested this assessment, to my mind unsuccessfully, though, as noted earlier, Descartes' writings are not fully consistent on the topic.

Descartes tried to bridge this divide in the manner of the higher-order-thought theorist,[5] by taking the phenomenally subjective to be infused with concepts, that is, as involving propositional conscious awareness *that* pain is present or anger or fear or whatever, where this awareness is thought-like in its character. Since the capacity for thought is essentially tied to the capacity to use language, it follows that nonhuman animals, all of which lack a language for Descartes even if some of them can emit sounds that might be mistaken for words by the untutored, lack phenomenally subjective states. So nonhuman animals are merely organic automata. For Descartes, then, it's got to be human to enjoy experiences and feelings.

There are three fundamental problems with Descartes' position. First, the essence of the mind is not thought/consciousness. There are mental states I have when I am unconscious, for example, the belief that $2 + 2 = 4$. It is true, of course, that when I am unconscious, I have no reason to believe that my mind exists, as Descartes notes. But it does not follow from this that I do not exist when I am unconscious! One might as well argue: I have no reason to believe that there are daffodils at the bottom of your garden; therefore, there are no daffodils at the bottom of your garden. Secondly, the tight connection Descartes sees between thought and language and which he needs to cross the objective/subjective divide does not exist. Thirdly, the phenomenally subjective does not inherently involve thought-like awareness. These last two points need some elaboration.

Recall the earlier definition in chapter 1 of a triangle: a triangle is a closed, three-sided figure. We can see this definition as providing an analysis of the concept or idea of a triangle, one that equips us to decide very easily whether given figures are triangles or not. Descartes may be seen as offering an equally objective definition of what it is for a being to be capable of thought: a being is capable of thought if and only if it is capable of using language. An alternative, somewhat weaker definition in the same spirit is this: a being is of a kind that is capable of thought if and only if mature, normal members of that kind are capable of using

5. See chapter 2, section 2.

language. This has the advantage of not *ruling out* babies and mutes from having the capacity to think.[6]

This proposal is reminiscent of a proposal made by the father of the modern computer, Alan Turing, in the twentieth century. Turing was a remarkable man. In the Second World War, as a member of the British government codebreaking team at Bletchley Park in England, he deciphered the secret code the German U-boats were using to communicate with one another as they wrought havoc upon the Allies' shipping, thereby shortening the war by at least two years, by some estimates, and perhaps more strongly actually altering the outcome. Turing was also a founding father of the discipline of cognitive science, holding that at birth the cortex is an "unorganized machine" that is then later organized through training. In addition, he developed computers to model biological growth and in so doing he was one of the founders of the discipline of artificial life.

Turing had many eccentricities, including long-distance running while wearing a gas mask (in case the Germans dropped poison gas as he was exercising in the English countryside) and a bizarre early death of cyanide poisoning. The usual view is that Turing killed himself by taking a bite out of a cyanide-laced apple,[7] but it may be that the actual fact of his death was more mundane. Turing kept a chemistry lab in his house containing cyanide. One possibility is that cyanide gas escaped (it is odorless to 50 percent of men), and Turing accidentally died by inhaling it. The apple that was found in Turing's kitchen table with a bite taken out of it was never tested for cyanide.[8]

Turing was interested in the question of what constitutes intelligence of the sort that humans generally share, and he proposed a test,

6. If the capacity in the first definition is understood in a suitably forward-looking way as the capacity to use language either now or in the future, given normal development, the first definition also allows in babies.

7. In one version of the story, Turing was a great admirer of the story *Snow White*, and he decided to kill himself in the way that the Evil Queen tried to kill Snow White.

8. I have heard it said that the Apple computer logo derives from Turing's death, but what really happened was that Steve Jobs commissioned graphic designer Rob Janoff to produce something striking, and the "bite" in the apple was included so that people would realize that it represented an apple and not a tomato. The original Apple logo, incidentally, was designed in 1976 by Robert Wayne, and it shows Sir Isaac Newton with an apple dangling over his head.

now known as the Turing test, for deciding whether a machine is truly intelligent. According to Turing, a machine is to be counted as intelligent, as capable of thought, if and only if the machine cannot be distinguished from a human being, going on its linguistic responses, during the course of an extended conversation.

This proposal is behavioristic in character: what matters to thought, reasoning, intelligence—indeed, the *only* thing that matters—is a certain sort of behavior: linguistic behavior in the course of ordinary conversation. As with other behavioristic proposals, there are decisive counterexamples. To see this, we can construct a thought experiment—a scenario that is perfectly coherent and in this case physically possible, even if it is quite fantastic. So here goes.

Any test takes a finite period of time. Whatever that time is, there is a huge but finite number of sentences that can be typed or uttered in that time. Let us imagine that programmers write down each of these with a time tag by it. Then they write down a reasonable response to that sentence with a tag for the total time of the first sentence to which it is a response and the response. For each of these, there is in turn a finite number of further responses. These are written down, again keeping track of the time. So a huge tree structure results covering the entire time of the test. It is then stored in a machine.

You now come along—we can suppose that you are the judge in the Turing test—and you type string 5971, which then appears on your computer monitor screen. The machine grinds through the tree and produces a reasonable response, which shows up below your sentence on the screen. This happens for each string you type in, so the machine passes the Turing test. Even so, it is not at all intelligent. No thought or reasoning is going on (Block 1981). Everything is stored in advance—a matter of "memory" alone.

The broad point here is that the core of intelligence is mental competence, not behavioral performance. Performance is evidence for competence, but they aren't the same. A failure to distinguish these two is the root of the trouble with philosophical behaviorism generally (according to which mental states are no more than dispositions to produce characteristic behavior). And it gives rise to jokes at the behaviorist expense: for example, two behaviorists are walking down the street. One says to the other: "You're feeling fine. How am I feeling?"

Turing's problem is Descartes' problem too. Imagine that our technology is vastly more advanced than that of today and that we can travel to distant parts of the galaxy. In the course of our space explorations, we come across alien beings that use language apparently as we do. According to Descartes' proposal, these beings, or at least normal, mature members of their kind, are capable of thought, but the thought experiment above shows that *conceivably* they are not. Their linguistic behavior is very strong evidence for the claim that they think, but it does not guarantee it. Conceivably, their responses are controlled by internal programs as "dumb" as the tree structure in the machine envisaged above.

In one way, then, the tight conceptual connection Descartes alleges to hold between thought and language is too liberal, for it lets in machines and alien beings incapable of thought. In another way, it is not liberal enough, for it denies intelligence to nonhuman creatures lacking in a language but capable of intelligent behavior. Take the case of crows. It has been shown that if offered a variety of tool options, crows will examine them and pick the one of the right length or width for the task at hand. Indeed, they will even design a suitable tool of the correct dimensions, if needed. For example, in order to get bugs or other difficult-to-reach food in cracks and crevices, crows will use sticks, and they will even whittle sticks to make them thinner to fit into the cracks and crevices. Crows have even been known to bend a piece of wire into a hook to retrieve food that could not be acquired without it.[9]

Of course, Descartes would have insisted that, lacking a language, crows are not intelligent. Instead, they are organic automata designed by nature—automata totally lacking in thought. Leaving aside the fact that there is no conceptually tight connection between thought and language of the sort that Descartes held to be the case, supposing that a crow has psychological states gives us a satisfying explanation of its behavior: the crow *wanted* to eat the bug but it was out of reach, so it *decided* to whittle a stick, *believing* that doing so would enable it to reach

9. See chapter 7, p. 121.

the bug.[10] This it successfully did. What is the alternative explanation of the crow's actions that Descartes would favor? That nature designed an organic automaton to act *as if* it had such psychological states even though it didn't? Why would nature do that?

3.3 CONCEPTUALISM ABOUT EXPERIENCE

The last problem with Descartes' view I distinguished earlier is that it makes experience and feeling—the phenomenally subjective— implausibly conceptual or thought-like. I want now to say something more about this. Of necessity, the discussion for the remainder of this chapter will be less easy to follow for nonspecialists than what has gone before. Those who are not philosophers may skip this without missing much of significance to the following chapters.

One way to understand the conceptualist view of experience is as holding that subjects of experiences, in undergoing experiences, have a thought-like awareness of themselves *as* such subjects. So, for example, for me to feel pain, on this view, I must be able to think or somehow conceptualize *that* I am in pain, and this involves the idea or concept of myself.[11] Animals lack such self-awareness, it might be held, so they do not really feel pain.

The trouble is that a range of animals *have* self-awareness, or at least act in a way that is strongly suggestive of their being self-aware. This is shown by the mirror test developed by Gordon Gallup Jr. in 1970 (as noted in the last chapter). To date, animals that have passed the test are as follows: European magpies, bottlenose dolphins, gorillas, chimpanzees, bonobos, orangutans, orcas, and elephants. So if Descartes' view was that nonhuman animals are *not* self-aware and so cannot meet the

---

10. Correct attributions of the above cognitive states to crows do not require that the crows themselves exercise the very concepts we, the attributors, use in reporting those cognitive states. See here Sainsbury and Tye 2012.

11. As noted above, this is a version of the HOT theory of experience discussed in the last chapter.

conceptualist self-awareness condition on experience, he was straight-forwardly mistaken. Worse still, at least for Descartes' purposes, on this view some humans cannot have experiences either, for children prior to eighteen months fail the mirror test, as initially do adult humans whose sight has been restored.

There is an alternative way of understanding the conceptualist approach to experience. Experiences provide reasons for empirical beliefs. For example, my current visual experience supplies me with a reason for believing that there is a laptop computer in front of me. According to some philosophers (see, for example, Brewer 2005 and McDowell 1994), this is possible only if experiences are judgment-like: they must involve concepts or ideas, and they must be either true or false. Only then can they enter into the "space of reasons." On this view, experiences are a bit like sentences. In the case of vision, the visual experience one undergoes "describes" the scene before one's eyes via a complex structure of concepts or ideas, itself evaluable for truth or fal-sity (as is a sentence made up of words), and in so doing, it serves as the starting point for the formation of beliefs as to what is really out there. Effectively, visual experiences are premises in arguments or patterns of reasoning the mind goes through as it comes to conclusions as to how the nearby external world is.

Let us look at this proposal for experiences in more detail and why it seems very implausible. Consider my current visual experience. It contains a wealth of information. I am conscious of my laptop, the papers on its right, a pen, a desk, a bunch of keys, a number of books on the bookcase behind the laptop, and an art deco lamp, to men-tion just some of the more obvious things in my visual field. I am also conscious of the colors and shapes of these items. This consciousness is not just of such general colors as brown and red or shapes such as rectangular and cylindrical. I am conscious of determinates of these determinables. The desktop has variations in its shades of brown as well as irregular markings with shapes that I find impossible to cap-ture in words. The same is true for the books on the shelves behind my computer. Perhaps ten of the books have blue covers, but they do not look exactly alike in color: there are subtle variations in their shades. The lamp is in bronze, and it features a fairy-like figure holding a glass bulb shaped like a flower. The curves on the fairy and the undulations in the curves of the bulb again escape my power to describe. But they are part of my conscious awareness. If they had been only slightly different, what it would have been like for me subjectively would have been different too.

The richness of my experience, the fineness of its grain with respect to the features of visible surfaces, seems to go far beyond the concepts I possess. These concepts I can put into words, but any description or sentence I might come up with, no matter how complicated, would inevitably leave out much of the determinacy of detail in my experience, or so at least it seems.

This point about experience has sometimes been put by saying that experiences have nonconceptual content. The key claim here is that experiences, by their nature, are such that their subjects need not possess the concepts that the theorist would use in a careful and precise and full statement of the conditions under which the experience is accurate (or true). In the case of the experience above, the accuracy conditions would of necessity be fantastically complex, for there is a fantastic complexity of detail in the experience, each part of which contributes, if only minimally on an individual basis, to its overall conscious character.[12]

In the next few paragraphs, I'm going to consider some replies that the conceptualist might make about experience. These philosophical subtleties can safely be skipped by readers with more general interests.

The first reply that has been made to the above point about the complexity and richness of experience is that the relevant details are conceptualized in the experience by very specific but nonetheless general recognitional concepts for shades of color like red_{19} or $blue_{31}$ and correspondingly general but very specific recognitional concepts for shapes and other surface features.[13]

---

12. Some philosophers hold a stronger version of the nonconceptualist thesis. They hold that the content of experience itself is not the sort of content that can belong to a thought. On this view, you can't literally think *what* you or anyone else experiences. The content of your thought is a different sort of beast from the content of an experience.

13. A recognitional concept is a concept or idea stored in memory and used in recognizing something. The recognitional concept *dog*, for example, is a concept stored in memory and matched to the perceptual stimulus in recognizing something as a dog.

The trouble with this proposal is that human memory is limited. We abstract away from details to avoid information overload. We have recognitional concepts such as *red, green,* and *blue,* and more specific ones such as *scarlet* and *bright scarlet*. But we do not have recognitional concepts for minimal shades. The ordinary person cannot recognize red$_{27}$, even after having just seen it.[14] People who are shown a patch of color and then very shortly afterward are asked whether a second patch has the same shade of color or a minimally different one do not do well at the task. Of course, if the original patch is re-presented before the original experience is over, then the match will be made successfully. But this does not show a recognitional concept, for possession of that requires the capacity to recognize the given hue when it comes again after the initial experience ends.[15]

A second reply the conceptualist might make to the alleged fineness of grain in visual experience is to allow that the subject of an experience of a minimal shade lacks a general recognitional concept of that shade, but to insist that it does not follow that the experience has a nonconceptual content, since the subject can conceptualize the given shade in the experience via a general, fine-grained perceptual concept that is automatically manufactured on the spot, as the subject undergoes the experience; the concept is then lost as soon as the experience is over. The obvious trouble with this view is that if such concepts occur in the subject's experience, then they must be concepts the subject possesses and hence concepts that the subject is capable of exercising in thought. But if these concepts can occur in the subject's thoughts as well as in her experiences, and they really are general concepts, then the subject should be able to think thoughts that use the concepts even when the experiences are not present, and this conflicts with the hypothesis that the relevant concepts are lost once the experiences end.

---

14. See here Hurvich 1981 and Halsey and Chapanis 1951. See also Raffman 1996.
15. Another objection is that there cannot be recognition for a first-time experience of a property, but that experience still has a specific representational content: the world still appears a certain way to the subject of the experience (Peacocke 2000).

This brings me to the third reply that the conceptualist might make, namely, to suggest that the concept for a shade employed by visual experience is demonstrative. The obvious immediate question for this reply is: What form does the demonstrative concept in the experience take? John McDowell, in *Mind and World* (1994), appeals to the demonstrative *that shade*. To experience a particular shade, red$_{27}$, say, is to have an experience of something as being of that shade, where the latter is to be understood as involving the application of the demonstrative concept: *that shade*. The difference, then, between seeing red$_{27}$ and red$_{28}$ is the difference between applying the concept *that shade* to red$_{27}$ and applying it to red$_{28}$. The concept *that shade*, in the context of the one experience, refers to red$_{27}$; the concept *that shade*, in the context of the other experience, refers to red$_{28}$. The two experiences thereby have different correctness conditions and thus different contents.

This is problematic, as has been noted by several philosophers (but most forcefully by Peacocke 1998, 2000). First, which concept exactly is exercised in the experience of a particular shade of red? The concept McDowell appeals to is the concept *that shade*. But why not *that shade of red*? Or *that color*? Or *that red*? There seems no nonarbitrary way of deciding between these candidates—they all seem equally eligible—and thus no fact of the matter as to which one is applied in the experience.

Secondly, McDowell's proposal appeals to a demonstrative concept *that* as well as a general sortal, *shade*. The latter is a recognitional concept. The idea that in order to undergo an experience of a particular shade of red, something a child can do from a very early age, one must possess the concept *shade*, is absurd. To possess the concept *shade*, one must possess a cognitive grasp of the difference between a shade and a color that is not a shade, classifying red$_{27}$ as a shade, for example, and red as not. It seems to me quite likely that even some high schoolers do not grasp the concept *shade*.

One way to handle these problems is to appeal to a pure demonstrative *that*. But what is the referent of the demonstrative in the color case? The obvious answer is: the particular shade. Which shade? Suppose I am viewing a color patch with the shade, red$_{18}$. Pointing at the patch and the shade, on the basis of my experience, I say, "That patch has that." Should we suppose that the concept *that*, exercised in the experience with respect to a shade, refers to the shade of the patch the subject is viewing? Then both my remark and my experience are accurate. However, if I am misperceiving the patch and experiencing it as having a shade different from the one it actually has, my experience will not represent the patch as having *that*, understood as the actual shade of the patch, at all.

The conceptualist might respond that the demonstrative concept exercised in the experience is a concept of the shade the given surface *appears* to have. But how, in the case of misperception, is the referent of the concept fixed? The nonconceptualist about experience can say that if the subject of the experience goes on to apply a pure demonstrative concept, the concept gets its content fixed via the content of the experience: the concept refers to the shade the given experience represents the surface as having. However, this reply is not available to the conceptualist about visual experience, for the content of the demonstrative concept is supposed to be part of the content of the experience, and so the concept cannot have its referent fixed by that content (Heck 2000, p. 496).

The conclusion I draw is that the conceptualist view of experience is implausible and unworkable. Experiences just aren't like beliefs or judgments. The basic experiences we undergo—states like feeling pain or having a visual sensation of red—are phylogenetically fixed. On this view, through learning we can change our beliefs, our thoughts, our judgments, but not our basic experiences. Having acquired the concept *microscope*, say, we can come to see something *as* a microscope, but we do not need concepts simply to see. Once the receptor cells are matured, it suffices to open the eyes. No learning or training is involved. Basic visual experiences are nonconceptual, as are other perceptual experiences. Small children see pretty much what the rest of us see. They differ from us in *how* they see things, in what they see things *as*. They do not see that the kettle is boiling; they do not see the house as being dilapidated, the computer as malfunctioning.

What, then, of the claim that experiences provide reasons for empirical beliefs? The nonconceptualist about experience can accommodate this claim by holding that experiences carry information and, in so doing, imply or make probable some beliefs but not others. For example, my current visual experience carries information about what is before me even if it does not carry that information in conceptual form. The information carried makes it probable that there is a cup before me (but not that there is an iPhone, say). Here is a parallel. Suppose I have a picture of the scene before me. That picture carries information. It tells me things even if I do not appreciate all that it is telling me. In so doing, it supplies a reason to believe that the scene before my eyes is a certain way. Of course, the picture does not carry information in the way that a sentence or a description does. It is not a conceptual or linguistic representation, but it carries information nonetheless.

I should add that my experience can *provide* a reason for believing that things are thus and so even if I do not *have* a reason for holding that belief. *Having* a reason q to believe that p requires that one believe q; q's *providing* a reason to believe that p does not.[16] Suppose, for example, that Edgar has a heart condition. Edgar having a heart condition provides a reason to believe that Edgar will die early, but it may not be a reason Edgar actually has to believe that he will die early. Perhaps Edgar has never seen a doctor and is unaware of his heart problem. Accordingly, the visual experience of a small child might provide a reason for believing that a microscope is present, say, even if the subject of that experience, a small child lacking the concept *microscope*, does not *have* a reason for believing that a microscope is present.

The overall conclusion I draw is that Descartes' attempt to restrict the realm of experience to human beings is completely unpersuasive. His arguments rest on a variety of mistakes. The view that it's got to be human to have experiences is without merit.

---

16. Cf. Byrne 2005. See also ibid. for further discussion of the reason-playing role of experiences.

[4]

OUR FRIENDS AND NEIGHBORS

Let's forget nonhuman animals for the moment and reflect on other human beings. We take it for granted that other people experience pretty much what we do, that they feel joy and grief and anger and fear, that they experience pain, that they are conscious of colors and shapes and smells and sounds. What entitles us to suppose that?

4.1 BELIEFS AND DESIRES

This question is best approached indirectly by focusing initially on beliefs and desires. We all have a huge number of beliefs and many desires. These beliefs and desires are often a product of our backgrounds, our culture, our learning. You and I have many of the same beliefs, but we also have many different beliefs too. For example, we both believe that Obama was elected president of the United States, but perhaps only I believe that there are sentient beings on other planets in our solar system. Likewise for our desires; we both want to live for a long time, but perhaps only I want to buy a Maserati.

Many of our beliefs and desires are unconscious. Consider, for example, my belief that I will die. That's a belief I have when I am asleep or unconscious. Similarly, my desire to continue living. There is nothing inherently conscious about these mental states. Even so, they impact my behavior. My belief that I will die has caused me to make a will; my desire to continue living has led me to eschew very fatty foods.

Of course, beliefs and desires do not cause behavior in isolation. They work cooperatively to produce behavior. My desire to continue living has caused me to eschew very fatty foods *given* my belief that eating very fatty foods has a negative impact on longevity. My belief that I will die has caused me to make a will *given* my desire that my heirs have a fair share of my estate.

When we attribute beliefs and desires to others, we do so on the basis of their behavior. Suppose, for example, I see you walking toward a water fountain with an empty cup in your hand. One natural explanation of your behavior is that you want a drink of water and you believe that there is water available at the fountain. This is not the only possible explanation. You could be behaving in this way for an entirely different reason. Perhaps you want me to think that you want water and you believe that the water fountain does not work, and you further are curious to see how I will react when I witness your failing to get water.

The latter explanation is not as good an explanation as the former. For one thing, it is more complicated. For another, it raises further puzzling questions: Why should you be curious as to how I will behave? Why do you want me to think that you want water when really you don't? Furthermore, in my own case, walking toward a water source is usually caused by a desire for water along with a belief about the location of the source. Given the evidence from my own case and no evidence that your case is different, surely the best explanation of your behavior is the obvious, natural one. This explanation posits a causal story as to what is going on in you very like a causal story I already know about, namely, the causal story as to what usually goes on in me when I behave in the above way.

What other explanations are there? Here is one extremely fanciful one I might come up with: You have only an organic exterior. Internally, your head is hollow though you have all the other usual human organs. Your movements are controlled by Martians who send messages to the muscles in your body so that it moves in ways that do not mark you out as atypical. The Martians monitor every context you are in, and they get you to respond in whatever ways they deem appropriate for a human being in that context. You are thus a Martian marionette (Peacocke 1998). In reality, you have no beliefs or desires, but you certainly behave *as if* you do.

Explaining your movement toward the water fountain by hypothesizing that you are a marionette who is being caused to move in this way by the beliefs and desires of Martians is not at all plausible. Why not? The explanation is ad hoc. It posits a psychological difference between you and me on the basis of no evidence. It is also unnecessarily complex: Why introduce Martians when a perfectly sensible, much simpler explanation is possible? This sort of explanation would be dismissed in science. Why suppose it is appropriate here?

All that this case really shows is that behaving as if a certain mental state is present is no guarantee that it is present. After all, it is *possible* that you really are a Martian marionette. Nonetheless, this mere possibility does not undermine the superior status of the ordinary explanation of your behavior.

Here is one more alternative explanation I might conceivably propose of your behavior not only in the above instance but throughout your life. This explanation is different from the Martian one in that it posits internal states, but again it forgoes beliefs and desires, and it is sufficiently general that it will well predict your behavior throughout your life.

Let's begin the explanation with the example of chess. Chess is an enormously complex game. Each player can make roughly thirty moves on his or her turn, and each player has roughly forty turns in an average chess game. So, in the average game, there are roughly 30^{80} (or equivalently 1.48×10^{118}) moves—a mind-bogglingly large number. Suppose that chess grandmasters create a look-up tree that gives the best moves in response to all possible moves by a chess opponent. Forget how big this tree would be—indeed, forget whether creating such a tree would be physically possible. The point for present purposes is that the idea is coherent, just like the idea of the Starship *Enterprise* in Star Trek traveling at warp factor 5 (five times the speed of light), even though this is physically impossible. Now anyone with such a tree could play chess at grandmaster level without knowing anything about chess. Having such a tree, this person could play intelligent chess without being an intelligent chess player.

Life itself is a bit like a game of chess. For each person, at any time there are finitely many (effectively distinguishable) sensory inputs to the retina, the nose, the ear, the skin, and so on and finitely many (effectively distinguishable) muscle movements in response. So in principle one could make a look-up tree for any person—a tree that would perfectly describe their behavior as they go through life.

Suppose now I hypothesize that you are a normal human being except for one big difference: in place of your original brain, a silicon chip has been inserted on which the "game of life" for you is inscribed. This chip ensures that throughout your life, for the same sensory input, you produce the same muscle movements as you would have done had your real-life brain not been removed at the moment of your birth. In this scenario, you don't have any beliefs or desires.

It is important to realize that the fact that your responses can be predicted and are fully determined by the chip (and the inputs) is not relevant to this claim. After all, a fantastic, Laplacian demon[1] equipped with perfect knowledge of the physical structure of human beings and the laws of nature could predict how each human will behave at any given future time, at least if human beings are physical systems and the fundamental laws are deterministic.

What is relevant, rather, is the fact that the right internal causal and functional relations aren't present for beliefs and desires. For example, if you are in a classroom and the teacher says, "Think of the number 18," and then a bit later the teacher says, "Multiply that number by 2 and then work out whether that number divided by 3 is greater than 14 and give your answer," there isn't the right pattern of internal causal dependencies for you to be forming beliefs and reasoning through to the conclusion. There was, of course, in the people who set up the look-up tree, but not in you yourself. Given how the chip is constructed, there is a state of it that is responsible for your producing the right answer in response to the given input question, but you don't yourself work out the answer;

1. "We may regard the present state of the universe as the effect of its past and the cause of its future. An intellect which at a certain moment would know all forces that set nature in motion, and all positions of all items of which nature is composed, if this intellect were also vast enough to submit these data to analysis, it would embrace in a single formula the movements of the greatest bodies of the universe and those of the tiniest atom; for such an intellect nothing would be uncertain and the future just like the past would be present before its eyes" (Laplace 1814).

you don't first believe that 18 multiplied by 2 equals 36, then believe that 36 divided by 3 equals 12, then draw the conclusion that 14 is greater than this number, and finally express this conclusion verbally. Nothing like that goes on in you.

Similarly, when you walk over to the water fountain and press the button for water, the visual input generates your behavior via the silicon chip, but there is no intervening desire for water. The desire for water uses the concept *water* (that is, the idea of water), and that concept figures in the desire to refuse a drink of water as well as in water-related beliefs. But the silicon-chip state that is responsible for your reaching for the button on the water fountain need not have any common active component with the silicon-chip states responsible for the behavior that normally goes with the desire to decline water and the behavior manifesting water beliefs. That is not how the chip is constructed.

On the above silicon chip hypothesis, then, I can always explain your behavior and predict what you will do, but my explanation will not advert to your beliefs and desires. You don't have any. Still, the explanation is not as good as the ordinary, natural explanation. But why not, exactly? After all, in this case, unlike the Martian marionette one, the explanation does appeal to your inner states, and it does hold that they cause your behavior. Well, the explanation posits a scenario that isn't even obviously physically possible. The scenario is highly complex. It involves large-scale deception, which raises further explanatory puzzles of its own. For example, why would anyone want to do this in the first place, and what would be the point? It is also ad hoc. It posits a causal story in you for your behavior that is very different from the causal story underlying mine, and it does so with no evidence whatsoever.

The simple fact is that the everyday causal explanation of your behavior by reference to your beliefs and desires is the best available, and as such it is rational for us to prefer it.

It is important to realize that even though the everyday explanation involves supposing that a causal story is true for you that is like the causal story that is true for me, appealing to the explanatory virtue of the everyday account of your behavior in support of its rationality is not arguing by analogy that you have mental states like mine. This point is worth pursuing further.

One way to try to justify the claim that others have mental states is to argue by analogy as follows:

I have mental states that cause my behavior.
Other people are like me.

So:

Probably, other people have mental states like mine that cause their behavior.

This argument, famous though it is, has several deep problems. First, it is an inductive inference based on a single case. No one would think that it is rational to argue in this way:

That swan is black.
Other swans are like that swan.

So:

Probably, swans generally are black.

Why, then, suppose that it is rational to argue by analogy in the other-minds case?

Secondly, the inference in the other-minds case is an inductive inference to a conclusion that cannot be checked independently. In this respect, the inference is even worse than the inference in the case of swans, for there we can check independently on the color of swans generally.

Thirdly, the second premise of the argument from analogy in the other-minds case is questionable. Other people are like me in many ways, including their behavior, but they are also very different from me in many ways too, and they often do not behave as I would in similar circumstances. It might be responded that other people are *relevantly* like me, notwithstanding various differences, and that is all that matters. But the relevant similarities in analogical inferences must be between the cases in the evidential base and the case in the conclusion. Unless the new case is *relevantly* similar to the old observed case, why suppose that the feature found in the old case can be projected to the new one? Consider, for example, the following specimen inference:

Sebastian has red hair.
Tom is like Sebastian.

So:

Probably, Tom has red hair.

This inference is reasonable if Tom is relevantly like Sebastian—if, say, he comes from the same family and nearly everyone in the family has red hair. But if Tom is similar to Sebastian simply in his lifestyle and his job and his drinking habits, the inference is evidently weak.

The trouble with the analogical inference to other minds is that the evidence pertains only to me, whereas the conclusion pertains to others, to people who are not me. How can I be confident that the similarities between myself and other people are *relevant*, given that all the evidence pertains to me alone?[2]

The argument I have given—that the hypothesis that you have beliefs and desires is justified since it affords the best explanation of your behavior—is an example of inference to the best explanation. It is not an inductive argument by analogy. An analogy is effectively made, of course, in the hypothesis—that you are like me in having beliefs and desires—but that analogy does not figure in an argument by analogy.

Inferences to the best explanation are common in science. They form the basis for the kinetic theory of gases and the hypothesis that there are electrons. Further questions arise as to how we are to decide in certain cases when one explanation is better than others;[3] I shall return

---

2. This point is made by Robert Pargetter (1984). I am influenced above in several places by his discussion.
3. See here Lipton 1991.

to this issue in the next chapter. My point so far has been simply that the ordinary view that other people have beliefs and desires is the best available explanation of their behavior and that this fact entitles us to accept that view.[4]

Before I turn in the next section to the case of experiences and feelings, I want to mention another view that has been proposed with respect to our knowledge of the mental states of others, namely, that we directly perceive that these states are present both in other human beings and in some nonhuman animals (such as dogs), just as we directly perceive that there are tables and chairs in our immediate environments (Jamieson 1998; Cassam 2007, chapter 5). In the case of desires, the suggestion is that I can literally see the display of desire on your face and thus see that you have a desire for ice cream, for example, as you hungrily watch me eating a large cone filled with a chocolate swirl. If this is true, my justification for the view that you have this desire cannot rest on an inference *from* your behavior, for your desire is displayed right there *in* the facial behavior I see before my eyes, or so it has been claimed.

This proposal seems to me unsatisfying. The key question now becomes: What justifies me in supposing that I am seeing a display of such-and-such a mental state on your face? After all, you might be dissembling or controlled by Martians. And here the perceptualist model seems to have little to say. Furthermore, the motivation for the view seems based on a misunderstanding of the inferentialist view. Patently, in forming our beliefs about what others desire, for example, we do not consciously infer their desires from their behavior, at least in many cases. We just see that their desires are present. However, the question is what *justifies* our beliefs. Take the case of ordinary objects such as tables. Even if I directly see that there is a table before me and I do not consciously infer the existence of the table, the question of what justifies my belief that there is a table ahead remains open. After all, I could be hallucinating. One answer is that I am entitled to take my perceptual experience at face value unless I have a reason for supposing that in this instance it is

---

4. Whether this acceptance suffices for belief or merely preference to alternative views is a tricky issue. For the moment I ignore it. I return to it at the end of this chapter (and again in the next).

inaccurate. That answer (dogmatism: Pryor 2000) is perfectly compatible with the claim that I see the table directly.

In the case of the desires of others, granting that in some cases I do not consciously infer them from behavior, still there is behavior that I do witness, behavior that can be present in anomalous cases even if the desires are missing, the best available explanation for which is that it is produced by such-and-such desires. This being so, I am *justified* in supposing that others have those desires, or at least in preferring that view to its denial. That is the key claim of the view elaborated in this section.

4.2 EXPERIENCES AND FEELINGS

I see you lying on the road with blood trickling down your arm and your bicycle with a bent front wheel. You are groaning and you have a tense look on your face. You ask me if I have any aspirin. I take it that you are feeling pain. What justifies me in holding this view?

The obvious answer, given the discussion of beliefs and desires in the last section, is that the pain hypothesis, as we might call it, is the best available explanation of your behavior. I know that in my own case pain is caused by bodily damage and also that it causes the sorts of reactions you are having. I take it that a similar causal story holds for you. I have no evidence to the contrary. The pain hypothesis offers a straightforward explanation of your behavior, an explanation better than any other available. So I am justified in embracing it.

What goes for pain goes for other experiences and feelings. Here are two more examples. You are ashen-faced; I take your pulse and find that it is very fast. Your chest is heaving. You keep looking at the door, and you move so that I am in front of you and you are hidden by me from whomever might enter. Patently, you are doing your best to protect yourself. You tell me that there is a man in the next room who is intent on killing you. The best explanation available for your behavior is that you are feeling extreme fear and that you believe that you are in imminent danger.

You are in a room with me. I ask you to walk around it and use your eyesight to pick out as many red things as you can find and put them in the green box in the corner. This you do with great success.

I hypothesize that you want to comply with my request, you believe that placing red objects in the box does so, you believe further with respect to the objects you place in the box that they are red, and you hold this belief on the basis of your visual consciousness of their redness. This again is the best available explanation of your behavior. It adverts in part to your visual consciousness, to what you consciously see.

So far, it seems that there is no difference between these cases and the earlier ones in which experiences and feelings did not directly figure. Unfortunately, appearances can be deceptive. There is a serious complication.

Consider the pain case first. Pain has two aspects to it. On the one hand, there is the unpleasant, subjective felt quality: pains *hurt*. On the other hand, there is the causal role pain plays: pain is a state that is normally caused by bodily damage and normally causes a variety of psychological and physical reactions. For example, it causes bodily tension, attempts to protect the body from the damaging stimulus, the desire that it go away, irritation, distractedness, and anxiety. These two aspects of pain seem distinct from one another, at least to the following extent: we seem to be able to imagine a state—let us call it "ersatz pain"—that has all the usual causes and effects that pain has but that does not feel any way at all. In this way, pain is unlike belief. There is something it is like to feel pain. Pain is an inherently conscious state. But there is nothing it is like to have a belief, although, of course, given beliefs may immediately prompt other psychological states that do have a felt quality to them. For example, my belief that I am about to die may trigger in me an immediate experience of fear, and the latter state certainly has a subjective, felt aspect to it. The reason that there is nothing it is like to have a belief is that beliefs are not inherently conscious states. As I noted earlier, we retain many beliefs even when we are unconscious.

One alternative way I might explain your "pain" behavior, then, as I see you bloodied by your broken bike, is to hypothesize that you are undergoing ersatz pain and that is causing your behavior.[5] This explains

---

5. By your "pain" behavior here, I do not mean behavior caused by pain but rather behavior of a sort that competent users of the term "pain" take to be associated with pain in prototypical cases.

the facts as well as the hypothesis that you are in pain, and in one way it is simpler than the latter hypothesis, for it eschews the additional supposition that your state has a felt, subjective quality to it. So isn't *this* overall the best available explanation of your behavior? And if so, then isn't it rational to prefer the ersatz pain hypothesis?

Obviously, this argument generalizes. In the "fear" case, I should really believe that you have ersatz fear, and in the "visual consciousness" case, I should really believe that you are ersatz seeing the color of the red things you put in the green box.

This brings me to a second complication. Even if you are experiencing something in each of the above scenarios, why should I suppose that you are experiencing pain and fear and the color red instead of experiencing some other things that function as these experiences do? Take the color case. One hypothesis is that you experience green when I experience red, you experience yellow when I experience blue, you experience orange when I experience bluish-green, and so on, even though you react to these subjective experiences in the same way as I do to mine. This is possible, we may suppose, since your experiences might have been systematically inverted relative to mine from your birth, and you might then have associated your experiences with the same causes and effects that I have always associated with mine. So your experience of green is normally caused by red things and normally causes you to believe that they are red and to call them "red" and to sort them with other red things just as my experience of red does for me. Let us call this the inverted experience hypothesis.[6] What justifies me in accepting the same experience hypothesis? Why is it rational to prefer that hypothesis to the inverted experience hypothesis?

Note that the possibility of inversion is not applicable in the case of belief. Even if your experiences are inverted relative to mine, when you see a fire engine, say, you don't believe that it is green. You believe that it is red, just as I do. After all, you are a member of the same linguistic community as me; you learned color words in the same way as me. You are happy to defer to others if they all agree on the color of something

6. This hypothesis has a long history, dating back at least to John Locke in the eighteenth century.

and you initially disagree—if, say, you count something as red and everyone else says that it is slightly orange. Further, if you were later somehow to discover that your experience is inverted relative to the rest of us—perhaps you find out that inverting lenses were placed in your eyes at your birth and later you had an operation on your visual system to remove the lenses—you wouldn't say afterward, "I used to believe that fire engines were green, but now I believe that they are red." You believed that they were red all along. That's why then *and* now you say that fire engines are red.

What underlies these examples is what was called in chapter 1 "the apparent unbridgeability of the objective-subjective divide." Since no objective definition can be given of experience or of what it is like to undergo any specific experience, a gap exists between my knowledge of the objective facts for other humans and my knowledge of their subjective experiences. Consistent with my knowledge of the objective facts, I may hold that others are zombies, totally lacking experiences, or that if they have experiences, their experiences are inverted relative to mine. Moreover, these hypotheses are not more complex than the hypothesis that others are pretty much like me with respect to having experiences and also with respect to how their experiences "feel" subjectively. So how can they be ruled out?

Consider again the case of pain and the hypothesis that after your bicycle accident, you are undergoing a state that has no horrible felt quality to it—indeed, no felt quality at all. This state, nonetheless, was caused in this instance by bodily damage, as it normally is, and further causes all the various characteristic non-subjective effects of pain. Call the conjunction of these causal-functional qualities F, and call the felt quality of my pains Q. Your state, then, has F but lacks Q or any other felt quality. My state has both Q and F.

A question now arises: Why does my state have Q? Pain obviously is not a state that needs learning or culture to acquire. I am simply built so that from a very early age I experience pain. Why did Mother Nature see to it that I experienced Q? Why not just make me an ersatz pain feeler like you? What was added by having me experience Q or anything at all for that matter? Even without Q, so long as my state has F, I will behave just as you do in response to the same noxious stimuli.

It appears, then, that the hypothesis that you undergo ersatz pain is not as good an explanation of the facts as the hypothesis that you experience pain just as I do, for the former hypothesis generates a further explanatory puzzle with respect to me that the latter hypothesis does not. This puzzle is created by what was supposed to be a virtue of the ersatz pain hypothesis over the pain hypothesis, namely, its relative simplicity. We now see that this "simplicity" comes at a real explanatory cost. So, all things considered, the pain hypothesis is the best explanation after all.

There is a further point. As noted earlier, pain feels bad. That is why people in pain do their best to get rid of it, why in the first instance they want it to go away. Suppose that other people do not experience pain—indeed, more strongly, that the state they are in does not feel any way to them. Then why do they want that state to go away? It won't do to say that they want not to be in any state that is bad for them, and they believe that this state is bad for them, so on this basis they form the desire not to be in the given state. If there were reasoning of this sort going on, it would manifest itself in appropriate behavior (just as it would in you), and there is no such behavior. Nor is it plausible to suppose that in others the connection between the state they are in and the desire that it cease is automatic, something like a reflex. We don't always want our pains to go away. Suppose, for example, the pain I am suffering is the result of my having grabbed my beloved by her arms as she accidentally fell out of a tenth-story window, and she is now holding on to my hands for dear life. There is a clear sense in which I want the pain to continue until help arrives, for if I let go and the pain stops, the anguish I'll then suffer will be much worse. Moreover, if the connection were like a reflex, then functionally ersatz pain would not be just like real pain, as we are supposing.

The general point here is that if in someone else there is a mental state that tends to trigger the desire that it cease, we still would like a satisfying explanation as to why it does so. With pain, there is such an explanation. Pain feels bad. That's why it gives rise to the desire that it go away. But ersatz pain doesn't feel bad. It doesn't feel any way at all. So what is it about it that explains why it tends to trigger the desire that it cease? No satisfying explanation is forthcoming. What we have here, it seems, is a new explanatory gap.

Perhaps it will be replied that ersatz pain, like pain, has the function of indicating tissue damage. This functional feature explains why it causes the desire that it cease and also the desire to move away from the damaging stimulus. But if this feature is distinct from the felt quality of pain, as it must be in order for ersatz pain to lack any phenomenology, then why should that feature in you cause your desires when it does not do so in me? (In me, it is the felt quality that causes my desire that pain cease, my attempt to move my body away, and so on.)

The defender of the ersatz pain hypothesis may now respond by adopting a further auxiliary hypothesis, namely, that Q and other phenomenal (that is, subjective, felt) qualities are epiphenomenal: they have no causal power. On this view, Q is generated in me by some combination of underlying neural and physical facts, a combination that is lacking in you, but Q itself makes no difference to how I behave or react (or any other physical effect for that matter). What really explains my behavior is the underlying neurophysiology and the functional role F my state plays, just as it does in you. The difference between us is simply that my state tokens the causally inert Q, whereas yours does not.

As a partial illustration of what is involved in the case of a quality that is causally inert in producing a manifest effect, consider the case (due to Fred Dretske) of a soprano who is singing an aria and mouthing words in German that mean "I love you." The sounds she produces cause a wine glass placed on a table just offstage to shatter. These sounds have a variety of properties: for example, a certain pitch, a certain volume, and a certain semantic property. In virtue of which of its properties do the sounds cause the wine glass to shatter?

Not the semantic property, evidently. If German had developed differently so that the sounds she produced had meant "I hate you" or "Lo, a stranger approaches," the wine glass would still have shattered. The relevant properties are the pitch and volume. It is in virtue of *these* properties that the sounds cause the wine glass to shatter. The semantic property is causally inert in this instance (though not elsewhere, of course, as, for example, when Sally smiles widely at Tom as a result of his saying to her, "I love you").

The suggestion, then, is that Q plays the same role with respect to my pain behavior as the above semantic property does with respect to the shattering of the wine glass, namely, no role at all. It merely seems to me that Q has an effect here in the way it seems to the audience in a movie theater that the one actor on screen has hit another when the second actor falls down. In reality, appearances are deceptive: the falling down is coordinated without a genuine blow ever being landed.

The proposal that Q is causally inert with respect to my pain behavior encounters a number of difficulties. First, notwithstanding what has been said above, it simply isn't credible. Generalized, the hypothesis is that nothing I ever experience or feel makes any difference to how I behave. Even if I had experienced nothing whatsoever, I would have behaved just as I actually behave. That is preposterous. I avoid damaging stimuli because they *hurt*. I eat dark chocolate and I drink Burgundy wine because of the way they subjectively *taste*. I enjoy horror movies because I like *feeling* scared (in certain restricted contexts). I have painted my dining room red rather than brownish yellow because I prefer the way it *looks* to me when red, and so on. Further, it is plausible to hold that when we feel pain, we actually *experience* the subjective character of the pain compelling us to behave in certain ways, just as it is plausible to suppose that we *experience* the wave eating away at the sand as we stand on the beach watching the wave crash against the beach and the sand being dragged into the water. To be sure, error is possible. Things are not always as we experience them to be. But in ordinary life we are entitled to believe that things are as we experience them as being unless we have evidence to the contrary.[7]

Secondly, the proposal is ad hoc. It is put forward with no independent motivation: its rationale is simply that it saves the initial hypothesis. Thirdly, if Q, unlike the semantic property of the soprano's words, is causally inert across the board, then it cannot be a physical quality, for

---

7. The sort of entitlement I have in mind here is one that, in Crispin Wright's words, "we do not have to do any specific evidential work to earn" (2004). This is also the sort of entitlement or warrant that the dogmatist (Pryor 2000) claims we have with respect to the ordinary view of ourselves as living in a material world, the character of which is made manifest to us by our sense organs. According to the dogmatist, given the absence of a good reason to disbelieve this view, we are warranted in believing that such is our situation. My point is simply that this holds true with respect to experience in the pain case, as indicated above.

the physical qualities of my internal state certainly do contribute to its downstream physical effects, internal and external. So there is a further metaphysical complexity.

Perhaps it will now be replied that Q should be taken to be a physical quality. My internal state has Q since it has the relevant physical quality, P, and Q is identical with P. Your state does not, since your state lacks that physical quality and has another, P'. The result is that I experience pain and you undergo ersatz pain. Q in me, then, is causally efficacious after all. Q, for example, causes me to cry out, to nurse my damaged limb, and so on. Some other physical quality of your ersatz pain state does all that in you. This proposal, it may be urged, is just as simple as the pain hypothesis, and it explains all the pertinent facts just as well. So it just isn't true that the pain hypothesis is the best explanation of your behavior.

The trouble with this alternative view is threefold. To begin with, the ersatz pain hypothesis is certainly now no simpler than the pain hypothesis. In you, it is supposed, there is a physical quality P' that plays role F, and P' is not a phenomenally conscious quality. In me, there is a different physical quality, P, that plays role F, and P is a phenomenally conscious quality. Indeed, the ersatz pain hypothesis is not only *not* simpler, it is actually more complex. It posits two *kinds* of causes, a phenomenally conscious one (in me) and a non-phenomenally conscious one in you, whereas the pain hypothesis posits just one kind of cause, a phenomenally conscious one in both of us.[8] This is not only unmotivated; it also goes against considerations of parsimony standardly employed in evolutionary biology with respect to the attribution of character states to creatures with common ancestors (Sober 2000).[9] Secondly, the ersatz pain hypothesis introduces a lack of uniformity in the cases without any evidence of a difference. This is ad hoc.

As a way of bringing this out further, consider a scientist who explains the tracks in his cloud chamber by appealing to electrons as the cause but who, when asked to explain the tracks elsewhere in other

---

8. This was true of the ersatz pain hypothesis even before it was supposed that Q is a physical quality.

9. For more on this, see the next chapter.

cloud chambers, adopts the view that they are caused by schelectrons, where schelectrons differ in certain intrinsic properties from electrons but have the same pattern of causes and effects. Suppose that scientists generally agree that there are electrons and there is no reason whatsoever to introduce schelectrons *as well as* electrons among the causes of the relevant cloud chamber tracks. Surely, in adopting the schelectron hypothesis for other cloud chambers while retaining the electron hypothesis for his cloud chamber, the scientist is behaving irrationally. There is no evidence of a lack of uniformity in the cases and no independent explanatory virtue possessed by the electron *and* schelectron view over the electron-only view.

Here is a further example. Let us grant that we have unimpeachable evidence of the existence of water. Let us grant also that it is conceivable that there is some other substance, XYZ, that has all the same manifest properties as water even though chemically it is very different. There is no reason whatsoever to believe that there actually is XYZ, but the hypothesis that in the Himalayan mountains there is XYZ is a hypothesis that, if true, explains the observed facts about the colorless, tasteless, odorless, drinkable liquid that fills lakes, makes up glaciers, covers mountains, and falls from the sky in the Himalayas as does the hypothesis that there is only water with these properties throughout the globe. Still, were a scientist to propose without any evidence that there is water everywhere except in the Himalayas but only XYZ there, he would be laughed at. Why?

The answer is that multiple entities have been posited when one would do, and the second entity, XYZ, has been introduced without any evidence motivating it. So the explanation of the manifest watery properties found in all regions of the earth by reference to water *and* XYZ is not the best available explanation. The hypothesis that there is only water does better. That is the hypothesis it is rational for us to accept.

Returning now to the case of pain, the immediate upshot is that it is rational for me to accept the pain hypothesis over the ersatz pain hypothesis, and likewise for the corresponding hypotheses for the other cases of fear and the visual consciousness of red. These hypotheses offer the best explanation of human behavior.

There are other facts the pain hypothesis explains besides behavior of a sort that is known to all competent users of the term "pain" that should lead us to prefer that hypothesis to the ersatz pain hypothesis. Consider the effects of morphine and other opiate drugs. In my own case, I know that these relieve pain, and I know that they do so by acting on my nervous system, specifically by silencing nerves in the spinal cord that carry signals from my nociceptors (receptors throughout my body that respond to noxious stimuli). I know that you are a human being like me with a brain much like mine and that you have a physically similar nociceptor system (or at least I can find this out easily enough). I also know that the behavior that in me is a manifestation of severe pain is greatly diminished by taking morphine. Finally, I know that corresponding behavior in response to tissue damage is similarly diminished in you. I have no reason to suppose that your nociceptive system does not produce any feeling, no evidence whatsoever that there is any difference between you and me in the processing of noxious stimuli. So here I have further justification for accepting the view that the pain hypothesis applies not just to me but to you too. That is a better explanation than the ersatz pain hypothesis.

But is it also rational to accept the pain hypothesis over a hypothesis that postulates that in you there is a phenomenally conscious state that feels very different from mine even though it has the same biological function and the same causes and effects?

Yes it is, and for exactly the same reasons as it is rational to prefer the pain hypothesis to the ersatz pain one. The hypothesis that there is one phenomenal quality in me that causes groaning, bodily tension, withdrawal behavior, etc., and a different phenomenal quality in you that has these effects is more complex, and it is ad hoc. A difference is postulated without any evidence, without any reason to suppose that there is a difference.

In the case of color experience, the inverted experience hypothesis for you faces the same problem. Furthermore, there is likely evidence that goes concretely against this hypothesis. Here is why. There are more discriminable shades of green than red. So if I am looking at a green leaf against a minimally different green background and your experiences are inverted relative to mine, it may well be that in some instances of such a scenario you will experience the leaf and the background as having the same shade of red. So for you the leaf will not pop out from the background, whereas for me it will. So there will be a striking difference in our behavior. Were we to find such a difference in your behavior, that would be grounds to suppose that you experience red where I experience green and so to adopt the inverted experience hypothesis. But if you behave as I do, the inverted experience hypothesis is ad hoc and unnecessarily complex.[10] The same experience hypothesis then wins again as the best available explanation, and that is the hypothesis we should adopt.

My final conclusion, then, is that it *is* rational for me to accept that you feel pain when I see you bloodied by your broken bike, for it provides the best available explanation of your behavior. What goes for pain goes for fear and the visual consciousness of red. Indeed, it goes for feelings and experiences generally. The view that my friends and neighbors have experiences and feelings much like mine is *worthy* of acceptance—I am justified in accepting it—for the very same reasons that the generalizations of a scientific theory connecting unobservable entities to observable ones are worthy of acceptance. They have explanatory and predictive success; moreover, no other theory or network of generalizations does better. In very odd cases, for example, the Martian marionette or the individual with the "game of life" silicon chip, I make a mistake in attributing a mental life to another. Even so, I am not epistemically blameworthy. If something looks like a duck, walks like a duck, and quacks like a duck, without evidence to the contrary, I am justified in supposing that it is a duck.

There is one final complication that I have ignored thus far, which needs discussion. The conclusion I have drawn in the case of

---

10. Here is another problem for the inverted experience hypothesis. If you are shown two disks, one blue and one yellow, both with the same saturation, and you are asked to point at the one with the brighter color, you will point at the blue disk if the inverted experience hypothesis is true. But in actual fact, you won't do this (at least if you are like me)—you'll point instead to the yellow disk. So the inverted experience hypothesis does not do as well at explaining the behavioral facts as the same experience hypothesis.

pain—namely, that it is rational for me to accept that you are feeling pain when I am presented with certain behavioral evidence, since that hypothesis provides the best available explanation of your behavior—needs further clarification. The worry I have in mind here is this: a hypothesis may offer the best available explanation of a given set of data, and so it may be rational for me to *prefer* that hypothesis to any other even though it is not rational for me to *believe* it outright. Let me explain.

Given that one believes a claim just in case one is sufficiently confident of its truth, it is rational for one to believe that P just in case it is rational for one to have a degree of confidence sufficient for belief (Foley 2009). Whatever that level of confidence is, call it L. Suppose now that my level of confidence in hypothesis 1 is below L but greater than my level of confidence in hypothesis 2. Then it is rational for me to prefer hypothesis 1 to 2 so long as it is rational for me to have those levels of confidence, but it is not rational for me to believe hypothesis 1 outright.[11]

In the case of pain, then, we may wonder (a) whether it is rational for me, in believing that you are feeling pain, to have the degree of confidence I do in the hypothesis that you are feeling pain, and (b) whether it is rational for me to have *more* confidence in that hypothesis than in the hypothesis that you are not feeling pain. The claim that will play a key role in my discussion of other species in subsequent chapters is that to the extent that what I believe in believing that you are feeling pain provides the best available explanation of the behavioral data, it is rational for me to *prefer* the hypothesis that you are feeling pain to the hypothesis that you are not feeling pain and so to accept the former hypothesis, even if that acceptance is somewhat tentative (and so falls below the level of confidence required for belief outright). It follows from this that if I believe that you are not feeling pain on the basis of that data, I have an irrational belief and am myself, to this extent, irrational.

---

11. Suppose I am playing roulette. There are thirty-eight possible numbers the ball can land on, 1–36, 0, and 00. Obviously, it is rational for me to prefer the hypothesis that the ball will land on a number greater than 16 (there are twenty possibilities) to the hypothesis that the ball will not land on such a number (there are eighteen possibilities, 0–16 plus 00). But it is not obviously rational for me to believe that the ball will land on a number greater than 16. The odds are too close for that.

[5]

REASONING ABOUT
OTHER SPECIES

The problem of Other experiences is fairly straightforward for human beings, as we have seen. When we turn to the case of nonhuman animals, the situation is much more complicated. What makes it so is that many nonhuman creatures have brains that differ from ours in fairly dramatic ways. These differences threaten the viability of the reasoning used in the last chapter with respect to other human beings, for, given the neural differences, it is clear that the causal story behind my/our behavior will not be duplicated in them at the neurological level.

5.1 CUPCAKE'S PAIN

Consider again the case of pain. When I see you apparently in pain, witnessing your behavior, I assume that the same causal story applies to you as applies to me when I exhibit that behavior. So I take it for granted that you are feeling pain. I am justified in holding this view since, lacking any evidence that you are internally any different from me, I am entitled to reason from sameness of effect to sameness of cause.[1] This provides the simplest, most unified explanation of our common behavior. Of course, you might be dissembling, but I have no evidence that this is the case,

---

1. It is not being claimed here that I in fact go through any conscious reasoning when I witness your behavior and take you to be in pain—nor does there even need to be any commitment to unconscious reasoning here either.

and the hypothesis that you are dissembling and so in a different mental state is patently inferior to the shared pain hypothesis.

Now suppose that Other is not you but my dog, Cupcake. Am I entitled to reason from sameness of effect to sameness of cause in the same way? Here I know that Cupcake belongs to another species, and so I have evidence available to me that there is a potentially significant difference between us. On the other hand, we also have a lot in common neurophysiologically. So considerations of parsimony of a sort standardly used in biology count in favor of supposing that Cupcake undergoes the same mental state as me when she undergoes the same behavior. This is worth developing a little further (following Sober 2000).

Let Other be any dog exhibiting the same manifest "pain" behavior B as me.[2] There are two possible hypotheses: that Other is in pain and that Other is subject to some alternative internal mechanism (call it A). At the root of our shared ancestral tree, the behavior is missing, and the internal state is neither pain nor A (see figure 5.1 below). One possibility is that the posited mental similarity between Self and Other is a homology. That is, it is possible that the most recent ancestor we share also felt pain and that this state was transmitted unchanged to us, the descendants. On this view, there is only one change in the tree—from neither pain nor A to pain. On the alternative hypothesis, there are (at least) two changes, from neither pain nor A to pain in me and from neither pain nor A to A in Other. Ceteris paribus, then, parsimony favors anthropomorphism (De Waal 1991).

2. More on "pain" behavior below. Obviously, I do not mean by "pain behavior" behavior that is caused by pain. That would beg the question in the present context.

However, what if ceteris is not paribus? What if Other is an animal that shares an ancestor with me but differs from me at the neurophysiological level in very fundamental ways? Here the situation is a lot less clear. On the one hand, there is the everyday psychological explanation of Other's behavior. On the other, there is the fact that the neurophysiological story of what produces Other's behavior does not mesh at all well with the neurophysiological story of what produces mine.

5.2 SHARPENING THE ISSUE

Take the case of pain. Pain in me has both a distinctive set of behaviors resulting from it, some manifesting themselves later in time (as, for example, in my shying away from stimuli that have caused me pain in the past and in my behaving more cautiously and defensively shortly after having felt pain from an unknown cause), and a distinctive set of causes, most obviously tissue damage of one sort or another. It also has an impact on other mental states. For example, it normally causes anxiety; it distracts; and it causes the desire that it cease. These other psychological changes have behavioral effects. Consider the class of such causes and effects, as they are at least tacitly known to any ordinary person who is competent in the use of the term "pain." Suppose that Other behaves very much as I would in a range of situations in which I am feeling pain or I did previously as a result of tissue damage even though neurologically Other is very different from me. Should I attribute the feeling of pain to Other?

In my own case and that of other humans, the behavior that I explain when I attribute the state of pain in response to an encounter with a noxious stimulus S is not a specific bodily movement or complex of such movements. Rather, it is behavior that can be *realized* by a whole range of different bodily movements, such as the following: protecting/guarding part of the body damaged by S; withdrawing from stimulus S unless there is a strong need/desire for something else that requires enduring S (trade-off behavior);[3] decreased feeding; irritable and aggressive

---

3. An example of trade-off behavior is enduring the pain from a dentist's drill in order to get the long-term benefit of healthy teeth. Another example is holding on to a very hot

behavior (increasing with severity of noxious stimulus S); physical signs of stress; and avoiding (or behaving warily toward) other stimuli that have become associated with S.[4] Call this cluster of behaviors B.

What explains the specific movements? Answer: the detailed neurophysiological story. The two explanations are not automatically at odds, even though they are very different, for they operate at different levels and explain different things. The natural picture, then, in broad outline for me and Other, is roughly as follows:

In me:

Psychological level: the feeling of pain   -------->   Behavior B

Neural level: Neural states N, N' . . .   -------->   Bodily movement M

In Other:

Psychological level: ???   -------->   Behavior B

Neural level: Neural states O, O' . . .   -------->   Bodily movement M'

The question to be answered is this: Does my finding out that things are neurophysiologically importantly different in Other give me a good reason to deny that Other was feeling pain and thus to deny also that Other's behavior B occurred because Other was feeling pain? If it doesn't, then my original explanation of Other's behavior still stands as the best available: Other was indeed feeling pain.

Sir Isaac Newton formulated a rule (Rule 2) that helps to clarify further the dialectic here. He said: "The causes assigned to natural effects of the same kind must be, as far as possible, the same" (*Rules for the Study of Natural Philosophy* in the third book of his *Principia*). Thomas Reid

---

plate full of food when one is hungry, when one would have dropped the plate had it been empty.

4. When I used the term "pain behavior" earlier, I had in mind behavior of this sort, manifest behavior that we tacitly associate with pain in prototypical cases.

said something similar. In *Essays on the Intellectual Powers of Man*, he comments:

> As there are words common to philosophers and to the vulgar, which need no explication, so there are principles common to both, which need no proof, and which do not admit of direct proof. . . .
>
> *That similar effects proceed from the same or similar causes;* That we ought to admit of no other causes of natural effects, but such as are true, and sufficient to account for the effects. These are principles which, though they have not the same kind of evidence that mathematical axioms have; yet have such evidence that every man of common understanding readily assents to them, and finds it absolutely necessary to conduct his actions and opinions by them. (Reid 2002, ch. 2)

Newton's (and Reid's) basic idea was this: if a cause is assigned to an effect of a given kind, then if you assign different causes to other effects of that kind, you are introducing "superfluous causes." Neither Newton nor Reid explicitly includes a ceteris paribus or "other things being equal" clause. But it seems obvious that such a qualification is needed. Perhaps Newton had this in mind in adding "as far as possible" in Rule 2. Let me illustrate Newton's Rule (as I shall call it) first with respect to a case that has nothing to do with the mind.

Suppose that of the people I know, all who have contracted lung cancer were smokers, and smoking caused their cancer. I read that Jones, whom I don't know personally, has lung cancer. The simplest and most unified explanation of the condition Jones shares with the people I know is that he was a smoker and that smoking caused his cancer too. Another hypothesis: smoking caused the lung cancer found in the people I know and something *other than* smoking caused lung cancer in Jones's case. Which hypothesis is it rational for me to prefer, or is it rational for me not to prefer either (to be agnostic)?

Newton's Rule, as I understand it, entails that, ceteris paribus, I should prefer the simpler, more unified hypothesis. So, ceteris paribus, I should prefer the hypothesis that Jones was a smoker too. Now in this case, obviously ceteris is not paribus. Other things are not equal. I know that there are other fairly common causes of lung cancer besides smok-ing, for example, exposure to asbestos. This additional information *defeats* preference for the simpler hypothesis. Given this information, I should be agnostic.

The general point is that I am entitled to infer sameness of cause from sameness of effect in both the new case and the old ones, *unless I have evidence that defeats the inference*. In the above case I do. In effect, the princi-ple that Newton is applying is inference to the best available explanation, as elaborated in the last chapter, for where there is a common effect, the simplest, most unified hypothesis is that there is a common cause unless I have evidence that undermines the inference to a common cause.

However, the entitlement granted only gives me rational grounds to *prefer* the hypothesis that there is sameness of cause to its denial. It doesn't automatically give me grounds to *believe* the simpler hypothesis outright—the same-cause one. That will depend on whether the level of confidence in the simpler hypothesis suffices for belief,[5] and that may be influenced by a range of factors, including context and the cost of being wrong.[6]

The fact that the standards for rational preference are lower than those for rational belief is potentially important. For if in the case of pain it is rational for me to prefer the hypothesis that a given nonhu-man animal feels pain to the hypothesis that, unlike humans, it does not, then arguably it is rational for me to behave in certain ways toward the animal even if it is not rational for me to believe simpliciter that it feels pain. The connection between rational preference and behavior is not straightforward, however. To illustrate: it's rational for me to prefer the hypothesis that you will throw an even number with the dice to the hypothesis that you will throw a 6.[7] But that doesn't make it rational for me to act as if you would throw an even number (e.g., by placing a large bet I can ill afford on that outcome).[8] So more needs to be said here. The topic of how we should treat nonhuman animals will occupy us later in chapter 11.

---

5. See chapter 4, p. 68.
6. For more on context and cost, see pp. 211–212.
7. It isn't rational for me to believe that you will throw an even number, however, since the odds are 50/50.
8. I owe this example to Mark Sainsbury.

These points find direct application with respect to human and non-human animal behavior. Suppose as above that humans and nonhuman animals engage in the same or very similar behavior B, as summarized earlier, given the same noxious stimulus S. Why do humans produce behavior B, given S? Because S elicits the feeling of pain in them, and the feeling of pain causes B. There is, of course, no inconsistency involved in denying the latter causal claim. But, as noted in the last chapter, to do so is to go against what we all believe with respect to one another. It is a truism that we want to get rid of pain and that we behave in ways that reduce or eliminate it *because* of how it feels. It seems equally obvious that the felt character of pain distracts us so that it is difficult to give our full attention to other things.

Turning now to the case of nonhuman animals, I am entitled to infer that the feeling of pain causes behavior B in them too unless I have a *defeater* to that inference, that is, a reason to believe that a causal story is operative in those animals that cannot be reconciled with the causal story that adverts to pain. It follows that the existence of neurophysiological differences between the nonhuman animals and humans, and thus a different causal story at the neurophysiological level, does not threaten the common-cause story that adverts to pain, unless there is reason to accept that pain is not present, given those neurophysiological differences.[9]

Perhaps it will be replied that it *could* be that in the nonhuman animals, another state is present causing B, a state that lacks any felt character even though it functions in the very same way as pain—ersatz pain, as named earlier. This misses the point. It is certainly conceivable that ersatz pain elicits B in the relevant nonhuman animals, but the question is whether it actually does so. Supposing that in actual fact ersatz pain is responsible for B in some cases leaves us with a more complex explanation of the common behavior B than the explanation that adverts to the common cause, pain. Further, it generates a puzzle: if ersatz pain produces B in the relevant nonhuman animals, then why didn't Mother Nature content herself simply with making human beings subjects

---

9. These neural differences will result in different specific bodily movements (ceteris paribus). However, those bodily movements will be instances of B, and that common behavior will be the result of the same experience (again ceteris paribus).

of ersatz pain too? What was the point of making us pain *feelers*?[10] It appears, then, that the pain/ersatz pain explanation of B is not as good as the pain explanation, unless, of course, some reason can be adduced for denying that pain itself is part of the causal story for the nonhuman animals. That is what matters for present purposes.

Here is an example involving computers that may be helpful. Suppose that computer A works electronically and that it shows the number 32 on its screen after the 4 and 8 keys have been pressed. Computer B also shows the number 32 on its screen given the same input. You do not see what other keys are pressed, if any, but you form the hypothesis that both A and B are computing the product of 4 and 8. You then witness a number of other pairs of inputs and outputs for those inputs, all consistent with that hypothesis, again without seeing if other keys are pressed as well. You know that computer A works electronically. You are then told by a reliable source that B is unusual: it is a prototype of a new hydraulic computer designed by Elon Musk. Do you now have a good reason to treat the two computers *differently* and hold that while A is computing the product of two numbers, B is performing some other computation? Obviously not. The difference in hardware and design origin does not in itself provide any real evidence that the same computation is not being performed in both computers. The point here is that one and the same computation can be realized in any number of different ways physically. So the mere existence of physical differences does not in itself give us any reason to treat A and B differently at the computational level. So it is rational for us to prefer the hypothesis that A and B are both computing the product of the input numbers to the hypothesis that A is computing the product of the input numbers and B is performing some other unspecified computation that happens to coincide in its outputs for the observed range of cases.

The question to be addressed, then, is whether the neurophysiological differences between nonhuman animals and humans, *given the relevant shared behavior*, provide a genuine defeater to the inference, sanctioned by Newton's Rule, that there is a shared experience or feeling. The next section in this chapter is concerned with one specific

---

10. Take the case of fish. It is not as if we require a conscious jerk and fish don't. We are much smarter than fish.

neurophysiological difference that is often cited as supplying such a defeater.

Before I turn to this, let me close this section by responding to two general objections that have been raised to the methodology I am proposing. The first is that we cannot attribute even remotely the same behaviors to creatures such as crabs and bees that we do to mammals without either anthropomorphizing or begging the question, and so we cannot begin to apply Newton's Rule to their case. The second objection is that it is unclear whether Newton's Rule is true when applied to the behavior of living creatures/animals.

I find neither of these objections convincing. When we describe the bodily movements of human beings, one way we can do so is by specifying the physical details of the movements themselves through space— their speed, their direction, which limb is moving, and so on. We can also use specifically intentional language, for example, hailing a taxi or running toward safety. The first way of describing bodily movements is nearly always individual-specific: you and I, even when performing the same intentional action, rarely move our bodies in exactly the same first-order physical manner. The second mode of description has packed into it the assumption that the movement has an internal, mental (intentional) cause. There is a third way of describing bodily movements that is both general and does not presuppose a mental cause. We can say that a given individual is engaging in *a* bodily movement that tends to bring it about that so-and-so is the case. This mode of description allows you and me to engage in the same movement even though the movements of our limbs through space are different. For example, when Jones is hailing a taxi, it is also true that Jones engages in a bodily movement that tends to bring it about that a taxi stops by him if there are taxis nearby. And that can be true of me too even if I wave my arm in a different manner from Jones.

This third mode of description is unproblematically applicable to nonhuman species even when their first-order bodily movements are very different from ours; furthermore, the usage of it does not beg the question against those who doubt that members of the species have experiences. Thus, earlier, when I described behavior *B*, which is produced in typical cases by the feeling of pain in us, the terminology I used— protecting the body, guarding it, moving away from the damaging stimulus, etc.—should be understood in the third way. On this understanding, a creature protects its body from further damage, for example, so long as it engages in bodily movements that tend to bring it about that the body is not harmed further if damaging stimuli are nearby. So understood, it should be clear that the mere fact that some nonhuman creatures are physically very different from us does not entail that we are either anthropomorphizing or begging the question if and when we attribute the same behavior to them.

As for the second objection, to deny that Newton's Rule is applicable to living creatures is ad hoc. The rule is entirely general. It is another way of expressing the view that we are entitled to prefer hypothesis H to its denial so long as H provides the best available explanation of the observable phenomena. And it would be strange indeed to say that inference to the best explanation is a poor form of inference as applied to living creatures. As noted earlier, the entitlement we have to the view that other humans have experiences similar to our own seems best understood as resting upon the application of this inference.

5.3 IS THE ABSENCE OF A NEOCORTEX A DEFEATER?

In humans, in standard cases, the sensory aspect of pain is generated by activity in the primary and secondary somatosensory cortices of the parietal lobe (SI and SII). The unpleasantness of pain—what we might call its "felt badness"—is closely tied to activity in the anterior cingulate cortex (ACC). Human functional imaging studies show that there is a significant correlation between the felt badness of pain and ACC activation (Devinsky, Morrell, and Vogt 1995; Rainville et al. 1997). Further, when subjects feel pain from a stimulus that is held constant and a hypnotic suggestion is used to increase or decrease subjective unpleasantness, a correlation is found in regional cerebral blood flow in ACC but not in the primary somatosensory cortex (Fields 1999). Also, patients with ACC lesions say that their pain is "less bothersome."

If regions of SI and SII are damaged but not ACC, what results is an unpleasant sensation that is not pain. For example, a laser was used to deliver a thermal stimulus to a fifty-seven-year-old man with most of his SI damaged as a result of a stroke (Ploner, Freund, and Schnitzler 1999). When the stimulus significantly above normal threshold on the right hand was delivered to his left hand, the man reported an unpleasant sensation, but he denied that it was a case of pain.[11]

It appears, then, that the painfulness of pain in humans is based on activity in two different neural regions: the somatosensory cortex (comprised of SI and SII) and ACC.

Some animals, such as fish, lack a neocortex. So they lack these regions. This neurophysiological difference, it might be said,[12] makes a crucial difference. A related thought is that the causal story for animals lacking a neocortex that lies behind their behavior of type B cannot be reconciled with the story for humans. So we aren't entitled to infer a common cause, even given common behavior. The neurophysiological difference between the nonhuman animals and humans defeats the explanation of behavior that adverts to pain.

The claim that in humans pain and other experiences require a neocortex is widely accepted. For example, the American Academy of Neurology asserts (1989):

Neurologically, being awake but unaware is the result of a functioning brainstem and the total loss of cerebral cortical functioning.... Pain and suffering are attributes of consciousness requiring cerebral cortical functioning.

The Medical Task Force on Anencephaly (1990) says much the same thing in connection with congenital cases:

Infants with anencephaly, lacking functioning cerebral cortex are permanently unconscious.... The suffering associated with noxious stimuli (pain) is a cerebral interpretation of the stimuli; therefore, infants with anencephaly presumably cannot suffer. (pp. 671–672)

11. Asked to classify his sensation from a list of terms that included "hot," "burning," and "pain," the patient picked none.
12. And has been said. See Rose 2002.

And the Multi-Society Task Force on Persistent Vegetative State (1994a, 1994b) holds that any form of congenital decortication results in a "developmental vegetative state."

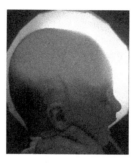

From D. P. Agamanolis, "Neuropathology," http://neuropathologyweb.org. Head of an infant with anencephaly.

These assertions do not sit well with the facts. It certainly seems to be true that adult humans who later in life come to lack a functioning cerebral cortex are then in a vegetative state. But this is not always true for children born without a cerebral cortex. Recently, Bjorn Merker (2007), who spent several weeks with decorticate children and their families, said the following:

> The author's impression from this first-hand exposure to children with hydranencephaly roundly confirms the account given by Shewmon and colleagues. These children are not only awake and often alert, but show responsiveness to their surroundings in the form of emotional or orienting reactions to environmental events . . . , most readily to sounds but also to salient visual stimuli. . . . They express pleasure by smiling and laughter, and aversion by "fussing", arching of the back and crying (in many gradations), their faces being animated by these emotional states. A familiar adult can employ this responsiveness to build up play sequences predictably progressing from smiling, over giggling to laughter and great excitement on the part of the child. The children respond differentially to the voice and initiatives of familiars, and show preferences for certain situations

and stimuli over others, such as a specific familiar toy, tune or video program, and apparently can even come to expect their regular presence in the course of recurrent daily routines. (p. 79)

In this connection, consider the hydroencephalic child described by Shewmon, Holmes, and Byrne (1999, p. 366) below:

> After only a few weeks her mother suspected her daughter could see. Between 4 and 5 months, she began to smile responsively, and thereafter vision was unquestionable. She was evaluated twice around age 2 by an ophthalmologist, who noted that fundi were normal and visual fixation was 'central, steady, and maintained'. . . . [At age five] she . . . tracked faces and toys, and oriented immediately to objects brought into the visual periphery.

Not only did the child track toys as they were moved before her, she would also react to them by smiling and laughing. See figure 5.3 below.

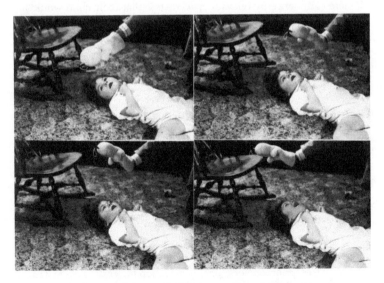

Shewmon, Holmes, and Byrne (1999). Decorticate child tracking the movements of a puppet and apparently showing pleasure.

In addition to displaying pleasure, as here, or at least appearing to do so, decorticate children also sometimes apparently feel pain, by rubbing an area that has been banged or pinched. Certainly, their behavior is nothing like that of children with congenital pain insensitivity (see chapter 9). Notwithstanding the absence of a neocortex, if the child above wasn't visually conscious of the toy, why did she find some of its movements pleasing?

Of course, one response that might be made to such cases is that the children may not have been completely without a cerebral cortex (Watkins and Rees 2007, in reply to Merker 2007). To this Shewmon, Holmes, and Byrne (1999, p. 371) say:

> The main point is that these children's consciousness can be inferred to be mediated subcortically *not* because there were absolutely zero cortical neurons, but because the few that were present could not plausibly subserve the *totality* of their conscious behaviors. That is why parents were invariably told—with complete confidence by relevant specialists—that their child would unquestionably remain in a vegetative state for as long as he or she lived. Experienced neurologists, to whom the authors have shown the CT and MRI scans with an invitation to guess the child's level of functioning, also typically predict vegetative state.

Given that the examples adduced by Merker and Shewmon involve congenital brain malformations, we may wonder whether developmental plasticity underlies the subcortical mediation of consciousness. In this connection, we should note the following comments from Shewmon, Holmes, and Byrne (1999, p. 371):

> The two children with vision despite fetal absence of occipital cortex had brain malformations arising *earlier in gestation* than the two with no vision despite occipital remnants. Presumably in the latter cases, prior to telencephalic infarction the visual system had developed so that relevant subcortical nuclei were already committed to a functional relationship with occipital cortex whereas

in the former the absence of occipital cortex all along allowed these subcortical nuclei "free rein" to organize *optimally* for functional vision.

If such vertical plasticity can occur with vision there is no reason to suppose it cannot also occur to some extent with other sensory and motor modalities *and with their mutual interactions mediating adaptive environmental relatedness*, i.e. *with consciousness.*

It is interesting to note that for those supposedly decorticate children where there is some occipital cortex left, the auditory cortex is almost always completely missing. Yet the vision of the children in these cases is significantly worse than their audition. This fact can be explained straightforwardly using Shewmon's vertical plasticity hypothesis: subcortical nuclei in the auditory case take over the job that would have been done by cells in the auditory cortex had there been any, whereas in the visual case, subcortical nuclei play a subservient role to the remaining cells in the occipital cortex, and the latter cells are typically glyotic or have other functional abnormalities, so vision is poor. A further fact worth noting is that rats that had been surgically decorticated a few days after birth and were subsequently reared by a normal mother seem impaired very little by removal of the cortex (Panksepp et al. 1994). Given the similarity in functional profile, if normal rats are subjects of conscious states, decorticate rats certainly seem to be such subjects too.[13]

13. One of the researchers who reported on these rats said later:

> The thing that stands out, in my memory, is how astonishingly normal these rats were. Without a cerebral cortex, these decorticate rats lacked fine motor control, but in most other respects, they were very similar to normal rats. For instance, we tested them on a test of finding individual pieces of Froot Loops brand cereal that had been hidden in little wells inside a special test chamber. Since they lacked fine motor control, the decorticate rats had trouble picking up the Froot Loops and putting them into their mouths. However, they were pretty good at locating the pieces of cereal. Indeed, I would say that searching for Froot Loops is a purposeful behavior that requires at least some degree of consciousness. It certainly isn't a reflex. If normal rats have consciousness—and there is no reason to think that they don't—then the decorticate rats had plenty of it, too. (Cox 2005)

I should emphasize again that no claim is being made that behavioral similarity *guarantees* similarity in experiences, painful or otherwise. There is no contradiction, no incoherence, in the idea that some creatures that are behaviorally just like creatures having experiences lack them. The point is rather that arguments to the effect that certain nonhuman animals lack a neocortex and that therefore their behavior is not best explained by supposing that they experience pain and a range of other conscious states, since a neocortex is necessary for all forms of consciousness, are unpersuasive. Even restricting ourselves to human beings, there is no good reason to grant the premise that in *all* cases where a neocortex is missing, there is no consciousness. Of course, the case of decorticate children is abnormal, and the range of behavioral responses of which they are capable is *much* more limited than it is for children with a cortex or adults. But they are certainly not all in a vegetative state. Moreover, the range of behavioral responses is limited for severely autistic children or very young children, and no one to my knowledge wants to claim that consciousness is missing in the latter cases.[14]

The conclusion I draw is that while the absence of a neocortex is something to take into account in the application of Newton's Rule to nonhuman animals exhibiting behavior *B*, it does not defeat the inference to the presence of the experience of pain. There is a further point that is worth making here. The absence of a neocortex does not in and of itself entail that cells homologous to those found in the neocortex are missing too. So if there is reason to believe that in certain animals lacking a neocortex there are such cells, this provides us with a further positive reason for supposing that consciousness is present. I shall return to the latter point in the next chapter.

5.4 SHOULD WE BE AGNOSTIC?

It is important to appreciate that the view that other animals are conscious and the view that other animals are not, with further hypotheses

14. I shall return to a discussion of brain structures that are found in place of the neocortex in some nonhuman animals in later chapters.

as to which animals are which, are not the only options with respect to animal consciousness. Another important option is agnosticism. This is the view that for some (maybe all) nonhuman species there is no more reason to say that they have consciousness than not—the matter of consciousness in animals is epistemically indeterminate. This is the line taken by the renowned biologist and animal researcher Marian Stamp Dawkins in her recent book *Why Animals Matter* (2012). She comments:

> Are animals conscious like us because they have many brain structures in common with us, or are they not like us because they lack some crucial pathway that prevents them from going that extra mile into conscious experience? Are they like us but only when we are using an evolutionary old unconscious route, or does a spark of what we would recognize as conscious experience flare in even the oldest of brains? On the basis of what we now know about human consciousness, both of these completely opposite views can be, and indeed have been, put forward as serious hypotheses. The elusiveness of our own consciousness and its infuriating refusal to be tied down to particular neural structures leaves us, at the moment, completely unable to distinguish between these quite opposite views of animal consciousness. (p. 91)

On the basis of her agnostic view, Dawkins goes on to develop a novel theory of animal welfare.

This agnostic attitude is not uncommon among scientists. The thought is that while we can draw conclusions about whether other animals have internal states that function in the ways that our experiences do, we are not entitled to go further and make claims about how those internal states subjectively feel. On this, some say, the only rational view is to remain silent.

I disagree. Consider again the case of other human beings. It is rational for me to prefer the view that you and other human beings undergo similar experiences and feelings to mine over the view that you and they do not, given the similarities in behavior. Agnosticism here seems absurd. But why? Not crucially because I know that you and they undergo the same sorts of neurophysiological processes as me, for even if I had not known this, I would still have been entitled to take the view that other humans experience pretty much what I do. Suppose, for example, I had grown up in a rural society isolated from the usual sources of knowledge. Or take the case of the ancient Greeks. To hold that two thousand years ago when nothing was known about the brain, no one was entitled to suppose that other humans feel fear, grief, anger, and pain; that they have visual experiences, auditory experiences, gustatory experiences, and so on is obviously absurd. What gave the ancient Greeks their entitlement? The answer is that they witnessed the behavior of their fellows, and, *lacking* a defeater, that is, a good reason to suppose that the behavior they shared with others was *not* the product of a common cause, they were entitled to hold that others had similar experiences.

The question that is relevant for other nonhuman animals, therefore, is this: Do we have a reason to suppose that the neural differences we discover defeat our inference to a common subjective cause as producing the behavior they share with us? If we don't, then the similarities in behavior and functioning, to the extent that they exist, justify us in holding that the animals have such-and-such states of consciousness. On this understanding of the epistemology of the situation, Dawkins is wrong. Lacking evidence that neural differences make a difference, we should not be agnostics but rather liberals about consciousness. We should take consciousness to be just where it appears to be, given the behavior and functioning. Again, it is certainly conceivable that this is not the case, that nonhuman animals are zombies. But conceivability is one thing; what it is rational for us to believe or prefer about what is actually the case is another.

5.5 ALTERNATIVE STRATEGIES

In chapter 2, I noted that some philosophers and scientists think that a fruitful way to proceed on the question of animal consciousness is via an investigation of their metacognition. If animals behave in ways that indicate that they have a cognitive grasp on how things appear to them, and not just on how they are, then the obvious conclusion is that things really do appear to them in various ways. And if things *appear* to them, then the animals must be conscious of those things—they must *experience* them. This is a strategy proposed by Shea and Heyes (2010) and also by Allen and Bekoff (1997). What would count as evidence that an animal has a cognitive grasp on how things appear to it? A complex form of behavior providing such evidence would be using appearances to deceive other animals. A simpler form of behavior would be recognizing how something visually appears color-wise (where that appearance is different from the customary and real color of the thing) and matching the appearance to the real color of something else in order to get a reward.

This seems to me a worthwhile and important field of research. However, it is important to be clear about what it shows. If a positive result is obtained, then that is evidence that the animal is indeed conscious. But if a negative result ensues, what follows is only that higher-order consciousness has not been found. And that is perfectly compatible with the existence of first-order consciousness—feelings such as pain, experiences such as the visual experience of red, etc. As already noted, no one wants to claim that a one-year-old child cannot feel pain because it is incapable of cognizing its state *as* painful.[15] That sophistication does not come until later.

The general point is this. Metacognition research proceeds via an investigation of animal behavior. This is what I am suggesting too. However, the behavior focused upon in metacognition studies is that produced with respect to tasks requiring relative cognitive sophistication (most generally, certain sorts of problem-solving behavior).[16] My proposal is less restrictive. For each of our feelings and experiences, there is a cluster of behaviors that are standardly or prototypically produced. These behaviors can be described at a number of levels—in terms

15. Well, almost no one. Carruthers (2000) says that consciousness goes with the capacity to make the appearance-reality distinction. On one reading of this claim (a cognitive one), his view has bad consequences for newborn babies.
16. The suggestion that animal consciousness be investigated by problem-solving behavior (and also communicative behavior) is to be found most notably in Griffin 1976, 1984, 1992. Griffin's examples of the relevant behaviors are very interesting, but the conclusion he comes to, namely, that consciousness has as its function to compensate for limitations in neural organization/apparatus, is very hard to swallow.

of specific bodily movements of limbs or other body parts, in terms of intentional action or in terms of behavior I characterized very generally as engaging in a bodily movement that tends to bring it about that P if Q obtains, where P and Q are specified without mental vocabulary. My suggestion is that behavior, understood in the last way, is what is crucially relevant, and that if we find that behavior (or most of that behavior) in an animal where in humans it is normally produced by experience E, then, ceteris paribus, it is rational for us to prefer the view that the animal is subject to E or a similar experience over the hypothesis that it is not.

Another strategy for investigating animal consciousness is via a preferred theory of the structure and function of consciousness. Consider, for example, the view of Cabanac, Cabanac, and Parent (2009), summarized as follows:

> The brains of animals show chemical, anatomical, and functional differences, such as dopamine production and structure of sleep, between Amniota and older groups. In addition, play behavior, capacity to acquire taste aversion, sensory pleasure in decision making, and expression of emotional tachycardia and fever started also to be displayed by Amniota, suggesting that the brain may have begun to work differently in early Amniota than in Lissamphibia and earlier vertebrates. Thus we propose that emotion, and more broadly speaking consciousness, emerged in the evolutionary line among the early Amniota. We also propose that consciousness is characterized by a common mental pathway that uses pleasure, or its counterpart displeasure, as a means to optimize behavior. (p. 267)

Amniota are made up of all descendants of the shared ancestor of today's birds and mammals, including reptiles and extinct animals such as dinosaurs. So, according to Cabanac, fish are not conscious, and neither are insects.

These claims naturally lead us to ask how Cabanac understands the term "consciousness." He says (2009, p. 267):

> What is consciousness? Bering and Borklund [2005] define it as "a higher-order cognitive system enabling access to

intentional state." That new property may have emerged because of the increasing complexity of life in a terrestrial environment. In this new adaptive landscape, existence required more and more stimulus-response pathways; eventually, a point was reached where it became more efficient, in terms of speed and flexibility, to route all decision making through a single mental space. Within this space, different possible responses could be simply matched according to the criterium of maximal pleasure.

Consciousness, so understood, is not consciousness as I am understanding it. Rather, it is a version of what Block calls "access consciousness," and, as I explained earlier (in chapter 2), the term "access consciousness" is a misnomer. So-called access consciousness is just access. So Cabanac's theory is really a theory of how a certain sort of cognitive access arose in living creatures. But putting this to one side, the theory is still controversial, and the best way to investigate whether nonhuman animals have a range of conscious states cannot be by drawing conclusions from a controversial theory. Surely a more promising way to proceed is by delineating pre-theoretically the class of conscious creatures as best we can and asking what those creatures have in common that could ground the attribution of consciousness. Think, for example, about a different scientific case, that of water. We began our inquiries by supposing that water is the colorless, odorless, tasteless stuff that comes out of taps and fills rivers and falls from the sky. We then inquired further as to the nature of the stuff with these manifest, observable features and concluded that water is H_2O. Somewhat similarly, in my view, we should begin, in the case of consciousness, by supposing that conscious state S is what causes behavior M (ceteris paribus), given that S causes M in humans, and *then* we may go on and inquire as to the nature of S (and likewise for other conscious states). To proceed otherwise by articulating a theory of the nature of S first and then drawing conclusions *from that* as to which creatures undergo S is to put the horse before the cart.

Another strategy worth mentioning is one that engages in informed speculation as to what consciousness is for in our case and then uses that speculation to generalize. Bjorn Merker (2005), for example, comments:

Consciousness presents us with a stable arena for our actions—the world—but excludes awareness of the multiple sensory and sensorimotor transformations through which the image of that world is extracted from the confounding influence of self-produced motion of multiple receptor arrays mounted on multijointed and swivelling body parts. Likewise excluded are the complex orchestrations of thousands of muscle movements routinely involved in the pursuit of our goals. This suggests that consciousness arose as a solution to problems in the logistics of decision-making in mobile animals with centralized brains, and has correspondingly ancient roots. (p. 89)

Merker then goes on to elaborate a theory of the structure of consciousness consistent with these speculations.

My point for present purposes is just this. Merker begins with *us*, our case, and what consciousness does for *us*. He then suggests that if this is what consciousness does in our case, it is reasonable to suppose that it does something like the same thing for other creatures, and with that as his starting point, he goes on to develop a theory, albeit a controversial one, as to the nature of consciousness—a theory that explains why consciousness does what it does. Methodologically, this approach is more in keeping with the methodology I am proposing, in that it uses the human case as the foundation for further inquiry (leaving aside issues as to what Merker means by the term "consciousness" and whether he really is referring to the phenomenon I am focusing on). My primary interest in what follows is in the question as to whether animals as different from us as fish and insects are subject to conscious states like ours. The question as to the nature of these states and whether Merker's theory or some other theory is the correct one is left for another occasion.[17]

17. But see Tye 1995, 2000.

[6]

A FISH CALLED WANDA

"It's OK to eat fish
'Cause they don't have any feelings"
Nirvana, "Something in the Way"

In the famous British movie *A Fish Called Wanda*, Kevin Kline desperately wants to discover the location of some stolen jewels, and so, in an effort to get Michael Palin to talk, he takes Palin's beloved tropical fish out of their tank one by one and slowly eats them, as Palin is forced to watch. (The fact that Kline also jams French fries up Palin's nose gives the scene a nice sort of fish-and-chips symmetry.) It is obvious that Palin thinks of the fish as creatures with feelings. He desperately wants them not to experience pain or fear or anxiety. Kline couldn't care less. For him, they are zombies (or at least they should be treated as if they are). Is Palin right? Or Kline (and Nirvana)?

There are, of course, some significant physiological differences between fish and humans, but there are also some very important similarities that result from a common distant evolutionary heritage with mammals (some four hundred million years ago). For example, we know that the capacity to feel pain has been subject to natural selection and that it confers an advantage on those creatures that undergo it, for it causes them to avoid or minimize injuries.[1] Given the similarities in subcortical physiology and functioning and also in the nervous systems for

---

1. For more here, see chapter 9.

responding to noxious stimuli, similarities that then manifest themselves in similar behavior and reactions to opiates, the hypothesis that in us the feeling of pain is generated whereas in fish there is no such subjective response when it is manifest that the existence of this feeling improves the chances of a species' survival is prima facie an unwarranted combination of views—unless it can be shown that there are other behavioral and physiological differences that make a crucial difference.

It is also worth reflecting on the fact that fish (and other lower animals) frequently live in a hostile environment full of predators. Most fish fail to make it to adulthood. It would have been very odd for Mother Nature to confer on us the advantage of feeling pain while denying it to them, just as it would have been very odd for her to give them much more acute senses (in fish, notably, the sense of smell) while denying them any genuine awareness/consciousness of their hostile environment. Why would she have given with one hand while taking away with the other?

One reply that is sometimes made is that it is we who have the ability to think. The ability to think goes hand in hand with the ability to feel pain, to suffer. The more developed the former ability, the more developed the latter. This might make some sense if the higher-order-thought theory of phenomenal consciousness were true. But it is not (see chapter 2). Furthermore, if we ask ourselves what pain is *for*, the opposite reply beckons. Pain is there to help us to avoid injury. Its purpose is to jolt us into action that will protect our bodies. But we are smart, much smarter than fish and other lower animals. Why would we need a big jolt of pain and fish only a small one, or no pain at all? The stupider you are, the bigger the jolt you need (R. Dawkins 2011). The little child who runs across the road is on the receiving end of a loud and vehement warning from her mother; not so you or I. We should know better.

It might be replied that there would be no point in Mother Nature equipping fish with the subjective felt aspects of experiences unless fish were capable of cognizing those aspects. We have subjective qualities in our experiences to provide us with a quick and easy way to identify our states introspectively, but fish cannot do this. They are incapable of metacognition. All they need in order to behave adaptively in response to bodily damage are inner states with the right functional and informational roles. So-called qualia aren't necessary.

This is unpersuasive. Take the case of a one-year-old human being. Does anyone really believe that such a child cannot feel pain simply because it lacks a theory of mind at such an early age and thus cannot engage in metacognition? It is not necessary to be able to reflect on pain, to think to oneself that one is in pain, in order to feel it. To be sure, "qualia" give us a quick and easy way to identify our inner states introspectively. But, as already noted above in the case of pain, they do more: they also give us a guide to how things are. Bodily sensations indicate how things are in our bodies; perceptual experiences indicate how things are in the world. To be sure, our experiences have distinctive functional roles as well as subjective aspects. But they function in the ways they do precisely *because* of how they feel. There is no reason to think that the situation is any different for fish—or very small children, for that matter.

Let us begin our further discussion of these matters with some general observations about pain.

6.1 PAIN

You can feel hot without being hot. Perhaps an electrical probe is directly stimulating your brain, thereby triggering the experience, while your body temperature is normal. You can also be hot without feeling hot. Perhaps your body temperature is greatly elevated but your nerve endings are damaged and you are insensitive to the heat with which you are in contact. Heat is one thing, and the appearance of heat another.

It's not like this for pain. You can't feel pain without being in pain, and you can't be in pain without feeling pain. Why? Why is there no appearance/reality distinction for pain as there is for heat? The obvious answer is that pain, unlike heat, is a feeling. Being in pain and feeling pain are one and the same. For pain, esse est percipi.[2]

---

2. Arguably, it can seem to you that you are in pain when you aren't, as when you are expecting to feel a hot poker on your back and an ice cube is substituted without your seeing it. This is doxastic. You (briefly) believe that you are feeling pain, correcting yourself shortly thereafter.

But wait: if you feel a pain in a leg, you don't have a feeling in a leg! For one thing, feelings aren't in legs. If they are anywhere, they are in heads. For another, you can feel a pain in a leg even if you don't have a leg. You can have a phantom limb pain. And such a pain is not a feeling in a nonexistent leg. Something has gone wrong.

It has indeed.[3] If pain is a feeling, then pains are naturally taken to be instances (or tokens) of that feeling. A pain in a leg is then not a feeling located inside the leg but rather an instance (token) of the leg pain (pain in a leg) feeling.

The view that pain is a feeling nicely explains two features of pains: their necessary privacy and their necessary ownership. Pains cannot be shared for the reason that token feelings cannot be shared. You can't undergo my token feelings any more than you can laugh my token laughs or scream my token screams. Pains cannot exist unowned for the reason that token feelings require subjects. There can no more be an unfelt feeling than an unlaughed laugh or an unscreamed scream.[4]

But just what is the nature of pain, conceived of as a feeling? Well, pains are painful. They hurt. This is a matter of their phenomenology. This is not to deny that pains vary in how they feel. There are stinging pains, burning pains, throbbing pains, pricking pains, dagger-like pains. But one thing they standardly have in common is that they hurt. We can't define what it is for a feeling to hurt; we can only give examples (see chapter 1). But one thing we can say is that hurting is an aversive quality. Pains, in hurting, feel bad. This is why creatures try to avoid feeling

.

3. Some say that we need to distinguish pain qua feeling and pains qua intentional objects of pain (Harman 1998). The latter are nonexistent objects that enter into the contents of token pain feelings. They are like the dagger you hallucinate after reading too much *Macbeth*. This proposal has some virtues. For example, it explains why you can't feel my pains and why there can't exist a pain that no creature feels. These features flow from the nature of intentional objects. You can't hallucinate the dagger I hallucinate, and there do not exist any such items as hallucinated daggers. But there are three problems. First, there is no generally accepted theory of nonexistent intentional objects. Secondly, other things being equal, we should avoid bloating our metaphysics with nonexistent entities. Lastly, it must now be denied that pains are tokens of pain, for the latter are feeling tokens (see the next two sentences in the text) and the former are not. This seems very counterintuitive.

4. Token screams, laughs, and feelings belong to the general metaphysical category of event. A plausible requirement on all members of this category is that they cannot exist without some subject or other, and moreover that their actual subjects are essential to them.

pain and why, once pain is felt, creatures do their best to get away from whatever stimulus is causing it. By contrast, orgasms feel good. This is the obvious explanation of the popularity of sex.

It is interesting to note that some recent work by Palmer and Schloss (2010) supports the general thesis that some experiences "feel" better (or worse) than others, and it does so in a domain of experience that is not generally thought of as evaluative: that of color experience. In one experiment, subjects were presented with a colored square on a monitor, and they were then asked to rate how much they liked the color. It was found that they tend to prefer blue, red, and green, and they show the least preference for dark yellow and brown. These preferences are based on how the colors look to the subjects. Some colors just look better than others, it seems. This may be a reflection of the fact that blue is the color of clear skies and clean water, red the color of ripe fruit, and green the color of fresh vegetation, whereas dark yellow is the color of vomit and rotten food, and brown the color of biological waste. Perhaps these facts play a role in accounting evolutionarily for why some colors look better to us than others.

Be that as it may, we can at least say the following: Pain is a feeling with a distinctive felt character, at least part of which is negative. This felt character—hurting or painfulness—has certain characteristic causes and effects. It drives certain distinctive cognitive and emotional responses and also behavior. For example, it is in virtue of its painfulness that pain causes distress, anxiety, the desire to move away from what is perceived to be the damaging stimulus, difficulty in concentrating, and caution in dealing with similar stimuli in the future. Furthermore, the characteristic or most common cause of painfulness is tissue damage.

These comments are in keeping with the definition of pain given by the International Association for the Study of Pain, which defines it as "an unpleasant sensory and emotional experience associated with actual or potential tissue damage, or described in terms of such damage." Neither this "definition" nor my comments above should be taken to imply that pain cannot ever occur without being unpleasant.[5] In certain

---

5. The "definition" is not intended to supply necessary and sufficient conditions but to indicate prototypical features of pain.

pathological cases it can (see later, and also Grahek 2007 on pain asymbolia). Let us begin our further discussion of these matters with some observations about fish nociception.

6.2 FISH NOCICEPTION AND FISH BEHAVIOR

Nociceptors are specialized receptors that respond to potentially damaging, noxious stimuli. They are associated with free nerve endings, and their operation in birds and mammals is well understood. The fibers that are linked to these nerve endings in the skin are of two types: A-delta myelinated fibers that convey information at a faster rate and that are associated with the initial brief, well-localized sharp pain—for example, that associated with a pinprick—and C-fibers that are unmyelinated and that convey information much more slowly. The latter fibers are associated with the second, more long-lasting pain that goes along with, for example, a crushing injury or burns or a headache. If you put a hand under a tap of very hot water, the initial pain is due to a signal from the A-delta nociceptors. The subsequent phenomenally distinct and more unpleasant pain results from C-fiber activity, as does the persistent pain from a burn or a crushing injury.

It has been found that fish have nociceptors—in the case of trout, for example, the nociceptors respond to mechanical, chemical, and thermal stimulation—and these nociceptors are linked to both sorts of fibers (Whitear 1971; Sneddon, Braithwaite, and Gentle 2003).[6] Since nociceptors transmit signals that generate pain in humans and other mammals, it seems plausible to hypothesize that fish feel pain too—if indeed fish respond behaviorally to activation of their nociceptors in the same sort of way as humans.[7]

---

6. At least in teleost fish.
7. In making this claim, I am relying on the general reasoning articulated in the last chapter.

Some twenty-two different nociceptors have been discovered on the face and head of the rainbow trout, as shown in figure 6.1 below (Sneddon, Braithwaite, and Gentle 2003).

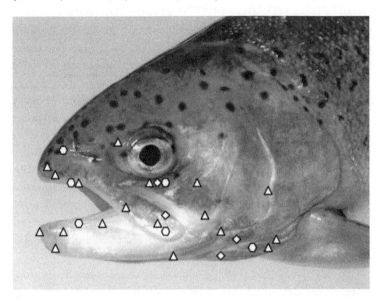

Some of these nociceptors are activated when trout are caught on hooks by anglers. Their response is to struggle and try to get away. Why should they do this? A plausible hypothesis is that the nociceptors trigger pain in the trout, and they then do their utmost to free themselves just as you or I would if we were suddenly to find ourselves attacked in a similar way.[8]

It could be that the reaction of the trout here is simply reflexive, the result of interference with free movement. However, fish can also change their behavior in response to noxious stimuli. A plausible hypothesis again is that this learned behavior shows that fish feel pain, for the behavior fish produce in such cases is not merely a simple automated reaction to a stimulus, like withdrawing a hand that has been pinched while under anesthetic. It is a product of a

8. Similar behavior is also found in elasmobranch fish. See here my comments on p. 103. One important difference is that elasmobranch fish lack nociceptors.

learned association between *pain* and the stimulus, an association that changes the fishes' behavior. One example of this is provided by an experiment by William Tavolga in which toadfish were electrically shocked (Dunayer 1991). They responded to the shocks by grunting. Through time the toadfish came to grunt simply at the sight of an electrode. Apparently they had come to associate a noxious stimulus with pain, and that association grounded the alteration in their behavior.

Fish also exhibit trade-off behavior. In one experiment (Millsopp and Laming 2008), fish were trained to feed in a part of an aquarium where they subsequently got a shock to the flank. It was found that the number of feeding attempts decreased with increased shock intensity. However, with increased food deprivation, the number and duration of feeding attempts increased, as did escape responses as the zone was entered. It appears that fish balance their need for food against the avoidance of acute noxious stimuli (just as we do—for example, when we are hungry, we continue to hold on to a very hot plate laden with food, but we drop the empty hot plate).[9]

David Papineau has objected to me that fish are not really choosing their actions here. In his view, they are incapable of reasoning through what to do, evaluating alternatives and forming action plans. This is an overly pessimistic view of the intelligence of fish. Not only has it been found that fish can find their way out of mazes using cognitive maps,[10] but there is also evidence that they can make transitive inferences. The latter is especially interesting, so let me quickly summarize one relevant experiment involving cichlids.

---

9. Interestingly, trade-off behavior is found in hermit crabs too. See chapter 8.
10. Monkeys, humans, fish, and birds can use basic geometric cues to recall object locations. Fishes' ability to use such cues exceeds that of toddlers (Brown 2015). Here is an example of complex spatial learning in small fish. Rock-pool-dwelling gobies can not only find their way back to their home pools when removed and located some thirty meters away, but they can also jump correctly into neighboring pools when startled, and they can remember the locations of these surrounding pools forty days after being removed from their home pools. To do this, they make use of a cognitive map that is developed during high tide as the water level rises, and they can swim from one pool to another, a map that remains intact and functional for long periods of time (White and Brown 2013).

Cichlids are fighting fish. They regularly fight over territory. A male spectator cichlid was placed in a tank surrounded by five other tanks, each containing a similarly sized male cichlid. Call the latter cichlids A, B, C, D, and E. Initially, B was placed in A's tank (as shown in figure 6.2) and was roundly thrashed by A for having come into A's territory. This was in plain view of the male spectator fish. Then the spectator fish saw B thrash C, C thrash D, and D thrash E, following corresponding transfers of each fish into another's territory.

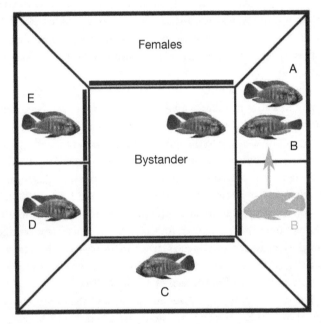

Grosenick, Clement, and Fernald (2007)

After this, the spectator fish was moved to a longer and narrower tank, at one end of which was a further small tank containing male B and at the other end a second small tank containing male D. It was found that the spectator fish spent its time hovering at the end of its tank, close to male D. Why? It was already known that cichlids like to hang out with worse fighters. But how did it know that D was a worse fighter than B? After all, it had seen B win one fight and lose one fight, and likewise for

D. The only explanation seems to be that the spectator fish reasoned that since B beat C and C beat D, B would beat D if they fought. So D must be the weaker fighter. The procedure was repeated with eight different spectator fish and the same result achieved each time. Moreover, in some of the experiments the set-up was changed so that D beat C and C beat B (Grosenick, Clement, and Fernald 2007). In each case, the spectator fish chose the weaker individual.[11]

Returning now to the case of pain: fish react to morphine much as we do. For example, fish reactivity to electrical shocks is reduced if they are given morphine, just as is the case in humans (Sneddon 2003). Why should this be? We know that morphine is an opiate analgesic drug used to relieve severe pain. Subjects given morphine no longer feel severe pain. The horrible felt quality of pain is greatly diminished or disappears altogether. Since the administration of morphine to fish decreases their response to a stimulus that is known to be painful in humans, namely, an electrical shock, a plausible hypothesis is that the fish were feeling intense pain in response to the shock but no longer are.

One objection to this hypothesis is that the application of morphine might be expected to decrease reactions to a stimulus regardless of whether pain is present (Ehrensing, Michell, and Kastin 1982). This objection is not relevant to some other experiments involving the administration of morphine. Consider, for example, an experiment conducted by Janicke Nordgreen and Joseph Garner on the basis of which they concluded that goldfish do feel pain and that their reactions to pain are much like those of humans (Nordgreen et al. 2009). The fish were split into two groups. One group was given morphine and the other saline. The temperature in their tank was then slowly raised until both groups of fish started to wiggle at around the same temperature, but later on (some two

11. It has been suggested that in some cases of apparent transitive reasoning in animals, what is actually going on is that simple associative mechanisms are in play (Shettleworth 1998, p. 229). According to value transfer theory, if a stimulus S is associated with a stimulus that is never a negative stimulus in any discrimination in a series of discriminations, S has the highest value, whereas if another stimulus S′ is associated with stimuli that are both positive and negative, then innate mechanisms ensure that S is to be preferred to S′. However, it is not clear how this applies in the above case, for both B and D are associated with positive and negative stimuli.

hours after injection), when the temperature returned to normal, a difference in the behavior of the fish in the two groups became evident.[12] The fish that had been given saline reacted with defensive behaviors, indicating anxiety, wariness, and fear, according to Nordgreen and Garner. The fish that had been given morphine swam around as they always had. Nordgreen and Garner concluded that the first group of fish "consciously perceive the test situation as painful and switch to behaviors indicative of having been through an aversive experience."

In another experiment, Lynne Sneddon (2003) injected bee venom and acetic acid into the lips of trout under anesthetic. (Acetic acid is the main ingredient of the vinegar that often goes with fish and chips, incidentally.) After the trout came to, they rubbed their lips against the sides and base of their tanks. They also rocked from side to side while resting on the tank base. Sneddon proposes that this behavior is to be explained by hypothesizing that the trout feel pain and attempt to relieve themselves of it. In an alternative version of the experiment, Sneddon conditioned trout to approach a food ring in response to a light cue in the tank. They were then anesthetized and divided into four groups. The first was allowed to recover; the second was injected with saline, the third with acetic acid, and the fourth with bee venom. Trout injected with acetic acid or bee venom (noxious stimuli) took the longest to start feeding again in response to the light cue indicating that food was available (around three hours on average).[13] Trout given saline or nothing took around eighty minutes to approach the food ring and start feeding. The disparity of feeding time, according to Sneddon, is best explained by supposing that the trout feel pain in response to the acetic acid and venom injections, and this suppresses their motivation to feed.

Sneddon also found a greatly increased beat rate of the opercula (the hard bony flaps protecting and covering the gills) in these trout as compared to the others. This is usually taken as an indicator of stress, and

12. This wiggling itself might be a reaction to the feeling of pain. However, if it were such a reaction, then the later distinction in the behavior of the two groups of fish is harder to explain. A more likely possibility is that the wiggling is reflexive rather than pain-induced, an automatic response to the increased temperature.
13. Humans take on average about three hours to stop experiencing pain from the acetic acid test.

Sneddon takes it to add further support to her hypothesis that the trout injected with bee venom and acetic acid feel pain.

6.3 IS THERE A BETTER EXPLANATION?

The hypothesis that fish experience pain offers a straightforward explanation of fish behavior in the above cases. If this is the best available explanation, then it is rational for us to prefer that hypothesis to the hypothesis that fish do not feel pain (as argued in chapter 5). But is it the best available? Let us look now at some potential problems, beginning with some differences between fish nociception and human nociception.

To begin with, only about 4 percent of all fiber types in teleost fish (fish with a bony skeleton such as trout) were found to be C-fibers, whereas in mammals up to about 50 percent may be C-fibers. Since humans with congenital pain insensitivity have a lower percentage of C-fibers (24–28 percent) than is normal, but still a much higher percentage than fish, there is reason to question the analogy with human nociception. Perhaps fish have nociception but no pain even though fish behavior in response to noxious stimuli is not that of a simple reflexive response, as already noted.

Still, is the much lower percentage of C-fibers in fish really of any great significance pain-wise? According to Sneddon, electrophysiological studies show that the functioning of trout A-delta fibers is much the same as mammalian C-fibers in reaction to a variety of noxious stimuli, with one difference: the former are faster. So the much lower percentage of C-fibers may simply be an indication that the pain responses of trout and other teleost fish are *slightly* different from ours. This should hardly be a surprise. Evolutionary histories are different, and so inevitably there will be differences in nervous systems in different creatures, but the commonalities in the human and fish nociceptive systems are many and there is no reason to adopt the radical view that the differences undermine the general hypothesis that fish nociceptors generate pain.

Having said this, a qualification is in order. Elasmobranchs (fish such as sharks that have cartilaginous skeletons) have a general lack of nociceptive receptors. One consequence of this is that they are able to feed on prey that would otherwise be noxious. For example, hammerhead sharks prey on stingrays. These sharks have been found with as many as ninety-six stingray barbs embedded in their mouths (Rose 2002)! Yet sharks react in the same way as teleost fish to being caught on a hook. They struggle and try to get away. What seems to trigger their escape response is interference with free movement. For elasmobranchs, so far as I am aware, there is *no* behavior, the best explanation of which is that they feel pain.[14] Let us then put the case of sharks and stingrays to one side.

A second worry with the appeal to the presence of a nociceptive system in teleost fish is that in humans signals pass along the A-delta and C-fibers to the brain stem and spinal cord, and from there information is relayed to the cerebral cortex. It is usually supposed that the experience of pain in humans results only after the cerebral cortex has been appropriately activated, notably the somatosensory cortex (SSC) and the anterior cingulate cortex (ACC) (see here chapter 5). In fish, nociception initially proceeds in the same way, via the brain stem and the spinal cord. Further, the organization of the brain stem and the subcortical cerebrum in fish shows much organizational similarity with humans (deriving from a shared vertebrate genotype). But there the similarity ends. Fish lack a neocortex. Since in us pain and indeed conscious activity generally result only *after* the relevant neocortical activity, and fish lack a neocortex, why suppose that fish feel anything at all as a result of noxious stimuli? To do so, it might be said, is like arguing that a non-turbo-charged car must be able to go as fast as a turbo-charged version, since prior to the turbo-charger kicking in, the two operate in the same way.

One problem with the above line of reasoning lies with the claim, discussed at length in the last chapter, that having a neocortex is necessary for consciousness. As noted there, at a minimum the case of decorticate children raises serious doubts about whether even all human beings lacking a neocortex are without consciousness. It is also worth noting that a strong

---

14. There are reports from whalers of sharks that they have split in two continuing to feed; likewise for sharks that have been disemboweled by other sharks attacking them. Apparently their fatal wounds do not cause them to feel pain.

case can be made that in some animals cells homologous to those in the neocortex can be present without a neocortex. I shall return to this important point and its relevance to the case of fish in detail in the next chapter.

Another supposed problem for the view that fish feel pain is that if the cerebral hemispheres are removed in fish with the brain stem and spinal cord left intact, this has little impact on the behavior they produce in response to noxious stimuli. The fish will continue to withdraw the stimulated body part, struggle, and locomote in an attempt to get away from a damaging stimulus (Rose 2002). Moreover, the case of pain in fish is supposedly not atypical. As David Ferrier notes (1890, p. 2), for fish with their cerebral hemispheres removed, "there is little if anything to distinguish them from perfectly normal animals. They maintain their natural attitude and use their tails and fins in swimming with the same vigour and precision as before."

These claims are an exaggeration. Some behavior associated with noxious stimuli is reflexive (one obvious example is that of withdrawing a hand that has touched a hot stove). Behavior of this sort can continue in the absence of the cerebrum, as can behavior of the sort Ferrier notes, since it is largely controlled by the brain stem and spinal cord. But behavior of the sort outlined in the last section in connection with noxious stimuli—trade-off behavior, for example, or rubbing of the lips or learned behavior—is much more complex. And there is *no* evidence at all that behavior of this complexity occurs in fish in the absence of a cerebrum.

Perhaps it will be replied that in the case of learned behavior, while it is certainly true that fish can learn things—and this learning can alter their behavior in response to noxious stimuli—such learning does not require consciousness, for it is well known that many complex nonreflexive behaviors in humans do not involve consciousness.

For example, in one experiment, Arthur Reber (1993) asked human subjects to memorize a set of letter strings, such as XXRTRXV and QQWMWQP, that were (unknown to them) generated by some rules. After the memorization phase, subjects were informed that the strings they memorized followed certain rules, and they were asked to classify new strings as following those rules or not. Typically, subjects performed this grammar-learning task at an accuracy rate better than chance, despite remaining unable to verbally describe the rules.

Here is another example (Esteves, Dimberg, and Öhman 1994). Subjects were conditioned to a backwardly masked angry face that was followed by electric shock;[15] they were also shown a backwardly masked happy face, but this time there was no negative reinforcement. Later the subjects were presented with both unmasked angry faces and unmasked happy faces. A galvanic skin response was found in the former cases but not in the latter. It was concluded that "with fear-relevant facial expressions as the conditioned stimulus, associative learning was possible even in conditions where the subjects remained unaware of the conditioned stimulus and its relationship to the unconditioned stimulus" (p. 375).

Since humans learn much without conscious awareness, why not fish? Perhaps, in the case of the toadfish mentioned earlier, an association is generated by a noxious stimulus (an electrical shock)—an association between the instrument of the shock (the electrode, which is visible to the fish) and grunting—so that later visual presentation of the electrode without the shock suffices for the toadfish to grunt. In this way, the fish are like Pavlov's dogs, who, having learned an association between the sound of a bell and being fed, come to salivate at the mere sound of the bell. In other cases where fish learn to avoid noxious stimuli, perhaps it is because they are unconsciously drawing a link between those stimuli and bodily injury and then, given the predisposition to avoid injury, learning to avoid the noxious stimuli. If this is what is going on, the experience of pain is not required.

The main point to make in response to this argument is that although it is certainly true that there is non-conscious associative learning, the learning that fish display is a result (in part) of their nociceptors being activated by noxious stimuli. So, given that the nociceptive systems in us generate the experience of pain, the *simplest* hypothesis is that nociceptor activity in fish causes pain too (same cause, therefore same effect).[16]

---

15. Backward masking occurs when one visual stimulus (a "mask" or "masking stimulus") is presented immediately after another brief "target" visual stimulus (lasting at most 50 ms), with the result that the first stimulus is not consciously perceived.

16. Furthermore, to reject this hypothesis is to create an explanatory puzzle as noted in the introduction to this chapter and in section 6 below.

It also cannot be the case that the association is between noxious stimuli and bodily injury. As noted earlier, in Tavolga's experiment, toadfish come to grunt at the mere sight of an electrical probe nearby, but there has been no bodily injury in the past. Rather, the explanation seems to be that the shock from the probe *felt* bad previously—that is what gets associated.

I turn now to the results of Sneddon's experiment involving bee venom and acetic acid (described in section 4.1). J. D. Rose et al. (2014) have objected that the rocking noted in the fish given venom or acid may well have been a result of anesthesia on the balance of the fish. This point of view is supposedly supported by the more recent experiment of Newby and Stevens which "duplicated" that of Sneddon without the use of anesthesia. In Newby and Stevens's experiment (2008), rocking was not observed. There was also no significant delay in feeding.

The trouble is that the latter experiment did not duplicate Sneddon's. Newby and Stevens's tanks had no bottom for the fish to rest on and no gravel substrate but instead involved cylindrical flow (Sneddon 2012). So it is hardly surprising that the fish did not "rock" or rub their lips against the gravel. Moreover, the lack of anesthesia coupled with forcible restraint while the venom and acid were injected would have generated high cortisol levels in the fish, thereby releasing endorphins, which function as painkillers in mammals. If they do the same in fish, the trout would not have experienced pain, and so there would have been no reason for a reduction in feeding.

Another objection raised by Rose et al. (2014) is that the lip rubbing observed by Sneddon was found only in the acid-injected fish and not the venom-injected ones. But the rubbing is supposed to be an effect of the pain the fish experienced, and pain is supposedly produced by both noxious stimuli (for in both cases the nociceptors are activated). So why was the rubbing observed only in the acid case? The problem this time is that it seems likely that the pain experienced in the two cases is different. In our case, getting vinegar (acetic acid) in a cut causes a severe sharp pain; venom, by contrast, causes inflammation and itch. So why should the very same effects be expected?

A further complaint raised by Rose is that the increase in opercula beat rate is not clearly due to nociceptive stimulation of the receptors in the lips, since venom and acid injections to the lips leak and circulate to the mouth and gills, thereby activating a more general set of receptors, including gustatory and olfactory ones. The difficulty this time (noted by Sneddon 2012) is that if the effect were a toxic one, it would not be reduced by the administration of a painkiller such as morphine. But morphine does reduce the beat rate, and normal feeding resumes in a shorter period of time.

I might add here that Rose et al. (2014) claim that when fish are caught on hooks and returned to the water, they resume feeding (or looking for food) immediately or within minutes and exhibit good long-term survival. According to Rose, their thrashing around on the hooks is simply an unconscious reaction, a reflex. If the fish were genuinely experiencing pain, they would not be expected to feed again immediately upon release. What fish are really equipped to do, then, is unconsciously detect injurious stimuli, but they cannot feel pain. Fish, on this view, are pain zombies. The literature suggesting otherwise, in Rose's view, is replete with anthropomorphisms: human-like capabilities have been erroneously projected onto fish.

The trouble with the claim about feeding is that it is largely anecdotal. No serious empirical study has been undertaken by Rose or his coauthors. The data cited is from one author who works for a fishing company that catches, tags, and releases fish, and that data is unpublished. As Sneddon has noted, there are published studies showing fishing does impact the behavior and physiology of fish (see review in Cooke and Sneddon 2007; see also Norwegian Food Safety Agency 2010). So far as I can see, there is no reason to take Rose's position seriously.

6.4 FISH FEAR

There are several experiments whose results are best explained by supposing that fish experience fear. Japanese researchers gave goldfish a low-voltage electrical shock every time a flashing light came on (Yoshida and Hirano 2010). The goldfish soon came to associate the light with a shock, and their heartbeats increased when they saw the light even without the shock. However, when lidocaine was injected into the cerebrum of the fish an hour before the experiment began, the fish did not react to the light in the same way: their heartbeat remained steady. Once the lidocaine wore off, the fish reacted as before.

The obvious explanation for this is that the fish came to experience fear when they saw the light as a result of its past association with an electrical shock that had caused them pain, and the experience of fear increased their heartbeat. The lidocaine calmed the fish, but when it wore off, the fish experienced fear again.

In another experiment, twenty-minute sparring sessions were arranged between male African cichlids, a freshwater territorial fish (Desjardins and Fernald 2010). The two fish matched against one another were kept apart by a clear wall. In some cases, instead of a wall, a mirror was inserted so that the cichlid was actually seeing itself. The fish tried to fight their foe, real or apparent, and they did so whether the wall was there or the mirror.

A betta fish (not itself a cichlid) fighting its own reflection. Malzees at Wikimedia Commons (https://commons.wikimedia.org/wiki/File:Betta_Fighting_Reflection.JPG)

The scientists then tested the cichlids' blood for testosterone and other aggression-linked hormones. They also dissected the cichlids' brains, including a brain region that is a homologue of the amygdala in mammals. They found high levels of testosterone throughout, but only in the cases where a mirror had been inserted did the scientists find especially high activity in the amygdala homologue.[17]

Why should this be? Obviously, the fish must have been able to make fine-grained discriminations between the real opponent cases and the reflected opponent cases. Given that in mammals the amygdala is primarily associated with fear and anger, a plausible hypothesis is that the especially high level of activity in the amygdala homologue in the mirror cases indicates that the fish were experiencing fear or more fear in these cases as a result of the anomalous moves of the opponent.[18] Desjardins comments online in the Stanford report in May 2010:

> In normal fights, [the fish] bite at each other, one after the other, and will do all kinds of movements and posturing, but it is always slightly off or even alternating in timing. But when you are fighting with a mirror, your opponent is perfectly in time. So the subject fish really is not seeing any sort of reciprocal response from their opponent.

Here is another piece of evidence that fish feel fear. When fish are injured, in many species a chemical substance is released from their skin into the water. One plausible hypothesis is that this serves as an alarm signal, causing fright responses in other conspecific fish. Researchers have identified this substance and found that if it is released into the water in low concentrations, zebrafish react by darting around, but if it is released in high concentrations, the fish "freeze" and float in place for more than an hour. What seems to be going on is that the fish detect the chemical via their sense of smell and are wired to experience fear as a result. This experience then causes them to dart around, but it can also become overwhelming and "paralyze" them. In this connection,

---

17. See chapter 8.
18. The elevated level of testosterone in all the fish indicates a constant higher level of anger.

the following remarks about human fear from the turn of the nineteenth century seem to apply to the zebrafish too:

> Fear produces an agony and anxiety about the heart not to be described; and it may be said to paralyze the soul in such a manner that it becomes insensible to everything except its own misery. . . . When the effects of fear operate powerfully without any mixture of hope, these passive impressions are predominant but where there is a possibility of escape, the mind reacts with wonderful energy . . . enabling the sufferer to precipitate his flight, by exertions that would have been impracticable in a more composed state of mind. (Cogan 1802)

It is sometimes argued that, without a neocortex, activity in the amygdala does not signify that there is any *experience* of fear or fear phenomenology (Rose 2002). Prima facie, this flies in the face of the escape-and-fear behaviors that can be exhibited by decorticate animals. Why not take such behaviors at face value as indicating an aversive experience?

Furthermore, it is very natural to think of fear itself as a primitive emotional *experience* that evolved to enable animals to handle dangerous situations. So if the amygdala is the basis of fear, as is widely agreed, it is the basis of a negative aversive experience. To respond that without an associated neocortex, the amygdala is really only the basis of "fear," or ersatz fear, as we might call it, is to adopt a position that is ill-motivated. It is also puzzling. Why would ersatz fear have the effects it supposedly does? It doesn't *feel* bad. It doesn't feel any way.

To be sure, it is sometimes said that in the human brain there are two fear systems, one conscious and one non-conscious (LeDoux 1996), and this might be held to provide grounds for denying that the *experience* of fear is generated by activity in the amygdala. But this is misleading at best. One fear system—the supposedly non-conscious one—goes from the senses to the thalamus and thence to the amygdala and the action systems. This system is fail-safe. It operates very fast and responds automatically to stimuli with a dangerous appearance. The other system—the conscious one—goes from the senses to the thalamus, and from there it goes to the neocortex before reaching

the amygdala and the action systems. This system involves delibera-
tion and thought. The former system operates when, for example, you
are at the zoo and a snake the other side of a glass barrier lunges at
you. The latter system is at work when, upon hearing of job layoffs at
your university and even in other liberal arts departments, you start
to reflect upon your own security and a twinge of fear grabs you.

The point to make here is that the supposedly non-conscious fear
system is really a *pre-reflective* fear system. When the snake lunges at
you, there is certainly something it is like for you subjectively as you
unthinkingly step back. There is a fear *phenomenology* to being startled,
even if it is automatic and beyond your cognitive control.

There is other relevant evidence. Scientists at Umeå University in
Sweden recently checked rivers for pharmaceuticals. What they found
was that a drug prescribed for anxiety, oxazepam, was accumulating in
fish. This is because wastewater treatment allows chemicals, pesticides,
and suchlike to pass through, and they end up in fish and other wildlife.
The scientists then replicated in the lab the concentrations of oxazepam
found in the wild (circa a microgram per kilogram of fish body weight),
and they then observed changes in the fish behavior (Brodin et al. 2013).
Basically, the changes were similar to those that occur in people. Jonathan
Klaminder, one of the scientists, offers the following plausible explanation:

> What the drug does is remove some of the fear that the very small fish
> experience. . . . [They] become less interested in staying close with
> others—staying close to others is a well-known defence system to
> avoid predators. They become less afraid of exploring new areas, so
> they just go out to search for food and become more effective in find-
> ing and consuming food. (Report in the *Guardian*, February 2013)

6.5 PERCEPTUAL CONSCIOUSNESS IN FISH

Fish generally have well-developed sense organs. Daylight fish have
good color vision; their eyes are similar to those of mammals, though the
lenses are more spherical. Fish can be made to undergo visual illusions

just as we can. They are also subject to color constancy. Opponent processing channels have been identified in goldfish; these are not the same as those found in humans. In goldfish, there are three such channels, whereas in humans there are two. Goldfish are tetrachromats, and they have receptors in their eyes that respond to light in the ultraviolet range (Bradley and Tye 2001). Vision in fish that live in the deep sea shows adaptation to the much darker environment.

Fish can also hear. They can determine the range and direction of sounds under water within certain frequencies. Fish do not have earlobes, however. Their ears do not open to the outside and cannot be seen. They are internal and allow fish to pick up sound vibrations in the water. In fish, the sense of smell is extremely well developed. Using it, they can pick up on distant odors. Fish have taste buds too. These are used in the identification of food.

Fish also have a sense we do not. Some teleosts are able to detect weak electrical fields through pit organs on their heads and faces. Since living things generally generate weak electrical fields, they can use this ability to locate prey in murky water.

Fish use multiple sensory cues to navigate much like we would if we were trying to find our way in an outdoor plaza full of tourists. We hear the clock in the clock tower strike on our left, we smell the pizza at the outdoor café by it, we see the tiny shop selling expensive jewelry some twenty feet in front of us, and we get our bearings. The same sort of thing is true of fish. This was shown in a recent set of experiments (Huijbers et al. 2012) using juvenile French grunts, commonly found in the Caribbean. These fish were chosen in part because they are small but also in part because they settle on plankton a long way out at sea and yet manage to find their way back to the mangrove/seagrass nurseries where they grew up.

In the initial set of experiments, the fish were placed in auditory chambers and given a choice of swimming toward the sounds of waves crashing on a coral reef and various other sounds. They showed a high preference for the former. Why? The suggested hypothesis was that far out at sea the grunts need a way of orienting themselves toward land, and the sound of crashing waves on coral is a way to do this.

However, the fish did not start out on coral reefs, and so what they needed next were some cues for navigating from the coral reefs to the mangrove swamps. These cues cannot have been visual, since the mangrove swamps are not visible from the coral reefs, so the second hypothesis was that here the fish use their sense of smell. To test this hypothesis, Huijbers and colleagues constructed Y-shaped olfactory mazes. Presented with various different scents, the fish chose the smell of mudflats, and mudflats are where the mangrove swamps are found.

The third experiment was one in which the fish had to choose between visual images displaying various different habitats and shoal mates. Here the fish chose the images of shoal mates. They did not discriminate via habitats.

The last experiment combined two of the earlier ones. The fish this time were placed back in the olfactory maze. Directly after they chose their preferred scent, they were shown visual images of shoal mates. These then were combined with other scents than the preferred one. It was discovered that once the fish have recognized a potential shoal mate, they tend not to be driven by preferred scents.

Do the fish in these experiments *really* see and hear and smell? One reaction is to say that they do, but that this does not guarantee consciousness. Consider the case of spiders. Tyler Burge (2010) has commented that we are sure that they see, but we are not sure that they have experiences. From this, he concludes that the ordinary concept *see* leaves open whether all the creatures that fall into its extension have visual experiences (see also Block 2010).

I am inclined to disagree with this conceptual point. Take the case of hearing. If I hear something, it must sound some way to me. If it didn't sound some way to me, I wouldn't hear it. But something's sounding some way to me requires that I have an auditory experience occasioned by it. Likewise, if I see something, it must *look* some way to me. If it didn't look any way to me, I wouldn't *really* see it. But something's looking some way to me—red or square, say—requires that I have a visual experience (of red or square) occasioned by it.

This is not to deny that there can be unconscious seeing. There can. But unconscious seeing is not seeing without experiences. Rather, it is seeing of which one is not conscious. In the case of the spider, to the extent that we have doubts about things around it looking any way to it, we have doubts about whether it is genuinely seeing those things. It may function to some degree *as if* it is seeing them, but if we picture the spider as lacking any visual phenomenology, we picture it as not really seeing the items with which it interacts (or so I would say).[19]

Leaving this point to one side, are the French grunts genuinely subjects of visual, olfactory, and auditory experiences? How are we to decide? Well, take our own case. If a human being has a sense that fails to generate any experiences as a result of some neurological abnormality, this is immediately evident in behavior. The person who has lesions in her visual cortex resulting in total blindness cannot find her way at all using the sense of vision. There is nothing like this for the fish in the above experiments. They exhibit rather remarkable skills in using their senses individually and together to map out a route to the mangrove swamps.

Fish, I might add, are subject to visual illusions, just as we are. One well-known example of an illusion for human beings is the Ebbinghaus-Titchener illusion shown below:

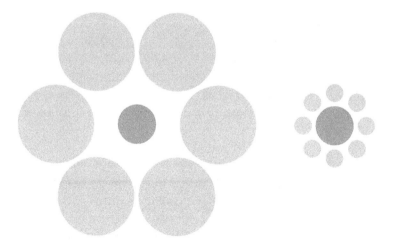

The circle surrounded by larger circles looks smaller than the circle surrounded by smaller ones. Yet the two circles are the same size. Guppies are

19. Of course, we are sure that normal spiders aren't blind, just as we are sure that zombie duplicates of humans aren't blind, even though we may not be sure that spiders have visual experiences and we are sure that zombies do not. But "not blind" here means something like "capable of finding one's way around using one's eyes."

subject to the same illusion. They have round patches on their sides, and the male guppies try to position themselves between other male guppies having smaller patches. The explanation is simple: female guppies are attracted to males with larger patches. Of course, no claim is being made here that the male guppies reason this through. It may well be that innate mechanisms are at play. But if the patches surrounded by smaller patches on the males did not *look* larger to the females, the behavior would be pointless.

As before, it might be insisted that, lacking a neocortex, fish cannot have perceptual experiences, so nothing can look any way to them. But then what are we to make of the guppy behavior? Furthermore, as already noted, this potential defeater to the inference from shared perceptual behavior to shared perceptual experiences is brought into question by the case of some decorticate children, as well as by the recent hypothesis that there are homologous cells in the human neocortex and fish brains (for more on the latter, see the next chapter).

It is perhaps worth noting here that there is another view that also enjoys wide support, namely, that having a functioning *primary* visual cortex is necessary for visual consciousness. This view is also suspect. What the evidence shows is that a certain region of the neocortex is the main locus of visual consciousness in normal adult humans. It does not show that visual consciousness cannot go on in the absence of that region either in humans or elsewhere.

This is demonstrated by a recent study by Ffytche and Zeki (2011). In this study, both fast- and slow-moving stimuli were presented on a laptop computer as three adult subjects without a primary visual cortex fixated on a cross on the screen. The subjects were asked to indicate the direction of the stimulus and also whether they had seen it. In addition, they were asked to specify a confidence rating of seeing (or not). These requests were made using a forced choice for responses as follows:

Question	Response choice
Did you see any motion?	Yes/no
How confident are you?	Certain/unsure
What was the direction?	Two or four direction forced choice

All three subjects were able to draw what they saw when they answered yes to the first question (with their drawings being compared with what they saw with respect to the same stimuli presented in their intact fields). The subjects did better with the fast-moving stimuli than the slow ones. Ffytche and Zeki comment:

> The subjects could prepare drawings of what they had perceived in their blind field, which compare favourably with the drawings of the same stimuli when presented to their intact fields. We did not ask our subjects to draw their experiences after every trial; however, we assume that every time a subject reported seeing the stimulus using the forced-choice responses, they had the type of experience depicted in their drawings and described in their verbal report. These descriptions left us in no doubt that the experiences they had were visual in nature and amounted to what might be called "visual qualia" and considerable doubts in accounting for them in other ways. This is not to say that the blind field experiences are identical to those in the intact field or to understate the poverty of the blind visual experiences. Indeed, Riddoch originally described his subjects as experiencing the moving stimuli in their blind fields as "shadowy." . . . When we first asked Patient G. Y. about his phenomenal experience, he described it in terms of shadows and thus in a way remarkably similar to the descriptions given by Riddoch. (p. 253)[20]

Returning to the case of fish, in summary (and drawing on the earlier discussion of reasoning about other species in chapter 5), the dialectical situation with respect to visual consciousness is as follows: we know that human beings are subject to visual illusions and color constancy effects and that the same is true of fish. We know that human beings are subject to visual experiences as a result of the operation of their eyes and visual systems and that these visual experiences cause discriminatory behavior. We know also that fish engage in a wide range of discriminatory behavior as a result of the operation of their

---

20. I take it that when Ffytche and Zeki refer to the blind field, they mean the portion of the field with respect to which the subjects are effectively blind (leaving aside the case of motion) as a result of loss of functioning primary visual cortex.

eyes and visual systems. The best available explanation of the behavioral similarities is that fish undergo visual experiences as humans do and that these experiences interact with their cognitive states much as they do in us, thereby generating the behavioral similarities. Admittedly, the behavior fish engage in does not guarantee that they have visual experiences (any more than in the case of pain). But the same is true for other human beings and for nonhuman mammals generally. And just as for the latter, lacking a genuine defeater (that is, a good reason that undermines or defeats the attribution of visual consciousness to other humans and nonhuman mammals on the basis of their behavior), it is rational to prefer the hypothesis that they have such experiences to the hypothesis that they differ from us in this respect, so too for the former.[21] The simplest, most straightforward explanation of a wide range of fish behavior in response to visual stimuli across both normal and illusory contexts is that those stimuli *look* various ways to them, as they do to us, and thus that they are subject to visual experiences. Accordingly, we should embrace this explanation. It is rational for us to prefer the hypothesis that fish have visual experiences to the hypothesis that they do not. One who believes nonetheless that fish lack visual experiences has an irrational belief and is herself at least to that extent irrational, and likewise (mutatis mutandis) for other perceptual experiences.[22]

21. Admittedly, in the case of fish, unlike that of other humans, there is a *potential* defeater (absence of a neocortex). But as already noted, that defeater is itself defeated by two further considerations: (1) cells homologous to those in the neocortex can be present without a neocortex, and, at least according to some scientists, fish have such cells and similar microcircuitry in their forebrains (see the next chapter), and (2) it isn't clear that such a structure in the brain is needed anyway even in the case of human beings, given the example of some decorticate children (indeed, it seems not to be the case).

22. Fish behavior generally is more flexible than is often supposed, and in some cases it is a reflection of the fishes' personality. Here are some comments by Bart Adriaenssens, a zoologist at the University of Gothenburg:

> My results show that it [is] not just humans and other mammals that exhibit personality. Also brown trout differ among each other in their level of aggression and react differently to changes in their surroundings. The release of a novel object in the aquarium causes very different reactions. Some individuals will immediately explore this object, whereas others will rather hide in a corner and try to avoid every contact. (*Science Daily*, December 7, 2010, https://www.sciencedaily.com/releases/2010/12/101206111445.htm)

6.6 YES, BUT ARE THERE REALLY FISH QUALIA?

One possible reaction to the above arguments is to grant that fish do indeed undergo states that *function* as pain, fear, and other phenomenal states do, but to insist nonetheless that their states have no phenomenal "feel" to them. On this version of the Nirvana view quoted earlier, fish undergo ersatz pain, fear, and so on. An alternative response is to say that the relevant states do indeed have a "feel" to them, but we do not have the slightest idea what their states are like subjectively (Rose et al. 2014, p. 26). There is no merit to either of these views.

Consider first the no-qualia alternative for pain. This proposal postulates a striking, radical difference between fish and humans, notwithstanding the commonality in nociceptors, nervous system responses, downstream functioning, and behavior. In us, there is a conscious "jolt" that is elicited by the messages that travel down our nerves from our nociceptors when our bodies are damaged and that prompts us to protect ourselves. In fish, there is no conscious "jolt" at all. In us, something *painful* occurs, something that *hurts*. In fish, there is nothing painful. Why then did Mother Nature bother to install a conscious felt quality in us in reaction to the impact of noxious stimuli, when she did not do so in fish? Why not just make us ersatz pain feelers too? What was added by having *us* experience something awful?

As I noted in the introduction to this chapter, it cannot be that we are less smart than fish and we require a nasty conscious quality to grab our attention so that we protect ourselves, whereas fish, in their relative wisdom, need no such thing. So why the difference? It seems that the hypothesis that fish undergo ersatz pain is not as good an explanation of the facts as the hypothesis that they experience pain just as we do, for the former hypothesis generates a further explanatory puzzle with respect to us that the latter hypothesis does not.[23]

---

23. Supposing that in addition to pain there is ersatz pain, or pain*, where pain* is a phenomenally very different state that functions in the same way, is no more warranted

It might be replied that the nasty "jolt" comes for free with having a neocortex. It doesn't really *do* anything itself, notwithstanding how it seems. Mother Nature didn't really install the jolt with the aim of getting us to protect ourselves. The jolt is simply a byproduct of activity in the neocortex, itself having no causal power. This is very hard to believe, and it seems inconsistent with our everyday experience.

An alternative reply is that in us the jolt has causal power; in fish, however, some non-phenomenal property of ersatz pain does the same job. But again, if the effects of the feeling of pain can be gotten without any feeling at all, why did Mother Nature see to it that humans feel pain? What was achieved by installing such a state if a non-phenomenally conscious state would do as well? Inference to the best explanation favors the qualia alternative for fish over the no-qualia one.

Suppose now it is held that in fish there is a phenomenally conscious state, but one that feels very different from ours even though it has the same biological function and the same causes and effects as pain. One mark against this hypothesis is that it is more complex than the shared pain hypothesis (and unnecessarily so). Another is that it is very perplexing. If the state fish are in as a result of bodily damage feels some way to them without feeling bad, then why do they react to it as we do to pain? Small children like chocolate. They reach for more after tasting some. Why? Because it tastes good. If it tasted bad, they wouldn't do that. Suppose that the state fish are in has a neutral or positive affect to it. Why then do they exhibit stress? Why does their opercula beat increase? Why do they try to escape from the damaging stimulus? It is hard to see how to give satisfying answers to these questions. To retort that they are in a state that normally causes stress and an increase in the opercula beat is to offer no explanation at all, any more than my saying that your being in a state that causes you to rub your leg explains why you are rubbing your leg.

than believing that in addition to electrons there are schelectrons (unobservable entities that are intrinsically different from electrons but that affect our measuring instruments in the same way). See here chapter 4.

Clearly these points generalize to other phenomenal states, including perceptual ones. It is rational for us to prefer the view that fish are conscious beings (and that their conscious states are often similar to ours) to the view that fish are zombies. In short, we should side with Michael Palin over Kevin Kline and Nirvana.

[7]

OF BIRDS AND REPTILES
(AND FISH)

Birds have small brains and no neocortex. We disparage someone's intelligence by calling him or her a birdbrain. We sometimes take pigeons' bobbing movement while they walk to indicate that they are stupid. Yet in reality birds are anything but dumb. The New Caledonian crow, for example, not itself the smartest of birds, if presented with food that it cannot reach in the bottom of a narrow jar, will look around for a tool to help. Finding a straight piece of wire, it will bend the wire into a hook by inserting part of it beneath a rock and exerting a suitable bending force using its beak. It will then reach again into the jar and pull out the food by means of the hook.

Pigeons can differentiate between cubist and impressionist paintings. They can classify objects, for example, as human-made or natural. Scrub jays can remember events from particular times and places. And many birds ranging from parrots to hummingbirds are capable of learning and teaching vocal communication.

How is this possible in the absence of a neocortex? The answer to this question tells us something not only about birds but also about reptiles and fish. And what it tells us provides further support for the conclusion already reached that it is rational to prefer the view that fish are not zombies to its denial.

7.1 THE ORIGINS OF BIRDS

In the 1870s, Thomas Huxley proposed in public lectures that birds are dinosaurs. This proposal was based in large part on the discovery of a transitional fossil between reptiles and birds, that of Archaeopteryx. Huxley made a careful comparison of Archaeopteryx and various prehistoric reptiles and concluded that it was most like certain dinosaurs. For a long time, Huxley's thesis that birds are dinosaurs was a subject of heated discussion, but in 1996–1997 a fossil bed was discovered in Montana in which there were dinosaur fossils with feathers. Since then, further dinosaur fossils with feathers have been discovered elsewhere, notably in northeast China, and Huxley's view has become widely accepted. Of the dinosaurs, the evidence suggests that birds are closely related to the meat-loving velociraptor, familiar to many from the movie *Jurassic Park.*

On the face of it, bird brains are very different from those of mammals. See the figure opposite comparing fish, pigeon, and human brains. Bird brains are also very small relative to human brains. Even so, the ratio of brain size to body size is the same for birds as it is for humans. Still, how can birds be as intelligent as they are without a neocortex? Moreover, how can birds undergo perceptual experiences in its absence?

In humans, the neocortex is a region of the brain made up of white and gray matter and ordered into layers. This highly laminated, layered structure making up the outer parts of the brain as shown on page 123 is the endpoint of messages from the thalamus (diencephalon), which itself serves as a relay station for messages from the senses. A structure of this sort, though much simpler, is found in rats. Indeed, it is present in all mammals. By contrast, in birds, while there are sensory pathways leading from their senses, which are not unlike ours, to the thalamus, the thalamus does not project onto a neocortex. Yet birds live in the same environment we do and solve some of the same problems (witness the example of the New Caledonian crow). So what is going on in birds at a neurophysiological level? One reasonable hypothesis is that there are homologous cells in bird and human brains (that is, cells that share a

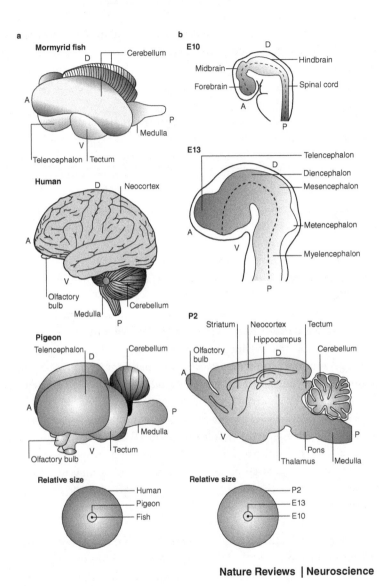

Ruiz i Altaba et al. (2002)

common origin) that mediate the behavioral similarities. But how can this be if humans have a neocortex and birds lack one? This question becomes even more puzzling if we think of the neocortex in the way it is often described, as a unique component of mammalian brains, something without a prior history.

The solution to the puzzle lies with the realization that the neocortex did *not* suddenly appear by magic in mammals. What happened with mammals was that certain sorts of cells present in non-mammalian brains and around for hundreds of millions of years were grouped together into layers to form the laminar structure of the cortex. This is what is genuinely new. But the constituent neuron types and the microcircuitry aren't new. Just as the insulin-secreting cells of the pancreas are not unique to mammals but are seen in all classes of vertebrates, so too cells in the neocortex are to be found in birds.

This hypothesis was first proposed by Harvey Karten in the 1960s (also Karten 1997). What Karten discovered directly was that the neural input and output pathways from a structure in bird brains known as the dorsal ventricular ridge (DVR) were extremely similar to the pathways traveling to and from the neocortex in mammals. Using genetic markers to identify neuron types, Jennifer Dugas-Ford, Joanna Rowell, and Clifton Ragsdale (2012) recently tested Karten's hypothesis. They confirmed that in chickens and zebra finches the cells in the DVR share the same physiological properties as the cortical cells. For example, there is a region of the DVR that is very similar to layer 4 of the auditory cortex. It responds to messages from the thalamus that are passed on as a result of incoming messages from the ears, and it has the same tonotopic organization as the auditory cortex.[1]

What is even more striking is that there is at least some evidence that a similar structure is to be found in the forebrains of teleost fish (Ito and Yamamoto 2009). If this is the case, then birds and fish have an area of the brain that functions in many ways like the neocortex, even though its location and shape are different. This is the result of

---

1. For more on the hypothesis that the cerebrum of birds and mammals is homologous (though differently organized), see Gunturkun and Bugnyar 2016.

convergent evolution. So the earlier argument that fish cannot be subject to a range of experiences since they lack a neocortex is seen to be problematic in a further way. Fish indeed are without a neocortex, but, according to a recent hypothesis, they have homologous cells within a brain structure that is awfully like the neocortex, both functionally and physiologically. Here, then, we have a further reason for supposing that the neurophysiology of fish does not defeat preference for the hypothesis that fish are like us in having experiences to its denial. And without a defeater, it is rational for us to prefer the former hypothesis, since it provides the simplest, most unified explanation of the various behaviors we share with fish and that result from experiences in us.[2]

It is also interesting to note that within the fish forebrain, the dorsomedial telencephalon (Dm) performs the same function as the amygdala. When this region is damaged, fish do not react in a fearful way to stimuli that previously generated fearful responses, just as is the case with the amygdala and mammals. A plausible hypothesis is that activity in Dm generates the experience of fear in fish.

In the next three sections, I shall summarize the behavioral evidence supporting the hypothesis that birds undergo a variety of experiences. The final section is concerned with reptiles.

7.2 BIRD EMOTIONS

When humans experience fear, they may run away in a panic or freeze in place. Their heart rate increases; they may call for help or to indicate a threat. Much the same is true of birds. Quick flight and escape is a common response, as is increased respiration rate. Birds may also call out in alarm or freeze as if paralyzed.

Birds sometimes hiss, slap other birds with their wings, and adopt threatening postures. Behavior of this sort is displayed when their territory is invaded by another bird or their nest is being

---

2. Another possible explanation as to why a neocortex has not evolved in fish is that it enlarges brain size, and a larger head is not advantageous in an aqueous environment.

approached by an intruder. In such cases, birds are naturally taken to be experiencing anger.

Birds also engage in gentle courtship behavior. They may preen one another, for example, and they seem to demonstrate parental love toward their hatchlings. They also share food with their mates, and those birds that mate for life may share companionship year after year as human mates do. Human beings behaving in these ways are taken to feel love. Why not too birds?

Birds seem to feel grief. Looking for a lost mate or a chick, they may behave in a listless fashion. They may also adopt a drooping posture. An example of complex behavior suggestive of grief is given by Marc Bekoff (2007) in his book *The Emotional Lives of Animals*. He says:

> A few years ago my friend Rod and I were riding our bicycles around Boulder, Colorado, when we witnessed a very interesting encounter among five magpies. Magpies are corvids, a very intelligent family of birds. One magpie had obviously been hit by a car and was lying dead on the side of the road. The four other magpies were standing around him. One approached the corpse, gently pecked at it—just as an elephant noses the carcass of another elephant—and stepped back. Another magpie did the same thing. Next, one of the magpies flew off, brought back some grass, and laid it by the corpse. Another magpie did the same. Then, all four magpies stood vigil for a few seconds and one by one flew off. (p. 1)

Another emotion indicated by bird behavior is pleasure or joy. Birds sometimes sing without trying to attract a mate; they make soft purring sounds, not unlike the humming noises humans sometimes produce when they are feeling happy. Magpies and other corvids engage in playful games.

One might respond that these behaviors, or at least many of them, are purely instinctive, not really indicating any emotions. Take the case of courtship behavior. Perhaps the birds engaged in it do not feel any love for one another; perhaps they are just wired to behave in this way so as to produce the healthiest offspring. In other cases, perhaps the behavior is produced simply because it is the best way for the bird to survive— to fight off a predator, to find a mate, to protect its territory. In still other cases, perhaps we are simply anthropomorphizing, as when we attribute the feeling of joy to birds.

Still, I might say the same about other humans. Why are you shouting at John Jones, who has just been propositioning your partner and who won't leave him/her alone? On another occasion, why are you smiling at your partner and holding his/her hand? Why are you taking out a shotgun as you hear the lock of the back door being forced in the middle of the night? Why should I suppose that you sometimes feel joy, as I do?

Perhaps the behaviors you display are simply the best way for you to survive. But this hardly seems an adequate reply. Take the first case. Suppose it is true that you are fighting off a predator by your action. Still, why not just walk away with your partner? Why not call the police or ask others for help? Why not calmly reason with the man who won't go away? These things need explaining, and the obvious explanation is that you are feeling angry and that this emotion has taken over and is controlling your specific behavior. Anger serves the purpose of aiding you to fight off predators and protect yourself in certain contexts, and it is doing so here.

Likewise for a bird that is hissing and slapping another bird with its wing. The bird could fly away; it could call for help; it could try to lead the second bird away to another place, to distract it from its present purpose. Why doesn't it do these things? Again, the obvious explanation is that the bird is feeling angry, and that is causing it to engage in aggressive behavior.

7.3 BIRDS AND PAIN

When animals damage a limb, they avoid putting weight on it or using it more than is necessary. This is known as pain guarding. For example, dogs, horses, and rats limp after they have damaged a leg. Chickens do something similar; after their beaks have been trimmed, they peck much less.[3] This (prima facie) is a kind of pain guarding.

Chickens also actively seek pain relief. Factory-farmed chickens are forced to grow abnormally quickly and to do so in overcrowded pens and cages. The result is that they are crippled. When these lame chickens are given a choice of two feeds, one of which has been laced with a pain reliever (carprofen) and the other lacking any pain reliever, a greater percentage of them opt for the former than is the case for chickens that are not lame. Moreover, the lamer the chicken, the greater its intake of feed with pain reliever. Researchers have also noted that lame chickens that eat this feed walk better (Danbury et al. 2000). Why? The answer is obvious: because it reduces the amount of pain they feel.

Recent studies seem to show even that female chickens exhibit hints of empathy with respect to pain felt by other chickens. In the relevant experiments, mother hens and chicks were chosen. The researchers ruffled the feathers of the chicks by blowing some air across them. The chicks showed indications of distress, and the mothers then reacted to this by becoming distressed themselves. Indications of distress in the mothers were increased heart rate, alertness, and lowered eye temperature (a well-known indicator of stress). Further, the mothers clucked more toward the chicks, and they preened less (Edgar et al. 2011). This has consequences for the treatment of chickens in battery cages and science laboratories, both places where chickens commonly witness the distress of other chickens that have leg fractures or bone disorders.

Consider also the case of feather plucking. Pulling out the feathers may cause a skin rupture, which in turn may lead to an infection. If pain is an adaptive mechanism for avoiding potentially harmful stimuli (for more here, see chapter 9), it should be expected that feather plucking is painful. And this is indicated by the physiological and behavioral responses of chickens to feather plucking (Gentle and Hunter 1991).

---

3. Chickens fight one another at the drop of a hat, and ranchers trim their beaks to stop them from pecking one another to death.

7.4 PERCEPTUAL EXPERIENCES IN BIRDS

Birds are like humans in having five senses. Their eyesight is acute. They have a much richer array of rods and cones on their retinas than we do. Moreover, some birds have cones that respond to ultraviolet light with the result that they can see colors that we cannot. Their eyes are also bigger than our eyes relative to their head size, and they are also spaced farther apart. This has the consequence that their field of view is wider than ours.

Hearing is important for birds. Their ears, which are placed a little behind and below their eyes, have soft feathers protectively covering them. Birds cannot hear as wide a range of sounds as we can, but they have very acute sound-recognition abilities that they put to work in differentiating changes in tone, rhythm, and pitch. This is important as far as determining whether a call is a warning of a predator nearby, a friendly greeting, a song, or an offering of food to share (among other things).

Birds have a sense of touch, but it is generally less sensitive than ours, most notably in their feet and legs. This permits them to stand or perch for long periods on icy wires or surfaces. Around their bills, however, their sense of touch is more acute. One explanation for this is that touch in this region is important for finding insects, as the birds probe through mud or water, and also for feeding on them. These touch receptors may also play a role in drumming against wood with the beak.

Birds have very few taste buds—up to only about five hundred, whereas humans have on the order of ten thousand. They are able to distinguish sweet, sour, and bitter flavors, but they rely frequently on other factors in finding the best foods. For example, they may prefer one food to another because it is easily available. They also use other senses, in particular sight and hearing, to find the foods that are the best nutrition for them.

When it comes to smell, birds are clearly inferior to humans, although there are exceptions. Vultures, for example, use smell to locate food from large distances—distances at which the food would be undetectable to humans.

The behavior that birds engage in using their five senses is complex. Here is one particularly striking example (from Endler, Endler, and Doerr 2010). Male bowerbirds construct bowers, structures with long entrances, to try to persuade females of their genetic fitness. The female birds come into the entrance avenues and see the males at the far end. The males meticulously place stones along the avenues, with larger stones at the back and smaller ones at the front. This creates a perspective illusion (as in the Ames room). See figure below.

Endler, Endler, and Doerr (2010). In the top case, visual angle varies in the usual way with distance; in the bottom case, visual angle is kept constant by carefully arranging the objects so that their size increases with distance.

The effect of the texture gradient in the lower panel is to cause an object placed on it to subtend a visual angle that makes it appear larger than it is. This results in the male bowerbird at the end of the entrance avenue appearing larger than he is from the perspective of the female bird at the entrance to the bower. The male bowerbird works hard to achieve this effect by placing stones of varying sizes and then going to see how they appear from the viewing position at the entrance to the bower, then going back, placing some more stones, and repeating the process until the overall desired effect is achieved—just as you or I might in trying to generate the same illusion.

So the male bowerbirds are perceiving and acting, and as they act, they are attending to how things look. The illusion they create is powerful, and it certainly strongly suggests that bowerbirds undergo visual experiences; for an illusion occurs when something *looks* other than it is, and for something to look some way, it must elicit a visual experience of it as being that way. To be sure, it is conceivable that the bowerbirds are merely functioning *as if* they are undergoing various visual experiences of size. But there is no reason not to take their behavior as indicating how things look to them, any more than there would be for you or me in the same circumstances.

This is not to deny that innate mechanisms may be in play. After all, the male bowerbird never sees himself down at the end of the bower. Furthermore, all male bowerbirds arrange stones in the same way (even when they make their bowers for the first time). Still, the point of the exercise is to make the male bowerbirds look larger than they are, thereby showing their genetic fitness to the females. If they didn't *look* any way to the females, the exercise would be otiose. But once there are visual appearances, there are visual experiences and thus visual consciousness.

7.5 REPTILES

Reptiles are cold-blooded, air-breathing vertebrates with scaly bodies. The first true reptiles emerged some 350 million years ago (Macphail 1982). Reptiles alive today include lizards, turtles, crocodiles, and snakes.

Reptiles show spatial cognitive abilities not dissimilar to those of rats. For example, Wilkinson, Chan, and Hall have shown (2007) that a tortoise (like a rat) placed in the central area of an eight-arm maze with food at the end of each arm went to get the food without revisiting arms previously visited. Where the maze was isolated from the room containing it by a dark curtain, the strategy used by the tortoise was to enter the arm next to the one just left. However, when the curtain was removed and the room contained clearly visible cues from the maze, the tortoise used these cues to determine which arms it had yet to go down (Wilkinson, Coward, and Hall 2009). Turn-by-one-arm behavior of the sort observed by Wilkinson, Coward, and Hall has been found in other reptiles too.

Visual discrimination has also been studied in a variety of reptile species. It has been found that reptiles can discriminate on the basis of color, form, line orientation, brightness, position, and size. Their position discrimination abilities are better than their color discrimination ones. For example, lizards given left-right cues to find their way out of Y-shaped mazes do better than lizards that are given color cues. In addition, tuatara have been found to be able to discriminate between a flickering light and a constant light for a food reward.[4]

Reptiles exhibit behavioral flexibility in their pursuit of food. In one experiment, young black-throated monitors were shown a clear plastic tube containing mice (Manrod, Hartdegen, and Burghardt 2008). The tube had hinged doors that snapped back into place if the monitors released them. Within ten minutes, they learned to open the doors and insert their heads to get at the mice. On the second trial, they were significantly faster, and ineffective strategies such as shaking the tube diminished.

Lizards can recognize other individual lizards and reidentify them. And tortoises have been shown to be able to follow the gaze direction of other tortoises. They have also been shown to be able to perform a task by watching the behavior of a conspecific. Thus, at least some reptiles are capable of social learning.[5]

As with birds, reptiles lack a neocortex. They also lack a hippocampus. In mammals, the hippocampus is central to performing navigational tasks. There is evidence that the medial cortex in reptiles operates in a similar way to the hippocampus in mammals, for when there are lesions to the medial cortex in reptiles, there is diminished navigational ability similar to that found in mammals with lesions to the hippocampus.

The absence of a neocortex does not prevent reptiles from engaging in a range of perceptual and social behavior, as noted above. Like birds, reptiles have a dorsal ventricular ridge (DVR) in their forebrain, and one possible hypothesis is that this plays the same sort of role as the neocortex in mammals (Lohman and Smeets 1991). To my knowledge,

---

4. Tuatara are reptiles endemic to New Zealand that resemble lizards but form a distinct species.
5. For a good summary of the evidence here, see Wilkinson and Huber 2012.

there has been no detailed physiological study of the neuron types in the reptile DVR of the sort conducted by Dugas-Ford, Rowell, and Ragsdale (2012) on birds. Furthermore, one important difference from mammals is that the visual, auditory, and somatosensory modalities in the DVR are almost entirely segregated from one another. This suggests that there is little or no integration between these modalities and thus that the kind of unity we experience when, for example, we hear thunder and see lightning, thereby experiencing a sound and a yellow flash *together*, may be missing in reptiles. Be that as it may, given reptilian behavior and what we know of their physiology, we are justified in preferring the hypothesis that reptiles undergo experiences (for example, that they have a limited visual consciousness) over the hypothesis that they lack experiences, notwithstanding the fact that they are without a neocortex.

[8]

TENSE BEES AND
SHELL-SHOCKED CRABS

Ninety-five percent of species in the animal kingdom lack a backbone. These include ants, roaches, bees, crabs, and octopuses. Octopuses have the most neurons—some thirty million, roundworms a mere three hundred. Insects form the most plentiful group of animals. It has been estimated that at any given time a quintillion insects are alive. Let us begin our discussion of invertebrate consciousness by considering whether insects feel pain.

8.1 INSECT NOCICEPTION AND PAIN

In general, nociceptors—receptors that respond specifically to a certain range of noxious stimuli—are missing in insects.[1] Nonetheless, insects do respond to noxious stimuli. Electric shock, noxious chemicals, temperature changes outside the usual range, and mechanical stimulations cause insects to withdraw or escape so as to reduce or prevent damage to themselves. In humans, these responses are mediated by the experience

---

1. An aside: the medicinal leech, not itself an insect but an annelid, does have nociceptors. Pinching, squeezing, or other similar mechanical stimulation of the leech body wall generates nerve impulses in certain cells, called the N-cells by Nicholls and Baylor (1968). In response, the leech pulls away as if it is trying to escape from something painful. This reaction is a simple reflex, however, no more indicative of pain than the reaction of an anaesthetized human patient pulling away an arm when pinched.

of pain. In insects, however, they appear to be simple stimulus-response reactions, the result of simple wired-in neural circuits—or, in some cases, the result of abnormal neural activity, as when an insect poisoned by DDT writhes and convulses in response to repetitive neuronal discharges.

However, insects can learn to avoid noxious stimuli. For example, when honeybees are presented with novel odors, they extend their proboscis to learn about them. But having learned to discriminate between two odors, when one of them is paired with an electric shock, the bees learn not to extend the proboscis. This is not a simple reflex but a plastic response, one explanation of which is that the electric shock causes the honeybees pain, they remember this and the pairing of the shock with a certain odor, and so, when presented with that odor again, they do what is necessary to avoid pain.

This is far from conclusive, of course. As noted in the last chapter, there can be unconscious associative learning. I shall return to this issue a little later.

Here is another consideration. In mammals, naturally occurring opioid substances such as endorphins are found. It is known that they moderate pain messages carried along the A-delta and C-fibers, thereby having an analgesic effect that manifests itself in a reduction in behavioral responses to noxious stimuli. Opioid compounds have also been found in insects (Stefano and Scharrer 1981). This may suggest that insects can feel pain like mammals. However, opioids mediate a variety of physiological and behavioral activities in mammals not connected to pain, and they have also been found even in the single-celled protozoa (Le Roith et al. 1980). So their mere presence in insects in and of itself establishes little.

Still, there are some intriguing experiments in which opioids are administered to insects. In one such experiment (Balderrama et al. 1987), bees were electrically shocked and their stinging response measured. Then some of the bees were injected with morphine and shocked again. Their stinging response diminished. Since morphine is a painkiller in humans, one explanation is that the bees were not feeling as much pain from the shock, and so their stinging response was reduced.

Another study supports this view. The sting-alarm pheromone is emitted by guard bees to warn the rest of the hive of impending danger and to stimulate them to sting attackers. Isopentyl acetate (IPA) is a major component of that pheromone. Núñez and colleagues (1997, p. 78) have shown that exposure to IPA activates a bee's endogenous opioid system. The result is that the defender bees in the hive keep attacking even if they are injured. One explanation again is that activation of the opioid system produces stress-induced analgesia, and this in turn permits the bees to battle on even in the face of injury—just as the soldier in the trench keeps fighting during the battle even though he has been shot.

In the Núñez study, the bees were electrically shocked to produce a stinging response. Producing a stinging response in bees that had been exposed to IPA (and consequently had their natural pain killers activated—if bees feel pain) required a higher-voltage shock than unexposed bees. The amount of stinging response also decreased as the quantity of IPA administered was increased. Moreover, giving the bees both IPA and naloxone, which blocks the opioid system, had the effect of the bees continuing to sting even at the lower voltages. As Núñez (p. 79) put it, IPA "chang[es] the threshold of responsiveness to a noxious stimulus."

Again, this is not conclusive. But, ceteris paribus, similar causes have similar effects. So if bees have a similar opioid system to mammals and they respond behaviorally to morphine and IPA in a similar way to mammals, it is tempting to conclude that the administration of morphine and IPA diminishes the bees' pain response, which in turn explains the absence of "pain behavior." Still, there is a reason to be cautious here: the reduction in sting response is not really very similar to the sorts of behavior mammals engage in with a reduction in pain—behavior such as diminished nursing, writhing, protection of the damaged limb, and withdrawal from the damaging stimulus. What a reduction in the sting response suggests first and foremost is a reduction in aggressiveness, and this may be simply because morphine in insects simply slows down and decreases behavioral responses generally.

There is evidence against this hypothesis, however. In some situations, analgesics actually increase activity in insects. For example, fruit flies placed in a glass tube in which there is a light gradient move toward the light. But if the center of the tube is heated, they are inhibited from going through it toward the light. Specific analgesics (agonists for $GABA_b$) diminish this inhibition, and the flies pass through the heated part (Dimitrijevic et al. 2005). These agonists are effective as analgesics in hot-plate tests on rats (Britto et al. 2012).

So a case can be made for insect pain. But there is also a case to be made against insect pain. Let me explain. In general, one of the things that is striking about the experience of pain is the effect it has above and beyond simple withdrawal from the noxious stimulus. For example, mammals feeling pain may stop moving, limp, protect the damaged part, show irritability, become aggressive if approached, feed less, and decrease their sexual activity (Morton and Griffiths 1985). They also learn from their experience by trying to avoid similar situations in the future. Much the same is true of fish, as we saw in the last chapter. Pain, by having these effects, permits the animal to recover from the damage it may have incurred and also helps it avoid getting damaged in the same way in the future. That presumably is the point of pain—why Mother Nature selected it.

It has been claimed that nothing of this sort is found in insects. Eisemann and colleagues (1984) comment in a review of biological evidence for pain in insects:

> No example is known to us of an insect showing protective behavior towards injured parts, such as by limping after leg injury or declining to feed or mate because of general abdominal injuries. On the contrary, our experience has been that insects will continue with normal activities even after severe injury or removal of body parts. (p. 166)

Eisemann continues:

> An insect walking with a crushed tarsus, for example, will continue applying it to the substrate with undiminished force. Among our other observations are those on a locust which continued to feed while itself being eaten by a mantis; aphids continuing to feed whilst being eaten by coccinellids; a tse-tse fly which flew

in to feed although half-dissected; caterpillars which continue to feed whilst taccinid larvae bore into them; many insects which go about their normal life whilst being eaten by large internal parasitoids; and male mantids which continue to mate as they are eaten by their partners. (p. 166)

Eisemann also points out that insects do not respond to pain by ceasing to move or protecting injured parts in the way that mammals do. In general, they do not react to treatment that would undoubtedly cause severe pain in mammals. This non-response does not prove the absence of pain, but it is a strong reason to doubt its presence, for the function of pain at least in part is to enable a creature to protect an injured part until it has healed—to rest up, as it were, as long as necessary. Why would Mother Nature have made insects feel pain if there is no adaptive significance to it, no adaptation in behavior?

One response to these claims is that they are too strong. Consider first the fact that if a bee leg is grasped by tweezers, the other legs will come to the rescue and push in a vigorous way against the tweezers in an attempt to pry it loose. However, this seems only secondarily to do with pain, if at all, for the primary impulse here is simply to free the trapped leg. Moreover, if the bee is decapitated, the bee will continue to struggle as before for five or six hours. This is because bee physiology is different from ours. In bees, there are nerve centers, or ganglia, from which nerves emanate, and some of these nerves extend along the legs. If a leg is touched, messages are transmitted up the nerves until they reach a ganglion. From there some messages go to the bee brain, but others go directly to the other legs. The result is almost instantaneous kicking. This kicking has no more to do with pain than does the jerking movement of a soldier's foot when it is pinched or tickled after he has been shot in battle and paralyzed from the waist down. Correspondingly, in the case of the decapitated bee, even if it wriggles for a long time, the bee is like the mud turtle with its head chopped off. The latter can continue to move in a pretty much normal fashion even though, as the boy (in the manner of Huck Finn) remarked, "He is dead and he don't know it" (Root 1886, p. 86).

Consider next the phenomenon of autotomy, or self-amputation. This is found in a range of insects in cases in which shedding the appendage is necessary for survival or reducing further damage in the rest of the insect, as, for example, in the case of noxious chemicals spreading from a sting (Fleming, Muller, and Bateman 2007). Getting rid of a limb has serious costs, of course, and it appears as if a "decision" is made by the insects concerning whether autotomy is worth the cost.

What is true of insects here is true of other arthropods. Orb-weaving spiders of the genus *Argiope* undergo autotomy (self-amputation) in natural conditions if they are subject to bee or wasp stings in a leg. In the laboratory, if they are injected in a leg with bee or wasp venom, they shed the leg. But interestingly, if they are injected with only saline, they don't (typically), so it is not simply the injection of fluid or the prick to the leg that causes autotomy. What is even more interesting is that if the spiders are injected with components of venom that cause pain in humans when they are injected (specifically, serotonin, histamine, and phospholipase A2) they autotomize the leg, but they don't do this if they are injected with components of venom that do not cause pain to humans. Here, it could be said, we have a case of arthropods protecting themselves in the same sort of way as do creatures that it is agreed feel pain (Eisner and Camazine 1983).

It seems to me that this case is more like that of the mammal with a trapped leg that decides to gnaw the leg off in order to survive. The mammal may well be feeling pain in the leg, but it isn't the pain that drives the action but rather the impulse to survive. Furthermore, the behavior of the spiders is perfectly well explained by supposing that they have innate physiological mechanisms that detect some of the main ingredients of venom in the same sort of way that an automatic door opener detects the presence of someone before it and opens in response. No psychological intermediary is required. It should also be noted that the common house spider never autotomizes even though it is just as susceptible to venom as orb-weaving spiders. Why should this be? The simplest explanation is that it lacks the relevant venom-detecting mechanism (possibly because, given its habitat, there is very low exposure to venom). Finally, it should be noted that two components of venom that definitely produce pain in humans, acetylcholine and bradykinin, don't cause autotomy in orb-weaving spiders, and one that does, melittin, doesn't cause pain in humans. So the match is not exact anyway.

Returning to insects, some insects (including bees, as noted earlier) do exhibit avoidance learning of a sort that indicates pain. So Eisemann's claim that insects are unlike mammals in that they do not learn from their experience by trying to avoid similar situations in the future is false. Consider the case of drosophila, or fruit flies. They can learn to associate an electric shock with an odor (as can honeybees, as I noted earlier). After six to twelve trials, if the odor is presented just before the shock, the flies avoid it for up to twenty-four hours (Yarali et al. 2008). Why should this be? One straightforward explanation is that the shock causes pain, which the flies associate with the odor. They remember the pain, and hence, when the odor is detected again, they avoid it. Interestingly, when the sequence of events during training was reversed, so that the odor followed the shock, the odor predicted relief from shock, and the flies approached it. Drosophila here seem to have managed what Yarali calls "pain relief learning" (Yarali et al. 2008). Again, it appears that pain and the memory of it are playing a role in learned behavior—just as they do in mammals.

These are not the only possibilities, however. Perhaps in the first case the flies come to associate the noxious stimulus with the odor that follows it after the two have been detected together a certain number of times, and then remember this association when presented with the odor again, thereby expecting the noxious stimulus. This then will produce retreat from the odor, if the flies are built to withdraw from any stimulus that has previously been linked with a noxious stimulus. In the second case, it could be that the flies again make an association, remember it, and infer that it is safe to approach the odor since the noxious stimulus has gone. On this proposal, non-conscious associations are what is driving the flies' behavior rather than pain.

Presumably, something like this is going on in the case of nereid worms that are shocked as they try to crawl through a glass tube. On successive trials, they go more slowly, eventually giving up altogether (Clark 1965). This behavior is remembered for a period of six hours, but by twenty-four hours, it has been forgotten and the worms repeat their initial attempts to crawl through the tube. Since worms have only around three hundred neurons, it seems a leap of great faith to suppose that they could genuinely feel pain!

Whatever the truth is here, the suggestion that fruit flies feel pain fits well with the claims made by recent researchers (Neely et al. 2010) about striking commonalities in gene pathways in fruit flies and mice, pathways that aid mice in sensing pain and fixing pain thresholds. If they do this in mice, why not also in flies? It turns out that there are 580 genes in these pathways in flies and 400 in mammals. The general suggestion made by Neely is that the gene networks are similar not only in flies and mice but also in other species and that this conservation of genes across species is what underwrites the ability to feel pain—an ability that prima facie is important to any animal's survival.

Returning to the case of bees, we may still find ourselves somewhat hesitant to say that they feel pain. To make further headway here, we need to turn to other aspects of bee behavior, and indeed to the case of crustaceans, and crabs in particular. These will occupy us for the next three sections.

8.2 INSECTS AND EMOTIONS

Even if insects *can* feel pain, it might seem incredible to suppose that insects can experience emotions such as anxiety or fear, but a recent experiment should give us pause. In this experiment (Bateson and Wright 2011), honeybees, strapped into little harnesses to render them immobile, were trained to associate one odor with a sugary taste and another with a bitter and unpleasant taste (that of quinine). The former taste was a reward, the latter a punishment. When the first odor was presented after a training period, the bees uncoiled and extended their mouthparts. When the second odor was presented, they retracted them.

Gabriela de Brito Sanchez et al. (2014). Honeybees strapped into harnesses.

The experiment next made use of the fact that when people are anxious, they tend to see the glass as half-empty instead of half-full. For example, if an anxious person hears the sentence, "The doctor examined little Emily's growth," she is less likely to conclude that Emily is OK and that it is just her height that the doctor is checking. In general, anxious people interpret ambiguous stimuli more negatively. This presumably is related to the biological function of anxiety. Anxiety arises naturally in potentially dangerous situations, ones in which it behooves its subjects to tread carefully, to play it safe.

In the case of the bees, the experimenters divided the bees into two groups, one of which was shaken vigorously for sixty seconds in the manner in which a hive might be shaken by a badger. If bees are capable of negative emotional states, this shaking should have sufficed to put them in one.

Within five minutes after the shaking, the two groups of bees were presented with in-between odors. It was discovered that the shaken bees were less likely to extend their mouthparts to try out the associated tastes than the unshaken bees. This was not because they were disoriented. When presented with the odor associated with the sugary taste, they extended their mouthpieces just as before. Rather, they interpreted the *ambiguous* stimuli as more probably punishment than reward. They saw the glass as half-empty. Since pessimism is behavioral evidence that a dog or another person is anxious, why not too for bees?

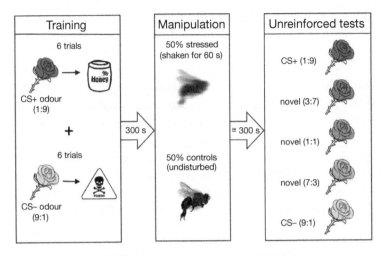

Bateson et al. (2011). The setup for Bateson and Wright's experiment.

Bateson and Wright also checked the shaken bees' systemic neurotransmitter levels. The shaken bees' serotonin and dopamine levels were diminished, as they are in humans who are feeling anxious.[2]

What are we to make of this? It does seem that the shaken bees were in a negative emotional state caused by the shaking and that this state in turn caused both stress-related physiological changes and a pessimistic cognitive bias, just as the experience of anxiety does in humans. But do they feel anxiety or distress? Here is what Bateson and Wright (2011) say:

> Using the best criteria currently agreed on for assessing animal emotions, i.e., a suite of changes in physiology, behavior, and especially cognitive biases, we have shown that agitated bees display a negative emotional state. Although our results do not allow us to make any claims about the presence of negative subjective feelings in honeybees, they call into question how we identify emotions in any nonhuman animal. It is logically inconsistent to

2. Likewise sheep; sheep with depleted serotonin levels judge ambiguous stimuli negatively.

claim that the presence of pessimistic cognitive biases should be taken as confirmation that dogs or rats are anxious but to deny the same conclusion in the case of honeybees. (p. 1072)

This seems to me incorrect. Either the bees have been made anxious by the shaking or they haven't. If they have, as Bateson and Wright assert, then they *feel* anxious, for occurrent anxiety is a feeling. Of course, someone can be anxious without feeling anxious at a particular moment, but that is because the anxiety is dispositional—a disposition to feel anxious. The experiment does not show that bees are generally anxious creatures. What it shows (arguably) is that they can be made to be anxious in a certain setting. And if they are genuinely anxious in that setting, they must feel anxiety then.[3]

One objection that might be raised to Bateson and Wright's experiment is that there is a confounding factor in the procedure. Perhaps the explanation for why the bees behave as they do is that there is a decrease in odor detection, which is itself brought about by the lower dopamine and serotonin levels. These lower neurotransmitter levels themselves may be due to some much more general negative psychological reaction to the shaking, or, for that matter, to no psychological state at all.[4]

However, this misses the point. If odor detection generally were diminished without any change in anxiety level, then one would expect the shaken bees to have a harder time distinguishing the CS+ odor, as shown in the figure on page 143, from the closest next odor (that is, the novel 3:7 odor) than the unshaken bees. So one would expect the response to these two odors (extending the mouthpiece) to be more similar for the shaken bees than the unshaken bees. But it isn't. The shaken bees extend their mouthpieces in exactly the same way as the unshaken bees for the CS+ odor but not for the novel 3:7 odor. This fact needs explanation, and the obvious explanation is that the shaken bees were feeling anxious and so were inclined to be more pessimistic about the 3:7 odor.

Another objection is that anxiety is a complex state functionally. Among other things, it involves anticipation of bad things to come

---

3. This is not to say, of course, that they must be conscious *of* the anxiety they are feeling. Consciousness of a mental state is itself a higher-order mental state (see chapter 2), and no claim is being made that bees are capable of such higher-order states.
4. I owe this point to Barry Smith.

(though no specific bad thing), and it is implausible to suppose that bees could anticipate future events.

But is this really so implausible? If so, why? After all, bees are very intelligent creatures, as I shall bring out later in this chapter, and it does not seem to me at all obvious that the bees could not be anticipating another shaking or something else threatening.

A third worry is that anxiety really has no distinctive phenomenology in the way that pain does. So what really does the claim that honey-bees *feel* anxiety as a result of the shaking come to in the end?

My response to this objection is to deny the premise. Think about what you feel when someone puts a gun in your back as you are trying to get some cash from an ATM. The phenomenology here is of a deep response in the stomach, a rearranging of the contents of the gut, as it were, together with an immediate increase in heart rate. This is the pro-totypical phenomenology of fear. Not all cases of fear are exactly like this phenomenally, but there is a family resemblance. The same is true for pain. And it is true for anxiety too.

Think of sitting by the phone waiting for the results of a medical test that will tell you whether you have cancer—the feeling of butterflies in the stomach, the general tension, the inability to concentrate on other tasks (or at least the great difficulty in so concentrating). This is a pro-totypical case of feeling anxious. The claim that bees feel anxiety is the claim that they feel something similar to this. Perhaps they are anxious about being shaken again as you are anxious about the results of the test, or perhaps their anxiety is generalized. Either way, there is something it is like for them, something akin to the distinctive feeling we undergo when we feel anxious.[5]

Another objection (due to Robert Lurz) is that there is a different, equally plausible explanation of the bee behavior. Here is how Lurz puts the objection (personal communication):

> Shaking bees causes them to go into attack mode, just as they
> do when you shake their hives. In attack mode, the bee's main
> focus is locating an intruder and attacking. The attack mode will

_____

5. I owe this objection and the final one below to Paul Boghossian.

obviously interfere with the bees' response to a positive stimulus (ones associated with food)—unless the stimulus is a sure bet. Too much is at stake to take a chance on a less than sure bet of food if you're defending the hive from a possible intruder. So the bees respond to CS+ because it's a sure bet of getting food, but they do not respond to novel (3:7) because it is less than a sure bet. The bees thus discriminate between CT+ and novel (3:7), but they don't choose the latter stimulus because it's not a sure bet of getting food (during a time of emergency).

This is an ingenious suggestion, but it seems to me to be unpersuasive. In general, under attack mode, food is of no immediate concern, even if it is a sure bet. Think, for example, of the soldier on high alert looking for armed enemy soldiers in an abandoned building. Even if he is in the kitchen and there is good food aplenty out on the counter, he is very unlikely to pause to taste it. The situation is too threatening for that. So Lurz has not adequately explained why the shaken bees respond in just the same way as the unshaken bees to CS+. Secondly, there is a five-minute delay after shaking before the tests are run. It seems unlikely that if there is an initial attack mode in response to the shaking, it would still be present after such a pause.

A final worry is that anxiety is a state of a sort that can only be experienced by creatures that are capable of feeling fear and/or pain. But this has not been established for the case of bees.

The claim that anxiety requires the capacity to feel pain is not at all obvious. Human beings with congenital pain insensitivity (see chapter 9) can still experience emotions such as joy and fear (though their fear is in reaction to emotional threats). Furthermore, there is behavioral evidence that bees can be fearful (Tan et al. 2013).

It is interesting to note that some bees engage in behavior that suggests the opposite of anxiety. These bees apparently are thrill seekers. They boldly go where other bees will not, fearlessly scouting out new food sources and potential hive locations. A recent study (Liang et al. 2012) found that there are large differences in brain gene expressions between scouts and non-scouts and that increasing the relevant chemicals in the brains of the timid bees make them into thrill seekers, and decreasing the chemicals in the brains of the thrill seekers makes them more timid. What is even more surprising is that the very same chemicals—catecholamine, glutamate, and gamma-aminobutyric acid—play a similar role in controlling thrill-seeking behavior in vertebrates, including humans. Robinson (2006) hypothesizes that the evolutionary history of the development of the underlying molecular pathways is similar in bees and humans. Since humans who engage in thrill-seeking behavior do so largely for the rush they experience, a plausible hypothesis is that something like this is true for bees too.

Going back to the case of anxiety, it might be replied that the bees are in a state that functions in the same way or a similar way to anxiety, but this state isn't *really* anxiety (likewise for the case of thrills). This reply flies in the face of the general reasoning laid out and defended in chapter 5. Even though bee physiology is very different from ours, this should not be held to count against the ascription of experiences, including anxiety, to bees—if bees behave in the same general way as we do and undergo similar changes in their neurotransmitter levels in response to stimuli that generate experiences, unless there is reason to suppose that the facts of bee physiology preclude them from undergoing experiences. I shall return to this point shortly.

Secondly, if it is denied that bees do indeed feel anxiety, then why does the state they are in function in the same way as anxiety? What is it about the state in virtue of which it generates the sort of functioning associated with anxiety if it isn't that the state feels bad in something like the way that anxiety feels bad? If bees are creatures of a sort that can undergo consciousness at all, any answer to these questions that eschews reference to the way the state feels is committed to denying consciousness a role where it certainly *seems* to have one. And so it inevitably leads to further puzzles: Why would this state not be conscious when others in the bee are? If other states in the bee act as if they are conscious, and they genuinely are, why would this state act if it is conscious and not be conscious? Why would Mother Nature have declined to make *this* state a conscious state when it acts as if it is? I see no satisfactory answers to these questions, unless a case can be made that bees are zombies, that is, creatures altogether lacking consciousness. It is to a further discussion of this issue that I turn in the next section.

8.3 ARE BEES ZOMBIES?

Bees have three pairs of legs, three body segments, and a pair of wings. They also have complex eyes and a highly developed sense of smell. Bee eyes are compound, made up of many tiny lenses known as facets. These facets are devoted to small regions of the visual field, and from the information they provide the bee brain generates something like a mosaic picture of the field of view. One advantage of the compound eye is that it makes movement detection very easy. Bees also respond to a range of colors, some not detectable by humans. This was established by Karl von Frisch in 1915.

Frisch placed a blue piece of cardboard on a table with honey on it to attract the bees to that color. He repeated this procedure several times and then removed the bees. Next he placed two more pieces of cardboard by the already positioned blue piece, the new blue one to the left, and the red one to the right. In neither case did he put any honey on the new pieces of cardboard. Finally, Frisch took away the first blue cardboard. Frisch then reasoned as follows: if the bees "remembered they found honey on blue they should fly to the blue cardboard" (Frisch 1915, p. 4). This the bees did. The conclusion to be drawn is that the bees can discriminate colors. But do they have a genuine color sense?

Frisch's next experiment was as follows. Frisch put a blue card along with a range of further cards of varying shades of gray from white to black, and he placed a small glass dish on each. Only the dish on the blue card had food in it. Frisch then switched the location of the blue card within the group. He found that the bees continued to land on the blue card with the food. Finally, Frisch removed all the cards and replaced them with new cards of differing shades of gray along with a new blue card, each with a small glass dish placed on top. This time, however, there was no food. Frisch found that the bees kept landing on the blue card, thereby showing that they remembered it and discriminated it from all shades of gray. Bees, then, must have a genuine color sense.

The same experiment was repeated for other colors. Frisch found that it worked for orange, yellow, green, violet, and purple but not for red. With red, the bees landed on the red card, but they also landed on the black and dark gray cards. So bees are red-blind. Interestingly, even though bees can distinguish colors from shades of gray, they have trouble discriminating orange, yellow, and green. They also see blue, violet, and purple as the same color.

More recently, it has been found that bees, unlike humans, are sensitive as well to colors in the ultraviolet range. Overall, the biggest difference between bee color vision and human color vision is that we can discriminate many distinct hues in the visible spectrum, whereas bees can distinguish only four: yellow, blue-green, blue, and ultraviolet.

Bees use their antennae for the purposes of touch and odor. The antennae have tiny sensory hairs on them that allow bees to feel things and recognize a wide variety of scents. It is known that bees have 170 odorant receptors, many more than fruit flies or mosquitoes, and in general their olfactory abilities are remarkable. They use these abilities to perceive pheromones, to recognize kin, to communicate within the hive, and to find food. In the last case, there may be a very large number of flowers encountered by foraging worker bees, distinctions among which are achieved on the basis of subtle differences in scent.

Interestingly, bees' sense of taste, which operates via hairs on their tongues or proboscises, is not so developed. This may be because in their natural habitat plants and bees get along well, and so plants don't need toxins to defend themselves, nor, correspondingly, do bees need ways of detecting toxins. Or at least they didn't until recently. Sadly, the recent decline in the bee population now widely traced to the use of pesticides manufactured by Monsanto and others may also have to do with the bees' weaker sense of taste.

Using their senses, bees are capable of a wide range of amazing behavior. Consider, for example, a recent experiment by Giurfu and colleagues (2005). Bees were trained (via sugar water as a reward) to fly into long cylinders with a single entrance and then out of one of two exits between which the bees had to choose. The exits of these cylinders then led to further similarly shaped cylinders, so that a maze structure was created at the end of which the reward was found. Where the branch point in a cylinder was colored blue, the bees had to turn right. Where it was colored green, the bees had to turn left. Amazingly, the bees managed to learn the blue-right, green-left rule so that when they were placed in a new, unfamiliar maze of cylinders, they could apply it and get to the reward at the end.

So bees are intelligent. And along with their intelligence comes a good working memory. One way to test working memory is to present subjects with a picture and then a little later present them with two pictures and ask them to pick the one that matches the previous picture. This requires the subjects to remember the earlier picture and to use that memory. When a subject is successful at this task (that of delayed matching to sample, or DMTS), this is standardly taken as an indication that the subject was conscious of the original sample and becomes conscious of it again via some sort of memory image in order to perform the match. A second version of this task (that of delayed-nonmatching to sample, or DNMTS) is a little more complex: it requires subjects to pick the new picture that doesn't match. So in this case there is an extra step.

Bees perform well at both tasks. If a colored disk is displayed at the entrance to the cylinder maze, and over one of the two exits to each cylinder a disk of the same color is placed, the bees can learn to take that exit (a DMTS task) or the opposite one (a DNMTS task). Moreover, bees can perform well at these tasks even when the stimulus is an odor rather than a color (Koch 2008).

If bees can discriminate colors and odors on the basis of their senses and use these discriminations along with their memories to perform well in DMTS and DNMTS tasks, then that is a reason to think that they are perceptually conscious, just as it is in the case of vertebrates. The appeal to behavior in DMTS and DNMTS tasks here, I might add, is not highly theoretical or scientific. It is part of our common-sense psychology that if subjects are shown a picture (for example) and then a little later they are presented with two pictures and asked to pick the one that matches the previous picture, their behavior, if they are successful, typically relies on remembering the earlier picture and using a memory image to meet the task demand. It is also part of common sense that memory images are laid down in memory from perceptual consciousness. The evidence is that bees conform to such generalizations just as human beings do.

Perhaps it will now be replied that although bees certainly behave as if they are perceptually conscious, there is a defeater to the inference that they undergo perceptual experiences. The defeater is provided by the absence not only of a neocortex but also of any homologous cells to those found in the neocortex. Bees just aren't like birds or fish. Indeed, in contrast not just to birds and fish but to all vertebrates, they have a fully distributed nervous systems (Ned Block, personal communication).

This is unconvincing. For one thing, bees do *not* have a fully distributed nervous system. For another, there are noteworthy facts about the neurophysiology of bees as well as their functional architecture that defeat the potential defeater cited above. So Newton's Rule is still applicable, as in the case of fish, and the conclusion to be drawn from bee behavior is that bees *are* perceptually conscious—or, more carefully, that it is rational to prefer the hypothesis that they are perceptually conscious to the hypothesis that they are not. This needs some explanation.

Bee physiology is certainly different from that of vertebrates, but there are important commonalities.

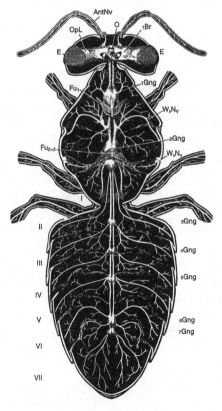

Snodgrass (1910)

In the figure on page 151, the two white parallel lines running from the base to the head of the bee correspond to the spinal column (though they are not structurally the same). The little white disks are nerve centers, or ganglia, from which signals are sent along nerves that reach into various parts of the bee body, including the legs. In our case, some of our functions, for example, our breathing and heartbeat, are controlled not by the brain but by subcortical mechanisms in the lower half of the brainstem. This relieves our brains of a significant amount of work. Ganglia do likewise for bees.

The bee brain itself has almost a million neurons in it, even though its size is less than one cubic millimeter. The result is that the neural density of the bee's brain is ten times greater than that of a mammalian cerebral cortex. The brain is composed of three regions: the protocerebrum (PC), deuterocerebrum (DC), and tritocerebrum (TC). The PC is by far the biggest, and it contains the mushroom bodies (so called because the cross section looks like two mushrooms). Attached to the PC, though not a part of it, are two large regions that receive inputs from the two compound eyes. These are the two optic lobes. They send visual information on to the mushroom bodies in the PC. Receiving input from the antennae within the DC are the antennal lobes. These too send information on to the mushroom bodies, as does the TC, which is the smallest part of the brain. It may have a role in tasting food. In addition, it links the brain with the ventral nerve cord. At the base of the tritocerebrum are two frontal nerves that link with a ganglion that controls swallowing as well as the actions of the heart and the gut.

So bees do not have a distributed nervous system. Moreover, even though a neocortex is missing in bees, as noted above, mushroom bodies are present in the bee brain, and these bodies function in a somewhat similar way to the neocortex. For example, in star-nosed moles, there is a huge region of somatosensory cortex (due to the fact that these moles find their way around and discover food using a large, star-shaped tactile organ on their snouts). There is a corresponding expansion in visual representation in the mushroom bodies of social Hymenoptera, including bees. This reflects the importance of vision to these Hymenoptera: more processing power has been devoted to this sensory modality, given its role in their behavioral ecology (Farris 2008). There is also integration of visual information with information from other sensory modalities within the mushroom bodies as well as the formation of short-term and long-term memories.

As noted earlier, bee brains and human brains, in addition, have important neurochemical commonalities. Catecholamine, glutamate, and gamma-aminobutyric acid play a central role in controlling thrill-seeking behavior in vertebrates, including humans. They do the same in bees. Serotonin and dopamine are diminished in anxious mammals. The same is true in functionally anxious bees. Humans have an endogenous opioid system (inhibited by naloxone). So too do bees.

Finally, there is evidence that the neural architecture of the bee supports a global workspace. According to some scientists, this suffices for consciousness. No such claim is being made here. The point I wish to make is simply that there is an important functional similarity in the underlying architecture of bee and mammalian brains. This point, together with the points made above, undercuts attempts to defeat the use of behavioral similarities as grounds for experiential similarities via an application of Newton's Rule and the same effect, same cause principle. Let me spell this out further by saying something about what a global workspace is. Sometimes those who write of a global workspace present the thesis in neurophysiological terms (Dehaene, Kerszberg, and Changeux 1998). There is nothing in the idea of a global workspace that is inherently neurophysiological, however. The key idea is that perceptual systems deliver representations "that are consumed by mechanisms of reporting, reasoning, evaluating, deciding and remembering, which themselves produce representations that are further consumed by the same set of mechanisms" (Block 2009). Perceptual information, once it is globally broadcast in the above way, is phenomenally conscious (Baars 1988). What crucially matters to phenomenal consciousness, on this view, then, is not the physical hardware but the functioning. In principle, global broadcast could be achieved via silicon chips or ectoplasm.

Here is an example to illustrate the view. Suppose I read out to you a seven-digit phone number. A little later, I ask you to give me that number. You do so accurately. What happens is that you initially commit the number to working memory. When you recall the number and repeat it to me, your initial representation of it is consumed by your mechanisms of remembering and reporting. In this way, it is globally broadcast, and at this time, your representation becomes conscious. It is subjectively experienced. There is, of course, controversy as to whether global broadcasting is really what matters to consciousness, but let us put that to one side. Is there anything like global broadcasting in bees? I have already mentioned the fact that bees can perform DMTS and DNMTS tasks and use their solutions to find their way to rewards. Moreover, they can do this using both colors and odors. This requires that they use information in working memory, just as you do in the above phone number example. Using the information to respond is a matter of the information playing a certain functional role—a role of the sort postulated in global workspace theory. This suggests that bees do indeed have a global workspace.

There is also an extraordinary variety in bee behavior based on sensory information. For example, bees use landmarks and celestial cues (such as the position of the sun) to navigate. They gather food by visiting hundreds of flowers one after another; they check out places for potential nests; they exchange information with one another about food and nest sites via "waggle dances." As already noted, they see the world in color; they also can recognize patterns, and they are highly sensitive to movements. Their olfactory sense is acute. They can identify orientations of items as such and respond to those orientations when present in new cases. For example, they can be trained to distinguish between horizontal and vertical black and white stripes and to transfer this distinction to things other than stripes.

According to Menzel and Giurfa (2001), the overall complexity of bee behavior is such that it cannot be explained simply by independent, domain-specific modules of the sort associated in philosophy with Jerry Fodor (1983). There are such sensory-motor modules in the honeybee, but they need to be integrated into a central state, and representations in that central state then drive behavior. They comment (p. 70):

> The question that we originally raised was whether the explanation of insect behaviour could be reduced to a stack of such vertical processing modules, or whether it is necessary to assume that horizontal combinations between modules occur at a central state.

Numerous examples show that the latter alternative is required for understanding the complexity of behaviour in the honeybee. Such an integration allows for consultation and comparison of different outputs corresponding to different contexts and stored in long-term memory, and thus for context-dependent decisions.

See below:

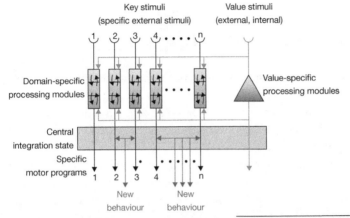

TRENDS in Cognitive Sciences

Menzel and Giurfa (2001)

If this is correct and there is indeed in bees a central integration state—a state that integrates information from a number of different modules and then uses that information cognitively to drive behavior—there seem to be all the ingredients in place for global broadcasting.

So bee physiology is not fully distributed; chemicals released in bee brains are very similar to the chemicals released in human brains that form the basis for a variety of human experiences, and bees have a global workspace. So the absence of both a neocortex and homologous cells does not carry much weight. Of course, it cannot be denied that bee brains are more different from human brains than fish brains or bird brains, for example. And so it seems rational to *more* strongly prefer the consciousness hypothesis to its denial for the case of fish and birds than for the case of bees. Still, the simplest, most unified explanation of a range of behavior in bees is that bees are conscious. This explanation stands as the best available, and so we should prefer it. Given the physiological differences, this rational preference pretty clearly does not come with a level of confidence sufficient for rational belief. Even so, it entitles us to hold that those who claim that bees merely undergo states that mimic anxiety and other experiences are, on this score, irrational. I turn next to the case of crabs.

8.4 CRABS AND PAIN

Crabs are crustaceans. Like insects, they are invertebrates having segmented bodies and limbs with joints. They are covered with a thick protective exoskeleton, or shell. Their sense of vision is poor. They search for food using their highly developed sense of smell (chemoreception). They also have a sense of taste.

Crabs have many fewer neurons than honeybees (around a hundred thousand). Even so, they react to analgesics and local anesthetics in the same sort of way that honeybees do. For example, when crabs are electrically shocked, they engage in a defensive threat display. Injection of morphine hydrochloride diminishes the crabs' display response, and it does so in a dose-dependent way; further naloxone injection inhibits the effects of morphine (Lozada, Romano, and Maldonado 1988). This is suggestive of the presence of pain. But as noted earlier, it could be that the morphine is not reducing the experience of pain but rather diminishing the crabs' response to all stimuli.

Still, there is evidence from some recent experiments that crabs feel pain, and this evidence is not so easy to explain away. In one of these experiments, Appel and Elwood (2009a, 2009b) rigged up some shells with wires that would deliver small shocks to hermit crabs.[6] The response of the hermit crabs to the shocks was to abandon the shells. Appel and Elwood then diminished the level of shock to a point at which the hermit crabs were prepared to stay in the shells. Other hermit crabs

---

6. Elwood was motivated to run this experiment by the question of a well-known British seafood chef who asked him if crustaceans felt pain. At the time, Elwood had no answer.

were not subject to any shocks at all. Next he made available new shells. What he found was that the only hermit crabs to check out the new shells were those that had been shocked. These were also the only crabs to abandon their old shells for the new (sometimes lesser) ones. Why? Evidently, this is not a matter of a simple nociceptive reflex.

The best explanation seems to be that the hermit crabs that had been shocked remembered it and the painful experience it elicited and chose the new shells, even if they were lesser, because they did not cause them any pain. The crabs thus were engaging in a kind of trade-off. Such trade-offs with respect to pain and other requirements are found in vertebrates too.

In another experiment Humans, for example, will typically break a promise if the cost of keeping it involves sufficiently great pain, and they will do so even if materially they are worse off as a result. Magee and Elwood (2013) exploited the fact that crabs like to hide in dark environments such as those found under rocks. The crabs were placed in a brightly lit tank with two separate darkly lit shelter areas. One of these areas delivered a mild electric shock to the crabs that had chosen it. All the crabs were then removed from the tank and returned to it a little later. This time around, the crabs returned to the areas they had selected before, even though some of them had been shocked in their region of choice. The crabs were then shocked again. The procedure was repeated once more. On the third return to the tank, most of the shocked crabs stayed away from their earlier shelter. And those that did return to it were now much more likely to leave it very quickly. The obvious conclusion to draw is that the crabs felt pain from the shocks and then learned to avoid it by choosing the other shelter. Those that took longer to switch were again engaged in trade-off reasoning: the unknown versus the familiar, where the familiar has a real cost. This evidently is not simply a matter of nociception. Pain provides for longer-term protection; nociception generates immediate reflex withdrawal but no more.

So the best available explanation of the crab's behavior seems to be that crabs feel pain. If this is so, then it is rational to prefer the hypothesis that crabs feel pain to the hypothesis that they do not. To my knowledge, no experiments have yet been performed that address the question of whether crabs can feel anxiety and other emotional states. There is, however, some recent work on the emotional lives of crayfish that suggests a positive answer.

In an experiment by Pascal Fossat and colleagues (2014), it was found that administering low-level shocks to crayfish and then putting them in an aquarium maze in which there were both dark pathways and well-lit ones resulted in the crayfish staying almost entirely in the dark pathways, whereas crayfish that had not been shocked or stressed went into both the dark pathways and the well-lit ones. Interestingly, Fossat found that the shocked crayfish had diminished levels of serotonin in their brains, as is the case with the honeybees in the experiment on anxiety discussed earlier and also with anxious vertebrates. Further, when crayfish were injected with serotonin, they responded in apparently anxious ways, and when the shocked crayfish were given the drug chlordiazepoxide, which in humans reduces anxiety, they relaxed and entered the well-lit pathways of the maze.

8.5 CRABS AND BEES

Arthropods are the largest animal phylum. This group include insects and crustaceans and spiders, also discussed in this chapter. Arthropods have segmented bodies with appendages and a strong outer exoskeleton. Arthropods all have a nervous system made up of ganglia that are connected by nerve fibers. Earlier, it was noted that insects have three parts to their brains: a protocerebrum that is connected to vision, a deuterocerebrum that is in charge of processing sensory information from the antennae, and a tritocerebrum that integrates processing in the other two brain regions and links the brain with the ventral nerve cord. This is true of arthropod brains generally.

So the brains of honeybees and those of crabs work in a similar way and are connected to similar nervous systems. Bees have a rich perceptual consciousness, and they can also feel some emotions, such as anxiety. Given this, and given also the fact that crabs feel pain even though they have only a hundred thousand neurons in comparison to the million of the honeybee, surely the most plausible hypothesis overall, consistent with what we now know, is that bees feel pain too, not just that they act upon occasion as if they do. Further support for this hypothesis would be provided by experiments similar in kind to those described above for hermit crabs, if they came out in the same way. But to my knowledge no such experiments have yet been done.

The general conclusion I draw is that experiences are not restricted to the realm of vertebrates. Creatures with different nervous systems than ours are phenomenally conscious. The inclination to suppose otherwise seems to rest on a reaction we might call "speciesism": no species as different from us as crabs and bees are could possibly feel what we feel. Speciesism is the opposite of anthromorphism, but it is just as much a form of dogmatism. What is needed is a middle ground, and that is what I have tried to supply.

[9]

THE GIRL WHO CAN'T FEEL PAIN

As a baby, Gabby Gingras slept through the prick of a blood test. She also seemed oblivious to the cold. Her parents would waken her in her crib and discover that she was freezing cold to the touch but uncomplaining and happy. Subsequently they discovered that she suffers from a rare abnormality: congenital pain insensitivity.

Her insensitivity to pain, which might first seem a blessing, is in reality a terrible curse. Why? Because Gabby hasn't a clue when she has hurt herself.

As a baby, when she was teething, she chewed on her tongue as if it were bubblegum, according to her mother. She also chewed on her fingers, mutilating them so much that her parents decided that Gabby's teeth needed to be pulled out to protect her. Learning to walk, she injured herself time and again. At age two, she broke her jaw but did not feel it, with the result that it was not diagnosed until much later when an infection resulted.

Gabby's eyes were a constant source of concern. If her parents looked away for a moment, she would put a finger in one or the other. They tried restraints, then goggles, but by age four she needed to have her left eye removed. Gabby's right eye was damaged too, but she still has it, although she need a lens covering the eye to improve her sight.

Gabby is not alone. There are around a hundred people in the world with congenital pain insensitivity.[1] A documentary was made

---

1. Congenital pain insensitivity is not to be confused with pain asymbolia. With the former, there is no feeling of pain at all. With the latter, there is, but its subjects do not mind it.

recently on children such as Gabby, and there is one thing it makes very clear: pain is a *gift* from Mother Nature.[2] It's a gift that none of us really want. But it is a gift we cannot do without, unless others are around to oversee our every move.

The job of pain, its function, is to protect us, to enable us to minimize injuries, to warn us of damaging stimuli. Without it, we as a species would not survive long—and neither would other species. Pain exists to help those who undergo it survive.

It seems plausible that what is true of pain is true in broad outline of other experiences, too. For example, the function of the feeling of disgust is to aid us in avoiding disease and contaminants. This is why we typically find rotting food, human waste, and animals that carry disease such as rats and cockroaches disgusting.

The experience of fear has as its function to enable us to tread carefully in dangerous situations; the job of anger is to get us to act aggressively in response to the threatening behavior of another; the experience of orgasm exists to promote reproduction; perceptual experiences have the task of informing us of features of things in our environments, features knowledge of which guides our actions and thereby improves our chances of survival;[3] the feeling of thirst has the job of getting us to drink water, and so on.

Experiences are states that Mother Nature has built into many of her creations. They are not states that were acquired by learning or culture. That would have made their subjects too vulnerable during the learning period. Now if experiences do indeed have functions of the sort just specified, then if their subjects did not have them, they would not be able to do the sorts of things experiences enable them to do. Thus the child who cannot feel pain is unable to do what the rest of us can do by virtue of experiencing pain. She cannot protect herself, minimize injury, and suchlike. Still, nonhuman creatures that lack a certain sort of experience we have, for example, the feeling of disgust, may have developed

2. See http://frozenfeetfilm.com/lifewithoutpain/.
3. Color experiences, for example, have the job of informing us of the colors of things. This was originally useful to our ancestors in helping them pick out ripe from unripe fruit in a forest setting.

other mechanisms for doing what that sort of experience enables us, its possessors, to do. Thus, animals such as dogs that lack the experience of disgust have developed grooming or wound-licking mechanisms that enable them to deal with contaminants and disease. Even so, where creatures of a certain sort do not display X, where X is what experience E enables its subjects to do, then that is reason to believe that creatures of that sort do not have E.

This is not intended as a metaphysically necessary truth. It has the same status as, for example, the claim that where a rock is dropped, it falls to earth. Of course, it is metaphysically possible for rocks to do otherwise. In some possible worlds, our laws of nature do not obtain. Still, in worlds with our laws, rocks that are dropped fall to earth. Likewise, many philosophers will say, it is metaphysically possible for an experience, understood as a state with a certain phenomenal character, to do other than what it actually does. Nonetheless, in worlds with our laws of nature, things retain their actual biological functions if they have any. So an experience that enables its subjects to perform a certain sort of action in the actual world will do the same in other nomically possible worlds, and hence if an actual creature cannot perform that sort of action, it is not subject to that experience. This gives us a condition—failing to be able to perform a certain sort of action—such that if creatures of a certain type meet that condition, we may conclude that they do not undergo a certain type of experience. This is a condition we have used previously in the earlier discussion of the question of whether insects feel pain.

There is another more general condition that can be extracted by reflecting on the role that mental states play. Mental states allow for flexibility in behavior. As the mental states of a creature change, so too does its behavior. And this is so even if the very same type of stimulus is present. Of course, non-conscious, non-mental learning can change how a living thing behaves too. But where there is no (or very little) flexibility in behavior in response to the same stimulus, that is evidence that no mental states are operative in the production of the behavior and thus no experiences in particular. This observation provides us with a kind of zombie test for living things, as we shall shortly see. But first I want to address a worry about my claims above concerning the function of pain and other experiences.

9.1 A COMPLAINT FROM BLOCK

In a well-known essay, Ned Block (1997) has argued that a number of philosophers and psychologists have been guilty of confusing phenomenal consciousness with what he calls "access consciousness" and that the reasons standardly given for taking phenomenal consciousness (and its various species) to have the sort of biological function(s) I earlier proposed are misguided. As we saw in chapter 2, according to Block, there is no single concept of consciousness. Sometimes, when we use the term "conscious" we are getting at phenomenal consciousness; at other times we are referring to access consciousness. I argued in chapter 2 that this is all wrong. There is only one concept of consciousness at play in our ordinary thought and talk. What Block calls "access consciousness" is really just accessibility (more below). For the moment, I shall ignore this point. What exactly is Block's argument?

Consider the case of blindsight. People with blindsight have large blind areas, or scotoma, in their visual field due to brain damage in the post-geniculate region (typically the occipital cortex), and yet, under certain circumstances, they can issue statements with respect to the contents of those areas (see Weiskrantz 1990). For example, blindsight subjects can make accurate guesses with respect to such things as presence, position, orientation, and movement of visual stimuli. They can also guess correctly as to whether an X is present rather than an O, or vice versa. And some blindsight patients can even make accurate color judgments about the blind field (Weiskrantz 1990).

It appears, then, that, given appropriate instructions, blindsight subjects can respond in a way that is significantly like normally sighted subjects with respect to a limited range of stimuli in the blind areas in their visual fields without anything experiential or phenomenally conscious going on. Blindsight subjects, however, do not spontaneously issue any public reports about the contents of their blind fields. In each case, they respond only when they are forced to choose between certain alternative possibilities. Moreover, they cannot identify objects in their blind field as falling into everyday categories: they cannot tell *what* is present except in rare cases (of the sort mentioned above). So, for example (it has been supposed), a thirsty blindsight subject will fail to recognize a glass of water placed before him and so will fail to reach out for it.[4] The result is that blindsight subjects are invariably "deeply disabled" (Weiskrantz 1990, p. 8).

Why should there be such failures of identification? The answer, according to some philosophers and psychologists (e.g., Marcel 1986, Van Gulick 1993, Flanagan 1992), is obvious. Blindsight subjects lack phenomenal consciousness. The function (or a function) of phenomenal consciousness is simply to enable creatures to use information represented in their brains in the guidance of rational action (as contrasted with guessing behavior). Blindsight subjects cannot use this information rationally in the way that the rest of us can.

According to Block, an obvious function of access consciousness has been transferred here to phenomenal consciousness. The blindsight subject who fails to reach for the glass lacks both sorts of consciousness. Block comments:

> There is an obvious explanation of why the patient doesn't reach for the glass in terms of information about it not reaching the mechanisms of reasoning and rational control of speech and action, the machinery of A-consciousness (access consciousness). ... A function of the mechanisms underlying A-consciousness is completely obvious. If information from our senses did not get to mechanisms of control and reasoning and of rational control of rational action and reporting, we would not be able to use our senses to guide our action and reporting. But it is a mistake to slide from a function of the machinery of A-consciousness to any function at all of P-consciousness. (p. 242)

So it could well be that the absence of phenomenal consciousness is *not* a factor in the patient's inaction. For all we know, it is empirically possible for access consciousness of the glass to be missing, while phenomenal

---

4. To my knowledge, the experiment has never been done. (Tony Marcel tells me that he tried something like this with a pint of beer, but the smell of the beer gave it away.)

consciousness is present; and in this case the patient will still not reach for the glass. This possibility is easy to ignore because access consciousness and phenomenal consciousness normally go hand in hand (and hence it is very easy to mistakenly identify them, according to Block). But it is a real possibility, certainly not one that can be ruled out a priori. The function of phenomenal consciousness, then, cannot be *obvious*.

There is no need for us to restrict ourselves to the recherché and hypothetical case of the thirsty blindsight subject. Consider again Gabby Gingrass (GG). Block's point with respect to GG is this:

1. GG does not act as those of us who feel pain do.
2. GG lacks the experience of pain (phenomenal pain consciousness).
3. GG also lacks relevant access consciousness: information from GG's nociceptors does not get to mechanisms of control and reasoning and of rational control of rational action and reporting.
4. It may well be that it is empirically possible for access consciousness to be missing while phenomenal pain consciousness is present, and in that case there will be inaction of the sort that GG displays.

So:

5. The function of the experience of pain is not obvious.

What Block calls "the absence of access consciousness," as applied to this case, is really just the absence of cognitive accessibility of the right sort. So Block's (4) may be restated as

4′. It may well be that it is empirically possible for the right sort of accessibility to be missing while phenomenal pain consciousness is present, and in that case there will be inaction of the sort that GG displays.

The idea that there could be a feeling of pain that is completely inaccessible to the individual's cognitive mechanisms is highly contentious.

After all, if I *have* such a feeling at a particular time, then I myself *feel* pain at that time. How could I really be feeling something and yet be *incapable* of registering it cognitively in any way? This question arose earlier in chapter 2 in connection with Block's example of the deeply repressed image of a red room.

Still, even if there is no incoherence in the idea of an inaccessible pain, what matters for present purposes is the following observation: if indeed an inaccessible experience of pain is empirically possible, still it cannot be denied that this is an abnormal case. Mother Nature surely did not design her creatures to feel pains that were inaccessible to them. What would be the point? Such experiences would be idle wheels. In the Normal case, that is, the case when everything is operating as it should, the experience of pain certainly is accessible. It is poised to make some cognitive difference. Accordingly, the case of an inaccessible experience of pain is abNormal. As such, it is irrelevant to claims about the *function* of pain. In general, the function of something is what it is supposed to do, what it is designed to do. And that is what it does do when everything is working Normally.

Block's empirical possibility—granting that it is a possibility—is a possibility occurring under abNormal conditions. So it has no bearing on the function of pain. The inference from (4′) to (5) is a non sequitur. This reply generalizes to other cases. The functions of experiences are indeed obvious, or at least relatively obvious after a little reflection.

I turn in the remaining three sections of this chapter to some examples of simple living things to which the zombie test presented in the introduction may be straightforwardly applied: protozoa, plants, and caterpillars.

9.2 PROTOZOA

Protozoa are one-celled micro-organisms, as shown in the figure opposite. They move and reproduce (by splitting in two), and they live in water or damp environments. Protozoa breathe too: they take in oxygen through their cell membranes and pass out carbon dioxide. They digest food by absorbing algae and bacteria from the water and storing it in tiny sacs.

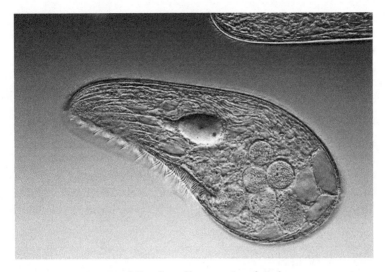

Frank Fox, http://www.mikro-foto.de

There is nothing it is like to be a protozoan. Protozoa are simple stimulus-response systems. There is no flexibility in their responses whatsoever. With human beings subject to the same stimulus, there is an enormous flexibility and variation in the responses produced. One may cry, another laugh, a third jump up and down, a fourth sit silent, a fifth run away, and so on. The response is a function not only of the stimulus but also of the psychological states generated by it and their interactions. And these psychological states may vary dramatically from one human to another.

Protozoa have no flexibility since they have no psychological states. Their responses are simple reactions to the stimuli that impinge upon them, just like the beeping noise that is emitted in my car, as I am parking it, in response to an object that is too close and in the car's path. This is not to say that all protozoa react in the same way. Some protozoa have no movement; others move by means of cilia, flagella, or pseudopods.[5] The

---

5. Cilia are slender protuberances from much larger cell bodies; flagella are lash-like appendages that stick out from cell bodies; pseudopods are temporary projections of the cell wall that enable some protozoa to locomote.

point is that they cannot change how they react through learning or life history. They are built by Mother Nature a certain way, though not all just the same way, and their responses to stimuli are thereby fixed. Protozoa no more have experiences than do cuckoo clocks or compasses or cars.

Even though protozoa are simple stimulus-response systems, they can protect themselves. If a protozoan finds itself outside of a host, it can form a capsule or cyst that enables it to survive. This is not an indication of pain or any other psychological state, however. There is no state of a protozoan that plays a functional role of the sort pain (or any other psychological state) plays. The protozoan is simply built so that in certain adverse environments, it automatically grows an overarching cover, just as the Wimbledon tennis facility does when it starts to rain on Centre Court.

9.3 PLANTS

It is not uncommon to read in the popular press today that plants think and have feelings. As surprising as this idea may seem, it has a long history. Charles Darwin's grandfather Erasmus Darwin (1800) describes some experiments in which barberry flowers were pricked with a pin, balsam was given an electrical shock, and apple trees were shipped to New York to find out how they would deal with the change in time zone! On the basis of the experiments, Erasmus Darwin comments: "Have vegetable buds irritability? Have they sensation? Have they volition? . . . I am persuaded they possess them all."[6]

Some fifty years later, Gustav Fechner, a German psychologist, hypothesized that plants undergo emotions and that our talking and being affectionate to them could make them healthier and also grow more quickly.[7] In 1900, Jagadish Chandra Bose, an Indian scientist, began conducting experiments on plants. Bose was of the view that plants have a nervous system and that they respond to pinching or other mechanical stimulation as animals do. In one of his experiments, Bose

---

6. Remarkably, Charles Darwin himself got his son to play the bassoon near a mimosa plant with the aim of finding out if there might be any reaction.

7. See Heidelberger 2004.

wired up a carrot to a galvanometer and pinched it with forceps. A journalist present tells us that the device registered "infinitesimal twitches, starts, and tremors." In this way, supposedly, "can science reveal the feelings of even so stolid a vegetable as the carrot."

Bose held that plants respond positively to pleasant music by growing more quickly and negatively to sounds that are grating or loud by slowing in their growth. He even held that plants can feel pain. This view did not go down well with the playwright George Bernard Shaw, who was a vegetarian. Apparently, Shaw was disturbed by a demonstration in Bose's laboratory in which a cabbage underwent convulsions as it was boiled to death!

Bose was a well-known scientist, subsequently knighted, but his experiments have not proved repeatable (though Cleve Backster, a polygraph specialist with the CIA, made some related claims in the 1960s).[8] Nonetheless, some scientists today call themselves "plant neurobiologists," and they hold that there are important similarities between animal nervous systems and information networks in plants.[9] This is shown, they claim (Karpinski et al. 1999), by the way in which plants transmit information about the light intensity and color shone on one leaf (for example, a leaf at the bottom of a plant) to other leaves (for example, ones at the top). The information is passed via electrical signals from cells of a specific type found throughout each plant (called "bundle sheath cells"). These cells function like nerves for plants, with the result that chemical changes induced by the light were found in leaves on which the light had not been shone. These changes continued in the dark when the light was turned off, indicating, according to Karpinski, a kind of memory.

What is especially interesting is that the chemical reactions varied with the color of the light (red, blue, white). Karpinski hypothesized that the plants use information in the light to induce chemical reactions that protect them against disease. Each day during the season has its own light quality, and there are diseases that attack the plants and that

8. These were later tested and shown to have no foundation by Horowitz, Lewis, and Gasteiger (1975).
9. They have a journal of their own, as well as their own professional society. Some botanists are strongly opposed, having signed a letter to a well-known journal in 2007 saying that plant neurobiology is "founded on superficial analogies and questionable extrapolations."

vary with the different parts of the season. So, according to Karpinski, what the plant does is to perform a kind of biological computation on the information in the light to generate a chemical reaction suitable to fight off diseases prevalent under that light condition.[10] This hypothesis was confirmed, in his view, by the discovery that infecting the plant with a disease (virus or bacteria) prior to shining a light on part of it an hour later left the plant unable to fight off the disease, but shining the light first and then infecting the plant during the following twenty-four-hour period enabled the plant to resist the infection.

Some other plant scientists, for example, Christine Foyer, have suggested that the plant here exhibits not only memory but also an appraisal of the situation, an appraisal that generates a suitable response. This shows a kind of intelligence.

Of course, intelligence is one thing and experience or feeling another. But these conclusions of Foyer and Karpinski are surely unwarranted. The fact that cascading chemical reactions to the light continue later in the dark no more shows that plants have memory than does the fact that knocking over a domino in a long line of dominoes, thereby much later causing a distant domino to fall over, shows that the sequence of dominoes has memory, and likewise with the ripple in a pond that results from a stone striking its surface and that continues afterward. The pond does not literally remember the stone striking it!

Moreover, even though plants contain cells, as do all living things, there isn't really the equivalent of a nervous system in the plant, at least of the sort found in animals with brains.[11] To be sure, cells have membranes, and where there are different concentrations of ions on the two sides of a membrane, as ions pass through channels from one side to the other, an electrical potential is generated. Still, plants don't have networks of cells put in place by Mother Nature for the purpose of fast, long-distance electrical signaling, as animals with brains do. Furthermore, plants don't have brains at all. So the similarity with the case of such

10. The idea here seems to be that in reaction to the strong light, plants absorb more energy than they need for photosynthesis, and the extra energy is converted to electrochemical activity that then has a positive impact on the plant's immune system.
11. Protozoa are sometimes classified as one-celled animals (I did so earlier), but they lack a brain.

animals is strained at best. And without that similarity, the case for plant mental states lacks any real foundation.

Admittedly, the behavior of the plants in Karpinski's experiments is striking and unexpected. But there are many examples of sophisticated changes in plant behavior in response to environmental changes. For example, trees can appear to communicate with other trees when they are in trouble! What actually happens is that when their leaves are damaged by insects, trees react by releasing volatile airborne chemicals. These cause changes in the nutritional quality of the leaves of nearby trees, thereby making those leaves less attractive to the insects attacking the initial trees. This at least is what is suggested by the findings in a series of experiments conducted by Orians and Rhoades (as reported by Kazarian 1983) on willow trees.

Consider also how some plants flower when the days get shorter while others come into flower as the days lengthen. This is not because the plants *know* the days are getting shorter or longer by, say, having kept a record of the length of each day and then having made the relevant comparisons. Rather, plants have circadian rhythms, and these dictate their flowering schedules.

Consider next the fact that plants grow up or that their roots grow in the direction of gravity. This happens even if the shoots of plants are kept in the dark or the plants are laid on their sides. Where the shoots are in the dark, even though the normal determinant of the direction of growth is missing, namely, light, the shoots use the force of gravity to give them an up-down axis and grow in the opposite direction of that force. Plants don't need to *know* which way to grow. It is determined for them by their environments and their nature as stimulus-response systems.

Plants have different parts and these parts may respond differently to the same stimulus. But each part will always respond to the same stimulus in the same way as determined by its being a part of a plant of a certain type. Plants are tropistic entities. They exhibit chemotropism, thigmotropism, phototropism, and geotropism, among others. The last two of these are movement or growth in response to light and gravity, respectively, as discussed in the last paragraph. Thigmotropism is movement in response to touch, as shown by the way in which a vine curls around a pole or a branch with which it comes into contact.

Chemotropism is movement or growth in response to a chemical stimulus. This is what enables plants to grow toward water and to avoid some toxins, for example.

Plants, then, are living things very different from human beings, or fish or crabs or honeybees, for that matter. Fish, even of the same species, in the same circumstances may react very differently, just as human beings may. Some trout, for example, are shy; others are bold.[12] Likewise, as we saw in the last chapter, some bees are thrill seekers; others are cautious. Plants are not like this. Their responses are rigidly fixed. Plants lack minds altogether. And lacking minds, they lack experiences and feelings—and indeed all mental states.

9.4 CATERPILLARS

The picture below is of a caterpillar on a branch of a plant. It is remarkably similar to a twig in appearance.

Geller-Grimm and Grimm (2006)

12. See chapter 6, note 22.

There is no evidence that caterpillars can experience pain or any emotions. But caterpillars have simple eyes composed of photoreceptors and pigments with which they can differentiate dark from light, although they cannot form any images. They also have a sense of touch given to them via long hairs that are attached to nerve cells. Further, they have taste cells that convey information about whether to eat various foods. And they have tiny antennae that provide them with a sense of smell. Can caterpillars hear anything? Well, they startle at loud noises. If you clap loudly near monarch larvae, they will rear up, although if you keep clapping, they will habituate to it and ignore the noise.

So are caterpillars perceptually conscious of anything? Do they have very basic visual experiences? Do they have olfactory experiences? What about tactual experiences? They have been called "eating machines," and they certainly do consume large quantities of leaves, but are they just "blind" eating machines?

I used to think so (Tye 1997), for I thought that caterpillars were incapable of any intelligent behavior, and so I was of the view that they are in the same camp as plants and protozoa: they are no more than stimulus-response beings. But recent scientific research has cast doubt on this assimilation (Skelhorn et al. 2011). Take the case of twig caterpillars. They look like twigs, and they use this fact to hide themselves from predators. During the day, when they are seen easily in an environment lacking twigs, they choose an environment, if it is available to them, in which twigs are in abundance. This is the case even if the latter environment is much lower in food than the former. They make this choice since it is much harder for predators to pick them out in the latter environment, and as the predators fail they become more inclined to search elsewhere. At night, when the caterpillars can't be seen, they go back to the food-rich environments, even if they are very low in twigs.

It is hard to explain the caterpillars' behavior here without attributing to them cognitive states of one sort or another. But what about the case of experiences? Are the caterpillars *conscious* of the twigs in the twig-rich environment? Do they really exploit the fact that they themselves look like twigs? Presumably not. How would they know that they *look* like twigs anyway? They can't see themselves in their entirety. Indeed, they can't genuinely see things at all, since they can only make out the difference between light and dark environments. Maybe there are innate mechanisms at play that drive them toward the twig-rich environments during the day as they gain information via their senses about the character of those environments. Whatever the truth here, it certainly is not obvious that these informational states are best taken to be phenomenally conscious.

Still, we can't argue either that, like plants and protozoa, the best account of the caterpillars' behavior has it that they are zombies, for there *seems* to be a kind of intelligence displayed in their choice of environments that certainly goes with the presence of conscious perceptual states in many animals, even if it does not require them. This is true, I might add, of other caterpillar behavior. Caterpillars of the large white butterfly (*Pieris brassicae*) vomit on their predators as a way of protecting themselves.[13] What is especially interesting is that when they are in a group threatened by a predator, they are less likely to vomit, and the likelihood diminishes as the group size increases. The reason for this seems to be that vomiting has a high cost: food is lost and so growth slows, as does reproduction in the female due to a lower number of eggs. So caterpillars seem to take into account group size in trying to decide whether to vomit. The bigger the group, the less likely it is that vomiting is necessary by a given individual. This means that some caterpillars seem prepared to cheat and rely on the likelihood that others in the group will vomit without them having to pay the high price of doing so. Moreover, since the caterpillars compete for food, as the group size increases, the cost of vomiting goes up, so some caterpillars "decide" not to pay it.

Here, given the same stimulus, there is variation in the behavior of individual caterpillars. And again, this is at least suggestive of the presence of mental states. But in the absence of strong evidence of the presence of phenomenality elsewhere in caterpillars, it is unclear whether this is due to some sort of sensory *awareness* of what is going on or whether non-conscious processing and innate mechanisms are responsible.

13. It may be wondered how caterpillars detect the presence of predators. They do so by vibrational cues. Caterpillars can distinguish the vibrations made by predators from those made by non-predators and also natural phenomena such as rainfall.

[10]

COMMANDER DATA AND
ROBOT RABBIT

So far we have been concerning ourselves with living animals. The world in which we find ourselves today contains artificial animals too. There are artificial "cheetahs" that can reach a speed of twenty-nine miles per hour, "dog" drones capable of carrying up to four hundred pounds, and robotic flies. There is even a robo-ape. To my knowledge, no one wants to claim that these actual robotic creatures are conscious. But now an interesting question arises. Could *any* robotic animal be conscious? What would we need to do to build such an artificial conscious being?

Consider, for example, Lieutenant Commander Data. Data is a character with a prominent role in the TV series *Star Trek: The Next Generation*. He is second officer and chief operations officer aboard the Starship *Enterprise*. Data is a fully functional android (a robot with a humanlike appearance). He has a positronic brain formed from an alloy of platinum and iridium. During his early years, he had significant difficulty in understanding various aspects of human behavior, and he was totally unable to feel any emotions. Later he was equipped with an "emotion chip," the result of which was supposedly to generate emotional experiences in Data and thus to make him better equipped to understand the human beings around him.

Let us suppose (for the purposes of this chapter) that the later Data's design has resulted in his undergoing a complex pattern of inner states that interact causally with one another and with sensory inputs and behavioral outputs in just those ways that our mental states do, as we (tacitly) understand those interactions in virtue of our everyday mastery of such terms as "anger," "pain," "belief," "desire," and so on. Functionally, then, we are supposing that there is no significant difference (except in intelligence and speed of reasoning) between Data and you or me. He is, as it is sometimes put, a perfect *common-sense functional isomorph* of normal human beings. Does Data really feel anything? Or does he just function *as if* he has feelings? If he does have feelings, does he feel what *we* feel?

These questions are interesting in their own right. But can they be answered? Given that Data's brain is physico-chemically radically different from ours, a case can be made (and has been made (Block 2002)) that we do not have any rational ground for the belief that Data has feelings (or experiences), nor indeed do we have any rational ground for the belief that he does not.[1] Take the emotion chip. It guarantees that Data functions as if he feels emotions, but, according to Block, beyond that we cannot say. Maybe he genuinely feels anger upon occasion or fear, but maybe he doesn't. There is no evidence that should sway us one way or the other.

Let us look at the case of Data in more detail. We will turn to Robot Rabbit later.

10.1 THE ORIGINAL CHINA-BODY PROBLEM

Ned Block, in his essay "Troubles with Functionalism" (1978), presented a thought experiment that has been much discussed. I want to begin with some remarks on this thought experiment. Its relevance to Commander Data will be explained in section 2. Block described the scenario he wanted his readers to consider as follows:

> We convert the government of China to functionalism, and we convince its officials that it would enormously enhance their international prestige to realize a human mind for an hour [artificially]. We provide each of the billion people of China with a

1. Indeed, Block holds that we have no *conception* of a rational ground for the belief that Data is conscious.

specially designed two-way radio that connects them in the appropriate way to other persons and to an artificial body ... [equipped with a] radio transmitter and receiver connected to the [body's] input and output neurons. ... [Finally] we arrange to have letters displayed on a series of satellites placed so that they can be seen from anywhere in China. ... The system of a billion people communicating with one another plus satellites plays the role of an external "brain" connected to the artificial body by radio. (p. 276)

As Block noted (p. 276), the China-body system seems physically possible. For some short period of time—one hour, say—it could be functionally equivalent to one of us. A more modern version of Block's example might involve billions of Chinese equipped with cell phones and huge books of instructions telling them which numbers to call when they get calls from so-and-so numbers.

The point of the example was to undermine a priori or analytical functionalism. Since the China-body system functionally duplicates a human brain at a neuronal level and therefore also a human mind at a common-sense level, according to a priori/analytic functionalism, it has a mind. Moreover, given the right internal interactions and inputs, the system experiences pain and other phenomenally conscious mental states. But, as Block says:

There is a prima facie doubt whether it (the China-body system) has any mental states at all—especially whether it has what philosophers have variously called "qualitative states," "raw feels," or "immediate phenomenological qualities." (p. 278)[2]

---

2. It is clear that Block's major worry concerned phenomenal states or experiences. He says:

Now there is good reason for supposing that [a homunculi-head system] has some mental states. Propositional attitudes are an example. Perhaps psychological theory will identify remembering that P with having "stored" a sentence-like object that expresses the proposition that P. ... Then if one of the little men has put a certain sentence-like object in "storage," we may have reason for regarding the system as remembering that P. But ... there is no such theoretical reason for regarding the system as having qualia." (p. 289)

A familiar reply by the functionalist is to claim that we are too small relative to the China-body system. We fail to see the forest for the trees. This seems to me to miss the point. We do not suppose that taking a hammer to the artificial body's foot would be doing something very wrong in the way that taking a hammer to another human being's foot would be doing something very wrong.

Why? The explanation, I suggest, is that we do not think that the China-body system would then *really* experience intense pain. To be sure, the system would *function* as if it is in pain (let us grant), but in reality no feeling of pain would be present.

Here is another case[3] that helps to make this point vivid. In China at the turn of the twentieth century a visiting English diplomat was being entertained by the emperor at a banquet. Dish after dish was served. Finally, the main course arrived: a large carp on a silver platter with a salad and various sauces displayed carefully and artistically around it. The dish was brought before the Englishman for further inspection. As he peered down, the fish suddenly flipped its tail. This last dying movement of the fish caused its skin to slip off. The poor fish had been skinned alive and the skin then put back in its original position!

To the extent that we think of the fish as capable of undergoing experiences, and pain in particular, we think of what was done to the fish here as very wrong. (And given what was argued in chapter 6, we should think of the fish in this way.) But surely we do not have a comparable reaction in the China-body case. Skinning the artificial body and then returning the skin to where it was originally while the Chinese people continue to communicate with the body (and one another) by radio does not evoke in us the same reaction of outrage and horror or disgust. These assertions are reinforced by the observation that, after Block's suggested time of operation has passed, there is patently nothing wrong in dismantling the China-body system, in destroying it, while keeping its parts intact (i.e., without harming the Chinese people). But this would be wrong if the China-body system experienced phenomenal states. It follows that Block was right: the China-body system does *not* undergo phenomenal states (and it does create trouble for a priori or analytic functionalism).

3. The origin of which, alas, I cannot recall.

One thing this shows is that if we were to encounter an alien robotic creature with a brain made up of tiny, living alien people so interacting that the robot spoke and acted as if it was fully conscious, it would not *really* be conscious, and likewise if we were ourselves to build such a truly huge robot with the participating Chinese people from Block's example inside its head.

10.2 REASONING ABOUT COMMANDER DATA

Turning now to Commander Data, what we know that is relevant to the question of his experiences is as follows:

a. By hypothesis, Data (or at least the Data of this chapter) functions at a common-sense level as we do, and so he behaves as we do when we undergo various experiences.
b. Data is not a homunculi head (a system with a brain made up of people).
c. Data has an artificial brain, physically radically different from ours.

Given (a), by an application of Newton's Rule, we have evidence that Data has experiences. Specifically, we have evidence that he feels anger, fear, and pain; that he has various perceptual experiences; that he feels moods such as depression and happiness. So we have (defeasible) reason at least to prefer the hypothesis that Data has the experiences and feelings he appears to have to the hypothesis that he does not. Given (b), we cannot infer from the case of the China-body system that Data lacks experiences. Of course, had Data been a homunculi head, our reason for preferring the view that Data has experiences would have been defeated, for we know a priori from reflection on the China-body case that homunculi-headed systems lack any experiences (assuming we are not ourselves homunculi-headed). But that is not how things are with Data.

Still, given (c), according to Block, we have reason to believe that Data *lacks* experiences; this is a consequence of Data's having a fundamentally different physical realization of our superficial functional organization. The result supposedly is that the epistemic value of Data's common-sense functional sameness with us is cancelled and we are left totally in the dark as to whether Data is conscious.

Let us look at this more carefully. Why should we agree that Data's physical makeup defeats the reason that (a) provides for preferring the hypothesis that Data is conscious? Clearly, physical makeup *is* sometimes relevant. In the case of a homunculi-headed system, there are huge physical differences between it and us in virtue of its being homunculi-headed and our not. But there is, in addition, an important functional difference, for the states of our own brains that play the functional roles commonsensically associated with sentience are not themselves entities having proper parts that also play those roles, as is found with the homunculi-headed system.[4] With Data there is no corresponding functional difference. So why should we suppose that his *physical* difference from us is of any significance?

Let us approach this question by looking at the alternatives as shown below. By "superficial" in the table and the following discussion, I mean what I meant earlier by "common sense" or "everyday."[5]

Table 10.1

	Superficial Functional Identity or Similarity (SFI)	Marked Superficial Functional Difference (SFD)
Physical Identity or Similarity (PI)	Yes	Yes
Radical Physical Difference (PD)	?	No

4. This is not the only further relevant difference. Block has another example involving homunculi (specifically, elementary particle people that come to make up the matter composing your body as you travel to another part of the universe) with respect to which our intuitions seem different than in the China-body example. For a discussion of why and how the two cases differ, see Tye (forthcoming). For present purposes, we can ignore the elementary particle people example.
5. The term "superficial" in this context is due to Block.

Where there is SFI and PI, we should agree that together they provide us with a reason to prefer the hypothesis that there is identity (similarity) in experiences and feelings to its denial (as indicated by "yes" in the table). Where there is SFD and PD, we should also agree that they provide us with no reason to prefer the hypothesis that there is identity (similarity) and indeed reason to prefer the denial of that hypothesis (as indicated by "no" in the table). Consider, for example, the case of a laptop computer. It is physically very different from us, and there is in addition a huge superficial/common-sense functional difference. It's *conceivable* that consciousness is present. We perhaps can conceive of a "phenomenal aura" attaching to a laptop. But patently we have not only no reason to accept that this is the case but also reason to deny it.

What about the case where there is SFD and PI? Take the man who is paralyzed and who also has Alzheimer's disease (McLaughlin 2003). Suppose that brain scans reveal that notwithstanding his inability to act in anything like the way normal adult humans do, he undergoes the very same brain states we undergo when we feel anger or fear or pain or when we experience a loud noise or the color bright red. Here, it seems, we have reason to accept that he is conscious and indeed that he experiences what we do. It is conceivable that he doesn't, but the physical identity gives us a reason to accept that he does.

Data fits the case of SFI and PD, as does the case cited by Block of partial physical overlap. Block says:

> Suppose . . . that we find out that *all* of the merely superficial isomorph's brain states are ones that—in us—are neural bases only of *phenomenally unconscious states.* For example, the neural basis of the functional analog of pain in the merely superficial isomorph is the neural state that regulates the pituitary gland in us. This would not *prove* that the isomorph is not phenomenally conscious (since the contexts of the neural realizers are different), but it would cancel or at least weaken the force of the reason for attributing consciousness provided by its functional isomorphism to us. (pp. 402–403)

There is no supporting argument offered for these remarks. Presumably, Block expects us simply to agree with him. I shall just say that I do not fully share Block's intuitions here. But let us put this case to one side for the moment. Block's view, in the case of Data, is that the striking PD provides a reason for *denying* that Data is conscious. The SFI, however, provides reason to *assert* that he is conscious. We are thus left epistemically in limbo, as it were—hence the question mark in the table. In my view, this is a mistake. What Block should have said is that even if PD in and of itself weakens to some degree our reason for supposing that Data is conscious, the SFI he shares with us trumps that reason. It is rational for us to prefer the view that Data is conscious to the view that he is not, even if our confidence in his consciousness is not as great as our confidence in the consciousness of a creature that shares both PD and SFI. So, in the table, we should have "yes" rather than a question mark.

Block will no doubt insist that this is mistaken. So the situation may seem to be a standoff. In the next section, I shall argue that the case of gradual silicon chip replacement of neurons shows that a silicon brain can undergo exactly the same experiences as you or me. This example calls into question Block's assertion that PD even in the context of SFI provides a sufficiently strong reason to deny consciousness that we are left entirely up in the air as to whether Data is genuinely conscious. Some of the issues in the section are complex, and readers who are not philosophers may wish to skip it.

10.3 THE SILICON CHIP ARGUMENT

The silicon chip argument is based on a thought experiment often associated with John Searle (1992), in which neurons in the brain of a normal human being are replaced one by one with silicon chips. David Chalmers (1995) describes the scenario in this way:

> In the first such case, only a single neuron is replaced. Its replacement is a silicon chip that performs precisely the same local function as the neuron. We can imagine that it is equipped with tiny transducers that take in electrical signals and chemical ions and transforms these into a digital signal upon which the chip computes, with the result converted into the appropriate electrical

and chemical outputs. As long as the chip has the right input/output function, the replacement will make no difference to the functional organization of the system. In the second case, we replace two neighboring neurons with silicon chips. This is just as in the previous case, but once both neurons are replaced we can eliminate the intermediary, dispensing with the awkward transducers and effectors that mediate the connection between the chips and replacing it with a standard digital connection. Later cases proceed in a similar fashion, with larger and larger groups of neighboring neurons replaced by silicon chips. Within these groups, biochemical mechanisms have been dispensed with entirely, except at the periphery. In the final case, every neuron in the system has been replaced by a chip, and there are no biochemical mechanisms playing an essential role. (p. 314)

It is important to emphasize that the complexity of the interactions between neurons does not undermine this thought experiment. Neurons do not simply relay electrical messages; they also manufacture chemicals, and the chemicals influence the signals that are produced and received. Still, even granting this (as Chalmers does), there seems to be no reason why the input-output functions could not be duplicated using silicon chips. The question to be addressed is whether the phenomenology *would* change under the above scenario. It is important to appreciate that this question does not presuppose that the original being still exists at the end of the process. What is being asked is whether the phenomenology would change, whether it is the original human being or a successor.

This is not the question whether it is metaphysically possible that the phenomenology changes—that it suddenly disappears or changes in its character or alternatively fades away. Rather, the former question is to be understood in the same way as the question of whether water heated to 100 degrees Celsius will boil. The relevant possibility is thus nomological.

Searle (1992) holds that the phenomenology might change. He suggests this possibility:

As the silicon is progressively implanted into your dwindling brain, you find that the area of your conscious experience is shrinking, but that this shows no effect on your external behavior. You find, to your total amazement, that you are indeed losing control of your external behavior. You find, for example, that when the doctors test your vision, you hear them say, "We are holding up a red object in front of you; please tell us what you see." You want to cry out, "I can't see anything. I'm going totally blind." But you hear your voice saying in a way that is completely out of your control, "I see a red object in front of me." If we carry the thought-experiment out to the limit, we get a much more depressing result than last time. We imagine that your conscious experience slowly shrinks to nothing, while your externally observable behavior remains the same. (pp. 66–67)

In Searle's envisaged scenario, as your experiences change, your beliefs change dramatically. For example, you believe that you are going blind. But how *could* new, radically different beliefs be formed, given that the functioning is the same at a very fine-grained level? Surely new beliefs (exercising completely different concepts from their predecessor beliefs) would require *some* change in functioning. To suppose otherwise is to suppose that the new beliefs arise from *just the same* patterns of causes as the old beliefs and that they have *just the same* patterns of effects. Perhaps this is metaphysically possible. Perhaps it is metaphysically possible that the introduction of silicon itself magically influences which beliefs are formed and further that the new beliefs have the same causal powers as the old ones. But it is highly implausible to suppose that this is what *would* occur.[6]

A second possibility (not considered by Searle), *if the phenomenology changes*, is that the beliefs stay the same throughout, including beliefs about phenomenology, but the latter beliefs are all false by the time the silicon chip replacement is complete. As with the first alternative, this is very implausible. It requires us to accept that the being at the end of the replacement process is *radically* mistaken about his own phenomenal life, even though he is fully rational. This is difficult to swallow. A more reasonable hypothesis is that rational conscious beings are not so mistaken. On

6. These points echo those made by Chalmers (1995, pp. 315–320) in his response to the thought experiment

this view, if the beliefs stay the same, the phenomenology would be left unchanged (or close to unchanged) by the silicon chip replacement.

There is another possibility. Perhaps (a) the phenomenology changes only very gradually, so that from moment to moment there is no discernible difference, even though by the end of the process the phenomenology has drained away altogether, and (b) the *new* beliefs, that is, the beliefs that were not present before the silicon chips started to be inserted, are all and only beliefs about the phenomenology, and they change with the phenomenological changes, resulting finally in beliefs that use concepts functionally equivalent to their predecessor concepts but picking out non-phenomenal states. In that case, it could well be that there is no change in functioning.

A fourth possibility is that the phenomenology would not change at all, and neither would the beliefs. Prima facie, this is a very reasonable response to the silicon chip thought experiment. Indeed, in my view, it is *the* most reasonable response, since the third alternative above is the only other option not immediately very implausible, and that alternative must deal with very tricky and puzzling questions concerning the individuation of concepts and whether the concepts operative in the final "phenomenological" beliefs really do refer to non-phenomenal states instead of failing to refer altogether.

This bears further elaboration. Suppose that the word "pain," as used by the individual in whom the chips are to be implanted, expresses a certain concept P that rigidly picks out a state whose essence is its phenomenal character. On the third alternative above, at the end of the silicon chip replacement, the word "pain" expresses another concept P' that rigidly picks out a *non*-phenomenal state whose essence is the pain functional role. On this alternative, then, both before and after the silicon chips are implanted, the concept the person expresses by "pain" has a referent, and first-person present-tense beliefs employing that concept (for example, the belief that I am in pain) are true. Still, there is a *new* concept introduced here: the concept at the end is different from the one at the start. How can this be?

In general, when a new concept is introduced, it is in one of two ways. It may be the first time the concept has ever been used. In this case, the use constitutes the introduction of the concept. Call such a use an "originating use." Alternatively, the concept may already be in existence, and the individual's first use of it constitutes his becoming a member of an existing concept-using community. In this case, the use is not an originating use of the concept. These non-originating uses are marked by both of the following features:

1. The use involves deference to other uses, by the same subject or other subjects.
2. The use makes possible the accumulation of information from other uses, by the same subject or other subjects.

To illustrate: when Murray Gell-Mann originated the concept *quark*, he was in no way deferring to other uses of the concept, whether by himself or by other scientists. (That's consistent with his having borrowed the word "quark" from James Joyce.) By contrast, our current uses of the concept *quark* involve deference in the following sense: we aim to conform in our usage to our previous usage, and to the usage of those in our conceptual community, especially to the usage of the scientifically informed. This is typical of non-originating uses. The deference takes the form of intending to use the concept as it has been used by oneself or others on previous occasions. Using it in the same way does not require one to use it to think the same thoughts, nor does it require one to believe that those to whom one defers are in a privileged epistemic position regarding the subject matter: one can change one's mind or disagree with others.[7] But this kind of change of mind or disagreement requires agreement in concepts.[8]

In the case at hand, the individual is happy to accept correction from others over his third-person uses of the word "pain" and perhaps also in some atypical first-person uses. So if the concept he expresses by "pain" at the end of the procedure is new in his thought, it is not because he

---

7. As I am using the notion of deference here, it has nothing special to do with expertise, nor even with superior epistemic position. In taking someone to have wrongly applied a concept (perhaps because she is in an epistemically inferior position relative to oneself), one still aims to use the very concept she used, and in that manner one defers to her usage.
8. In this paragraph and below I draw on views about concepts that are elaborated at length in Sainsbury and Tye 2012.

acquired it from others; the concept they express by "pain" is just the concept he expressed by "pain" initially. But neither does he introduce an entirely new concept himself. He intends to use the word "pain" in just the same way as he did previously.

Perhaps it is helpful to turn to the case of demonstrative concepts to illustrate this point further. Suppose I see an object from one angle and think of it as *that*. A minute or two later, I see and think of the same object, also thinking of it as *that*. Under what conditions have I used the same concept twice, and under what conditions have I used distinct concepts? Here is one feature that grounds the view that there is but a single demonstrative concept that has been tokened twice: the later use defers to the earlier one, in ways like the following:

- Information from the earlier use is treated as relevant in a certain way. Suppose earlier the subject formed the belief that that is F and is now inclined to believe that that is not F. If she sees that she rationally cannot give in to that inclination without abandoning the earlier belief, then she is treating her *that*-concepts as the same.
- Information from earlier uses is merged with current information. If she now forms the belief that that is G, she'll be disposed to form the belief that something is F and G.

It is easy to imagine situations in which these conditions are not met. A famous example is the case, first introduced by John Perry (1977, p. 483) and taken up by Gareth Evans (1982, p. 82), in which a subject, viewing a long ship from one window, forms a belief she is inclined to express by the words, "That ship was built in Japan," and, seeing the same ship from another window, but not realizing it is the same, forms a belief she's inclined to express by the words, "That ship was not built in Japan." The beliefs are related, as the belief that Hesperus is visible is related to the belief that Phosphorus is not visible. They cannot both be true, but they do not (in her thought) have the form of a contradiction.[9] The subject viewing the ship has distinct concepts of the ship,

---

9. Thoughts contradict just in case there is a structure of concepts that features un-negated in one and negated in the other.

and that is why the thoughts are not contradictory. The concepts were introduced on different occasions (though close together in time), and the second introduction was independent of the first. This is reflected in the subject's disposition to infer that there are two different ships, for example.

There is nothing like this in the case of the different concepts putatively expressed by the word "pain." Moreover, if we insist on subscribing to the view that there really are two concepts that are operative here, then it is difficult to see how we can stop at two. For the replacement process has many different stages involving states with a different phenomenal character from one another (and also from the initial state) as the phenomenology slowly drains away. To suppose that there are really many different concepts being exercised in the individual's beliefs and expressed by his use of the word "pain" is to suppose either that he would not defer to others in how to use "pain" in some cases (in the sense of "defer" elucidated above), as he had done in the past, or that he would repeatedly fail to intend to use the concept he expressed by "pain" in the way he had just previously. Neither alternative is at all plausible.[10]

It seems to me, then, that the most reasonable thing to say is that there is just a single concept expressed by "pain" and that during the replacement process the beliefs do not change, and neither does the phenomenology.[11] So if we wish to respect our initial intuitions and we also wish

10. If it is allowed that one and the same concept can change its content through time, it might be suggested that there is another nomological possibility here, namely, that "pain" expresses the same concept throughout but that the referent of the concept changes as the silicon chips are inserted. This seems extremely implausible, however. How could the content change if the same rigidly referring concept is operative throughout and the pattern of causes and effects associated with the exercise of the concept remains the same? Moreover, if the content does change, then it is false that pain is one and the same as such-and-such a neurochemical state, for pain is still present after the silicon chips have been inserted but the relevant neurochemical state is missing. So, on this proposal, the type identity theory, in its neurochemical version, has now been given up.

11. Nothing hinges on my use of the term "pain." If those who opt for the third alternative deny that "pain" rigidly refers to a state whose essence is a certain phenomenal character, the same points can be made for "this," as used to refer to the phenomenal character of pain, or for any new general term (e.g., R) the individual in the experiment is himself imagined to introduce, prior to silicon chip insertion, to pick out rigidly

to avoid getting embroiled in puzzles and problems that arise once we take the view that the phenomenology changes with the gradual silicon chip replacement, we should accept that, notwithstanding the absence of sameness in electrochemical mechanisms, there is sameness in phenomenology. If this is correct, it is rational to accept that a suitably constructed silicon brain *can* support the same experiences as a human brain.

10.4 REAL RABBIT AND ROBOT RABBIT

The claim that physical difference (PD) undercuts the evidential value of superficial functional isomorphism (SFI) for the hypothesis that Data is conscious is not made by Block alone. This is also the position taken by Brian McLaughlin (2003). Indeed, in McLaughlin's view, SFI is evidence for consciousness *only* where there is PI. So, in Table 10.1, in place of the question mark, we should have "No." It is to this stronger claim made by McLaughlin (and other related ones) that I turn in this section.

You live in a future era in which the technology of robotics is much more advanced than it is today. It is your daughter's ninth birthday. You decide to buy her a robot rabbit. Inside the pet store, there are rows and rows of such rabbits of varying colors and sizes, all motionless and deactivated. You pick one out and drive home. As you approach the front door of your house, you flip a small switch on the underside of the rabbit, hidden in its fur, and it comes to life. Your daughter is delighted. A pet rabbit at last!

Robot Rabbit has been designed so that it is a superficial functional isomorph of a real rabbit. It is subject to a complex pattern of internal states that interact with one another, sensory inputs, and behavioral outputs in all the same everyday ways that the mental states of real rabbits do. But Robot Rabbit does not have a brain like a real rabbit. Inside its head is an artificial brain, made of silicon, and inside its body are fine wires than operate in similar ways to the motor and sensory neurons of real rabbits.

that phenomenal character. For relevant general discussion of these topics, see Tye 2009. For a general theory of concepts and concept individuation, see Sainsbury and Tye 2012.

McLaughlin takes it to be obvious that Robot Rabbit has no experiences. It does not feel anything. It is a zombie that merely functions as if it is conscious. Here supposedly we have a case in which there is functional similarity to a being that is conscious (a real rabbit) but undercutting physical difference. McLaughlin's positive proposal is that functional similarity is evidence for phenomenal similarity *only insofar as* it is evidence for sameness of physical realization.

In the case of gradual silicon chip replacement of neurons in a human being, the argument that phenomenal identity would be preserved relied in part on the claim that the individual's beliefs putatively about his/her experiences would remain generally accurate or true. In the case of a rabbit, there are (let us agree) no higher-order mental states, and so the original argument, as applied to the rabbit, will not go through. Still, once it is conceded that beings with a very different physical makeup can nonetheless undergo the same experiences, it is hard to see why the absence of higher-order mental states should be a defeater.

The dialectical situation, as I see it, is this. Robot Rabbit behaves in just the same way as Real Rabbit. Applying Newton's Rule, we are entitled to prefer the hypothesis that Robot Rabbit, like Real Rabbit, is conscious unless there is a defeater. Finding out that Robot Rabbit has an empty head except for a radio receiver and that this receiver gets signals from Martians who control every movement that Robot Rabbit makes so that it behaves as if it is autonomous and intelligent and responds to sensory information in the same way as Real Rabbit would be a defeater. But that is not the case. In reality, Robot Rabbit has an economy of internal states that interact with one another and sensory inputs so as to produce behavior in just the same way as Real Rabbit. These states are realized in silicon, but we have no reason to think that this makes a difference to the presence of experiences and strong reason to think that it does not, given the silicon chip argument and the irrelevance to first-order consciousness or experience of the presence of higher-order mental states.

Admittedly, one salient difference is that Robot Rabbit is a product not of Mother Nature but of human design. But, again, why should this matter? What reason is there to think that design only generates consciousness when it is natural rather than artificial? None, so far as I can see.

Still, I grant that there is some intuition that Robot Rabbit could not undergo any experiences. It comes, I think, from two sources. One is that robots by their nature are unemotional beings who do just what they are programmed to do. This carries no weight in the present context, since it is assumed that Robot Rabbit functions as if it genuinely does have emotions just as real rabbits do. The other source lies with an oversimplified picture of how Robot Rabbit would behave. We imagine Robot Rabbit suddenly opening its eyes after it is switched on and then moving around in a restricted robot way much as current robot toys move. For example, we picture it letting out an artificial-sounding whimper if we stick a pin in it and then going on mechanically as before. *That* rabbit, we should all agree, experiences nothing. It does not feel pain. It is indeed a zombie. But the robot rabbit you buy for your daughter in the pet store is not like this.

Suppose that after Robot Rabbit is turned on, its on-off switch decomposes. There is now no way to turn it off. Suppose also that Robot Rabbit does not look like the rabbit below:

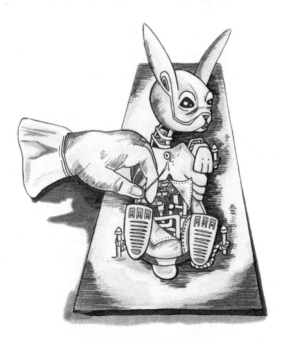

Fox (2014)

Instead, Robot Rabbit looks and moves just like the real rabbit you see here:

J. J. Harrison, jjharrison89@facebook.com

This is not especially far-fetched, I might add. The robot below from Japan exists today, and she is remarkably lifelike.

Wikipedia (https://en.wikipedia.org/wiki/Actroid)

In place of skin, she has flexible silicone; she appears to breathe; and she can move her hands and flutter her eyelashes in a humanlike way.

Now if Robot Rabbit is a common-sense functional isomorph of a real rabbit, there will be a vast number of common-sense causal psychological generalizations that apply to it as well as to real rabbits. No one has ever written down or tried to write down all these generalizations, though each such generalization we, the folk, would recognize as true were we presented with it. As an illustration, here are ten obvious generalizations pertaining to pain (leaving out the "normally" qualifier that is needed in each). These are certainly not intended to be exhaustive.

1. Pain is caused by tissue damage.
2. Pain causes a desire to get away from the damaging stimulus.
3. Pain causes anxiety.
4. Pain makes it harder to concentrate on tasks at hand.
5. Pain diminishes the desire to eat.
6. Pain causes guarding behavior with respect to the limb in which there is tissue damage.
7. If the same stimulus repeatedly causes pain, then new presentation of the stimulus causes fear and the attempt to get away from the stimulus.
8. Where a stimulus is associated with pain in a creature's experience, if the stimulus is presented again, the creature will be more wary of it than it was before the association developed.
9. Pain causes bodily tension.
10. If a creature is given a drug that relieves pain, the creature will subsequently behave in a livelier and happier way than before.

If Robot Rabbit has internal states with causes and effects that conform to these generalizations and all those other common-sense psychological generalizations that real rabbit does, it seems to me plausible to hold that they provide evidence that Robot Rabbit feels pain and other experiences.

Suppose next that Robot Rabbit only has a silicon brain. The rest of Robot Rabbit is like real rabbits. It has a blood-based circulatory system; it has a natural heart; it breathes and eats and produces waste. If you are like me, you will now have no intuition left that Robot Rabbit does not have experiences. But surely having a real biological heart and circulatory system and the like cannot be crucial to having experiences. After all, if I am kept alive without a heart via a machine that pumps blood artificially to my brain and body, we do not suppose that I lose my capacity to have experiences. Why suppose it matters crucially for Robot Rabbit then? Why not accept that even if Robot Rabbit is artificial through and through, it still has experiences?

Consider the case of Alien Rabbit. Suppose that Alien Rabbit lives on another planet and is a product of Mother Nature there. Alien Rabbit has a silicon brain and looks like earth rabbits, though Alien Rabbit's brain is not made out of silicon *chips*. Furthermore, Alien Rabbit is a superficial functional isomorph of Real Rabbit. Does the fact that Alien Rabbit's brain isn't made of the same stuff as Real Rabbit's brain provide a reason to *deny* that Alien Rabbit feels what earth rabbits do? Where there is striking physical difference without functional similarity, there clearly is reason to hold that the relevant being does not have experiences. But that is not the case here.

If this is right and it is agreed that Alien Rabbit is a conscious being, then we have reason to take what we might call "Alternate Robot Rabbit," the design of which is such that serendipitously it turns out be a microphysical duplicate of Alien Rabbit, to be a conscious being too. This reason may be defeated, of course. One possible defeater is the fact that Alternate Robot Rabbit has a human designer, whereas Alien Rabbit is the product of Mother Nature. But, as already noted, without a further case for the claim that this difference in origin is relevant, it carries no evidential weight. And if Alternate Robot Rabbit is conscious, it is difficult to deny that Robot Rabbit is conscious too.

10.5 A FURTHER REASON FOR PREFERRING THE VIEW THAT COMMANDER DATA AND ROBOT RABBIT ARE CONSCIOUS

Consider Commander Data again. Patently, it would be wrong to eviscerate Data while he screams and begs us to stop, just as it was wrong for the Chinese chefs to skin the fish alive and return it to the plate with the skin placed back on it again.[12] Why would this be wrong? The obvious explanation is that if we did eviscerate Data, it would *feel* very, very bad to him, and it is wrong to inflict intense pain gratuitously.

It might be suggested that the reason we deem it wrong to torture Data is not that he would feel intense pain but that he is a being whom we would then be disrespecting. Data has higher-order intentional states. Even if he is not conscious, he can pursue a life plan. If we torture him (or take him apart), we would prevent him from achieving his goals in life (McLaughlin 2003).

This seems to me not to come to grips with the heart of the issue. What if there are no lasting effects of torture, so that Data can go on and achieve his life goals? What if we are dealing with Robot Rabbit or Alien Rabbit? These creatures are sufficiently simple that it is likely that they have no life goals. But it would be wrong to torture Alien Rabbit, would it not? And if that's wrong, wouldn't it be wrong to torture Alternate Robot Rabbit and thus Robot Rabbit too?

Perhaps it will be replied that Alien Rabbit, even if she lacks life goals, is not a passive receptor but rather an agent. She acts in the world, and, in so doing, she deserves respect. But this seems too weak. Surely we do not have moral obligations to *every* creature in the world that is capable of acting, especially if that creature is not even conscious!

A further reply is that philosophical zombies lack consciousness. Yet they are like us in all physical respects. It is widely agreed that such zombies are at least *conceivable*. Yet these individuals could certainly have moral obligations to one another, and they could wrong one another as well. If zombie Smith were to eviscerate zombie Jones, for example, that would be a very bad thing, even though zombie Jones would not feel a thing. Correspondingly, it would be wrong for us to damage Data or take him apart or eviscerate him even if he felt nothing.

Let's take a simpler case. Evisceration, after all, would have all sorts of bad consequences later on for zombie Jones, if he survived the act. Suppose that zombie Smith violently sticks a pin repeatedly into zombie Jones's hand. Jones screams and rubs his hand, complaining bitterly

---

12. On the assumption defended earlier that fish feel pain.

as he does so. Suppose that there are no further significant effects and that Jones forgets the event shortly thereafter (as a result of taking a pill which obliterates the event from his memory). Did Smith do something wrong in repeatedly sticking the pin in Jones? It's not obvious that he did, for by hypothesis Jones didn't feel a thing, and the action had no further consequences. With Data, however, our *initial* intuition is that it would be wrong to do this, just as it would for me to repeatedly stick a pin in you, even if you retain no memory of it later on.

10.6 A FINAL CONSIDERATION

Here is a fantastic but conceivable possibility. We take it that in actual fact we human beings evolved from simpler creatures. But for all we know a priori, this is not the case. It is conceivable that the earth came into existence two hours ago and that all our memories of the past are mistaken. It is conceivable too that we "human beings" do not form a single species, that in reality there is no such natural species as *Homo sapiens* even though we believe that there is. The epistemic possibility I want to focus on is one in which we ourselves, totally unknown to us, are androids created by alien designers on another planet. It is certainly conceivable that this is the case. I have never seen my brain or anyone else's directly. I have certainly seen various photographs of brains, and I have read books and had conversations with knowledgeable scientists on the basis of which I have formed views about human brains. But suppose that these views are all mistaken. The alien designers very cleverly generate perceptual illusions whenever autopsies are done or MRI machines are used or a brain is exposed through some sort of accident. In reality, even though our scientists all agree that we have brains made of organic compounds and packed with neurons, our brains are artificial and of four different physical types distributed roughly equally among us, the result of a competition by the alien designers to see which brain would be the hardiest in an environment of the sort found on earth.

Totally fantastic, admittedly, but conceivable nonetheless. Now suppose that you discover that this scenario obtains. Brains, it turns out, are like blood types. Human beings have blood of types O, A, B, and AB. They also have brains of type silicon, platinum, iridium, and platinum-iridium mixture. Your best friend, you discover, has a brain of silicon, and your accountant one of platinum. You yourself have an iridium brain. With this information in hand, once you have gotten over the shock and accepted the reality of silicon, platinum, and iridium brains, do you now have any inclination to suppose that last year, when your partner fell over and twisted her ankle so badly that the bone protruded from the skin, she did not really feel pain as she went ashen in her face, clutched your hand, screamed very loudly, and begged you to stop the pain? Do you believe that it is now OK to go around sticking pins in other people if there are no lasting effects? Do you believe now that no one other than you and those with your brain type ever experienced fear or anger?

Perhaps you will reply that your confidence levels are now not quite as high as they were before this remarkable scenario was uncovered. Conceivably, you will even say that these levels are no longer high enough for unqualified belief in the experiences of others. But is this reaction really rational? After all, you are now forced to concede that you know from your own case that silicon supports consciousness and that carbon fibers and neurons are not required! Why not then platinum or iridium or a platinum-iridium mixture? You don't have any evidence that these *won't* do the job, and you do have the evidence provided by superficial functional isomorphism. In any event, given this, you *should* at least remain much *more* confident that humans feel pain, fear, and anger, that they have perceptual experiences and undergo felt moods of one sort or another than that they do no such thing. But then you should agree that physical difference does *not* undercut superficial functional isomorphism at least as far as rational preference goes. In that case, it is rational to prefer the hypothesis that Commander Data and Robot Rabbit are conscious to its denial, notwithstanding the physical differences.

Perhaps you will respond now that in reflecting on this thought experiment, your assessments are colored by anthropomorphic tendencies. You simply can't help but think that your fellows have experiences, even after the above remarkable discoveries, but this judgment is not one that should carry much weight.

I disagree. Suppose you were to find out that your fellows have empty heads and that their actions are controlled by Martians. This is the Martian Marionette case discussed in chapter 3. Would you still think of them as having experiences? Surely not. But why deny it in this case and not in the case I have been discussing above? Why don't you anthropomorphize in the Martian case too? The answer is that *some* physical differences make a difference, even given the same behavior; the ones I have described in the above thought experiment do not.

The examples we have looked at in this chapter are extreme and imaginary, though thought-provoking. Perhaps you find them *too* fantastic to know what to say. Still, the question of robot consciousness is an important one, and in my view it should be approached in the same general way as the question of the consciousness of real biological creatures.

[11]

THE ETHICAL TREATMENT
OF ANIMALS

In this book, I have argued that a very wide array of creatures have feelings and perceptual experiences: fish feel pain, as do crabs; honeybees feel anxiety; bowerbirds experience visual illusions; suitably constructed robots of the future may feel annoyed or happy.[1] If such creatures can share with us a range of perceptual, bodily, and emotional experiences, how ought we to behave toward them? Ought we to become vegetarians? These are the topics of the present chapter.[2]

It may seem that if nonhuman animals can experience pain and fear, we ought to behave toward them as we do toward other humans. But there is a simple thought experiment that should give us pause here. Suppose that you see a man standing on the edge of a cliff pulling hard on two ropes, each of which is dangling over the edge of the cliff. At the end of one rope is a child holding on for dear life. At the end of the other is a dog equally desperately gripping the rope in its teeth. The man lacks the strength to pull up either; you know that if you assist him, together you will both be able to pull up one of the two but not both. The unlucky creature will plunge to its death. Which rope should you help him pull?

The obvious answer is the rope with the child holding it. Apparently, then, the dog's value is not as great as that of the child. What if there are five dogs desperately gripping the second rope with their teeth? What

---

1. More cautiously, I have argued that it is rational to prefer the view that these beings have experiences to its denial.
2. In writing this chapter, I am very much indebted to Mark Sainsbury.

if there are a thousand? With a thousand dogs, the total quantity of fear and pain on that side will be much, much greater than on the child's side. So why prefer the child—if you agree, as many will, that the right thing to do is still to pull up the child?

11.1 ANIMAL WELFARISM

Animal welfarism corresponds to consequentialism in ethics. According to welfarists (e.g., Peter Singer), our behavior toward animals should be governed by the admission that they are capable of pain and pleasure. As such, they fall under utilitarian principles. So causing them pain or depriving them of pleasure is bad.

On simple hedonistic utilitarianism, which goes back at least to Bentham in the mid-nineteenth century, a right act is one that maximizes the net balance of pleasure over pain. So animals are counted in the utilitarian calculus simply by virtue of our taking into account their pains and pleasures as we do our pains and pleasures. All that is significant is the *quantity* of pain and pleasure, not what kind of creature experiences it. As Singer puts it (2000), on this view, "the pleasures of a mouse's life are all that the mouse has, and so can be presumed to mean as much to the mouse as the pleasures of a person's life mean to the person" (105–106).

To say that a particular right act maximizes the net balance of pleasure over pain is not to say simply that it has a positive score, but rather that of the acts available to the agent at the time, that one has the highest score. It follows that an act might still count as right even if it caused significant pain to animals, for that act might cause still greater pleasure to humans, and it might also be such that no alternative available act caused more pleasure. Suppose, for example, that there are five people left alive and three ducks. These people, all of whom are French, happen to get immense pleasure from eating pâté de foie gras, so they force feed the ducks, thereby causing their livers to become very fatty, and then kill them for the pleasure of eating the liver pâté. Of the acts available, that one might produce the most overall pleasure, and so by simple hedonistic utilitarian principles it would be right even if the feeding and its effects caused the birds very significant suffering.

So utilitarianism of the above sort is compatible with a carnivorous diet (as Singer concedes). If we kill the animals painlessly and we enjoy eating meat more than being vegetarians, eating meat is right. What about factory farming?

Well, factory farmers certainly behave badly according to the pure hedonistic utilitarian, for they cause much pain in animals that could be avoided without increasing pain much elsewhere (by generating minimally higher prices).

A second version of utilitarianism is preference utilitarianism. This replaces pleasure by satisfaction of preferences and pain by frustration of them. On this view, an act is right just in case it maximizes the satisfaction of preferences of all those creatures affected by the act.

Preference utilitarianism is associated historically with John Stuart Mill. According to Mill (1998), not all preferences count equally. Those that relate to the higher pleasures, for example, reading philosophy, count for more. Those that relate to the lower pleasures, for example, rolling around in warm mud, count for less.

What do these views say about the cliff case? Pure hedonistic utilitarianism says that if we generate more pleasure by pulling the dogs up, as well we may if we allow that there are several on the rope or simply one supremely grateful dog, then it is right to pull the dogs up and not the child. Intuitively, this seems the wrong result.

Preference utilitarianism may seem to have the resources to avoid this result, since humans have more forward-looking preferences than other animals (some of which may not have *any*). But what if the human on the rope is a newborn baby? It is hard to suppose that there are more forward-looking preferences here. Yet it seems obviously right to pull up the baby and let the dog go. So preference utilitarianism is in trouble here too.

Singer himself adopts interest utilitarianism. He begins with the idea that justice requires treating interests equally. He calls this the "principle of equality," and he says that it demands that *all* suffering be counted equally (1979). This is because in Singer's view the capacity for suffering and enjoying things is necessary (and apparently also sufficient) for having interests.

Still, why should all suffering be counted to the same degree? Presumably because to do otherwise would be unjust. But, again, this is not obvious, and intuitively it gets the wrong result in the cliff case.[3]

Singer's view also seems to have as a consequence that it is right to eat meat; for we can increase pleasure in the sense of preference satisfaction by increasing the number of creatures that have pleasure, and this we can do by breeding many animals that otherwise would not exist (so long as we make sure that they have at least minimal pleasure) and then slaughtering them for their meat. This is surprising, given Singer's commitment to vegetarianism.

Consequentialism need not focus on particular acts directly as candidates for right and wrong. Instead, it can take as its target act types or rules. Mill was an act-type utilitarian. He said (1998):

Acts are right in proportion as they tend to promote happiness.

Also:

It would be unworthy of an intelligent agent not to be aware that the action is of a class which, if practiced generally, would be generally injurious, and that this is the ground of the obligation to abstain from it.

On this view, an act type is right just in case it normally produces more pleasure than pain, and wrong just in case it normally produces more pain than pleasure.

---

3. Singer follows R. M. Hare (1981) in distinguishing between critical and intuitive moral thinking. The former is operative when we consider weird hypothetical cases such as the cliff or organ harvesting (see below). The latter is operative in our everyday moral thinking. Here we should follow "well chosen" general principles (e.g., don't lie). So in the organ harvesting example, even though we kill one for the good of five, and so, according to critical thinking, organ harvesting in this case is right, intuitively it is wrong. Where there is disagreement, according to Singer, we should go with the intuitive view. It is hard to see how Singer's double standard can be justified. The obvious reaction is that his theory gets the wrong result intuitively in certain cases and so cannot be correct.

One problem with this approach is that particular acts performed by particular agents fall under many act types, and so it may not help us to evaluate those token acts. Consider, for example, my killing Jones on Tuesday to harvest his organs. My act falls under the act type *killing an innocent human being* (itself a type that is wrong). But it also falls under the act type *saving five very deserving persons* (itself an act type that is right). So was my act right or wrong?

Another version of utilitarianism is rule utilitarianism, according to which an act is right just in case it accords with a rule that is right, and a rule is right just in case its "presence" in society would maximize happiness. This view is associated most notably with Richard Brandt (1963). It is not fully clear what it is for a rule to be "present" in society. Is it a matter of everyone accepting the rule? Or does acting in conformity with the rule suffice? Furthermore, what about supererogatory acts? These go beyond the rules, since they go beyond duty. So rule utilitarianism seems to have as a consequence that all such acts are wrong.

The upshot is that consequentialism, whatever its stripe, is problematic. And if consequentialism in ethics is problematic, so too is animal welfarism.

11.2 SPECIESISM

Speciesists (e.g., Ryder 1970) reject Singer's principle of equality. They do so by giving more weight to the interests of members of their own species simply on the grounds of species.

One virtue of speciesism is that it gets what is intuitively the correct result in the earlier cliff case. But why should species matter? Perhaps the answer is that it doesn't really. We think that it is right to pull up the child and let the dog fall to its death because we are reacting, perhaps unconsciously, to some other feature correlated with being human—a feature that *could* be possessed by some nonhumans but is not possessed by dogs or other actual nonhuman creatures. But what could this feature be? Here are some possible candidates:

being rational
being autonomous
being conscious
being a "member of the moral community"
being self-conscious, with a sense of one's past and future
possessing language
being tool users and makers

Unfortunately, there are various problems with this attempt to move away from speciesism to something prima facie more tenable.

First, many of the characteristics listed above are possessed by non-humans and so are not correlated with being human. Secondly, not all humans possess the above characteristics (e.g., the severely mentally and physically disabled), and some humans possess none of them whatsoever (e.g., humans in a vegetative state).

The initial reaction we have in the cliff case—a reaction that is rendered legitimate by the speciesist view—is not one that we can make go away by reflection as we can in certain other thought experiments within the moral domain. Consider, for example, the famous case of the trolley (Foot 1967). Here we are asked to imagine that there is a runaway trolley rolling fast down some railway tracks. Farther ahead there are five people tied up on the tracks and incapable of any movement. The trolley is going to hit them. You are standing away from the tracks in the train yard, next to a lever. Pulling this lever will cause the trolley to switch to another set of tracks. You observe that on this second set of tracks there is another person tied up. You have only two options (let us suppose): (1) you do nothing; (2) you pull the lever. On option (1), the trolley kills the five people on the first track. On option (2), the trolley kills the one person on the second track. What ought you to do?

Your initial reaction might be to say that you ought to pull the lever. But further reflection on the case might lead you to change your mind. Furthermore, we can easily understand someone saying that, placed in the situation, she could easily see herself *not* being able to bring herself to pull the lever and so opting for option (1) even though reflection told her that she ought to choose option (2). In the case of the cliff thought experiment, nothing like this seems likely or even possible. If there is a child on one rope and a myriad of rats, say, on the other, our initial reaction that we ought to save the child is not one that we can make go away by reflection. Nor can we imagine ourselves cogently deciding not to get involved and not doing anything. In this way, our initial intuitive judgment is robust and immovable.

This seems to me untroubling even if it leads us to embrace speciesism, for although speciesism tells us that we ought to favor our own species, it does not tell us that we shouldn't treat other species with respect. It's just that we can't help but see ourselves at the top.

Still, we may wonder now whether species is really *all* that matters in our thinking about the cliff case, for suppose that on one side of the rope is a normally functioning human being and on the other is an adult human with brain damage so severe that she is in a vegetative state. It seems to me intuitively clear that the right thing to do here is to pull up the normally functioning human and let the vegetative one go. But if this is so, then species *alone* is not what lies behind our moral judgment.

On the other hand, suppose that on one end of the rope is a normal human and on the other end is an intelligent extraterrestrial. I am inclined to think that, other things being equal, most of us would say that the right thing is to favor the human here. But what if an extraterrestrial of the same species is asked to make a corresponding judgment? It seems to me that what is right now shifts in favor of the dangling extraterrestrial. After all, we surely would not blame the extraterrestrial for making the choice she does in pulling up her fellow extraterrestrial. Does this mean that speciesism leads to relativism about right and wrong? I shall return to these issues shortly.

11.3 REGAN AND RAWLS

According to Regan (2004), people have "inherent value." This does not come in degrees, and it is not secured simply by being alive. Plants are alive, but they have no inherent value. Justice requires that anything with inherent value be respected. But what is required for inherent value? Regan's view is that it is enough that one be "subject to a life," that is, that one have plans, hopes, fears, and so on.

It seems to follow from this that all creatures that are "subject to a life" have the same value and thus that one cannot kill some to save others. However, in discussing a lifeboat example, Regan says that we should save the human by sacrificing the dog (even a million dogs!). The result is that the view is very hard to understand.

It is interesting to compare Regan's view to that of Rawls. Rawls (1971) tells us that animals are not owed anything as a matter of justice, since they are not "moral persons." Given Rawls's political liberalism, this ensures that the state cannot legitimately enact strong pro-animal legislation. So, for Rawls, hunting should be legally permissible, however much harm it causes animals.

This seems unacceptable. Surely we should not legalize practices that unnecessarily cause severe pain to animals. A theory that permits such legalization is a theory that should be rejected.

11.4 CENTERED SPECIESISM AND BIOLOGICAL PROXIMITY

Let me begin my presentation of this view by considering a totally different case: that of color. Many philosophers, in their theorizing about color, are moved by the fact that there is variability in the perceived colors of objects, depending upon background or perceiver. Something may look red to me and orange to you and purple to a pigeon and some other color to a Martian. Its apparent color may also change as it is moved from sunlight to fluorescent lighting. Who gets the color right? Which is the right set of viewing conditions? Prima facie, there is no nonarbitrary way of picking a unique perceiver and set of viewing conditions as being those in which colors are represented veridically.

This leads to the thought that colors are really relational properties that everybody gets right. If an object looks red to me in viewing condition C_1, it is red for me in C_1. If it looks orange to you in condition C_2, it is orange for you in C_2 (Cohen 2009).

Colors, however, don't seem to us to be relational in the above way in our experience, nor are color predicates in ordinary language relational in character. On the face of it, neither perceivers nor viewing conditions enter into the nature of the colors. One reaction to these points is to say that while colors aren't relational, the evaluation of whether an object has a given color is relative to an index. Consider the case of weight. The statement, "I weigh 170 pounds," is true on earth, but it is false on the moon. My weight there is about one-sixth of my weight on earth. But weight isn't obviously a relational property involving an environment, even though it is evaluated relative to an environment.

The relevant index for color ascriptions is a viewing index or a perspective. When we ascribe colors, sometimes we evaluate relative to some not very clear set of normal conditions and observers, and sometimes we evaluate relative to ourselves in our present viewing conditions. On this approach, colors themselves are dispositions to appear certain ways. Red is the disposition to look red*, green is the disposition to look green*, and so on, where red*, green*, and so on are the ways objects look to us when we are prepared to characterize them as red, green, and so on. These dispositions do not have as part of their nature either perceivers themselves or viewing conditions. But the *evaluation* of whether an object has a given color is relative to an index, comprising a viewer and a set of viewing conditions.[4]

I myself think that this approach to color is wrongheaded. If something looks red to me and green to you, it cannot really be both colors. The colors compete with one another just as the shapes do if something looks square to me and round to you. However, in the moral case, this approach seems to me very plausible. Let me explain.

The speciesist says that I ought to favor members of my own species over members of other species, that it is right to do so. So, as I ponder the cliff case, with the human and the extraterrestrial dangling from the rope, and I ask myself what is right, the conclusion I should reach is that

---

4. On this approach, colors are centering features. Formally, we can think of the color red, for example, as a function that takes ordered pairs of worlds and pairs of individuals and times $<w, <I,t>>$ as arguments and deliver sets of things that look red to individual I at time t in world w. See Egan 2012.

it is right to favor the human. However, if an extraterrestrial is pondering the situation, he will come to the opposite conclusion, that it is right to favor the extraterrestrial. It would be arbitrary to prefer one point of view over the other. Better to say that we are both correct. Relative to a human index, what is right is to favor the human. Relative to an extraterrestrial index, what is right is to favor the Martian. So, on this version of speciesism, there is a background index or center relative to which evaluations get made. It is not that there is such a property as being right for person P that is expressed by the predicate "is right." Being right is not relational in this way any more than weight or color is. So there is nothing in centered speciesism that involves us saying that it is right *for a human* to do so-and-so, or, for that matter, that involves a Martian saying that it is right *for a Martian* to do such-and-such. When I, as a human being, say that something, P, is right, if what I say is true, it is right *period*; likewise for a Martian, even if what is said by the two of us, if said together by one of us, cannot be true, for what is right is evaluated relative to an index. The index is not part of the semantic content of the assertion. Its role is to provide a context relative to which assertions of right and wrong may be assessed.

Intuitively, there is in additional "other things being equal" qualifier here. After all, if you know that favoring X, who is a member of your own species, over Y, who is not, will have terrible, disastrous results for the future of your species, your judgment about the cliff case intuitively will change. Suppose, for example, X is Adolf Hitler and Y is a friendly dog, and you know that if Hitler is allowed to live, he will exterminate every Jewish person in the world. Then, intuitively, it is no longer right to favor X.

Centered speciesism, as we might call it, gets the right results in the various cliff cases discussed so far. But it may seem that there is a further problem.

Suppose that on one end of the rope is a stranger's child and on the other is your own. If you can only save one (other things being equal), it would be wrong to save the stranger's child. But why? Both that child and yours are human. It seems natural to say here that in the case that the two individuals both belong to the same species as you, other things being equal, what is right is determined by intra-species factors, notably, how closely related the individuals are to you biologically. This suggests that there is an overarching consideration that enters into our evaluations, namely, how close individuals are to us biologically overall. The stranger's child is closer biologically than the dog, but your child is closer to you biologically than the stranger's. So your evaluation gets done relative to you biologically; mine gets done relative to me. So what is right as evaluated by me may not the same as what is right as evaluated by you. Still, both evaluations are correct, since what is right is relative to an index.

11.5 THE TREATMENT OF ANIMALS

It seems to me that the considerations adduced thus far support the view that it is right to favor others on a sliding scale of biological closeness or proximity. To make this vivid, imagine now that on one end of the rope is a single human child and on the other are a huge number of vast fish tanks filled with fish, millions of fish, swimming around happily. Suppose that you have amazing superhuman strength, but still you can only pull up one of the two ropes. Which ought you to choose? Obviously the one with the dangling child. But why? The total happiness extinguished by letting the fish tanks go will be huge, as will the total pain as the fish lie dying without water on the rocks below. The answer is that, evaluated relative to your index, the child has more value. Does she have greater *impersonal* value? If centered biological proximity is what matters, there is no answer, for moral values are relative to indices.

So it is tempting to conclude that looking after ourselves at animals' expense as we go through life is just like saving one's daughter at the expense of the stranger's. There is a difference, however. In the cliff case, the girl's dangerous situation is taken as given, whereas animals may be in a dangerous situation only as a result of our doing. So other things are not equal. But putting this to one side, even if it is correct for us to favor other humans over nonhuman animals, it does not follow that we should not treat them with respect. They experience pain and fear and anxiety, as we do, and we surely should do our best to minimize these negative mental states in our treatment of them.

Still, should we be vegetarians? There is an argument dating back to the third century AD that is worth reflecting on here. The argument, which is due to Porphyry (in his *On Abstinence from Animal Food*), goes as follows:

1. Brutes are rational animals, although their reason is less perfect than human reason.

This premise seems incontestable, given some of the evidence adduced earlier in the book. No need to stop at mammals. Fish are capable of transitive reasoning. Bees can learn and apply complicated rules in order to reach rewards.

2. The demands of justice extend to all (and only) rational beings—and so to brutes (but not to plants).

Porphyry supports this premise by noting that unlike plants, animals feel pain and fear. If we eat them, we *unjustly* ignore their pain; and we do not have the excuse that they are a threat to us. He comments:

> To destroy other things through luxury, and for the enjoyment of pleasure, is perfectly savage and unjust.

Moreover, a meat diet is not needed for subsistence, but serves only "luxury and pleasure." So

3. Justice requires us to abstain from meat.[5]

Here is an objection considered by Porphyry that is worth mentioning, namely, that God made animals for our use and pleasure. He notes that this is certainly not true of all of them. Consider mosquitoes, for example. Further, we have equal evidence that we were created for the pleasure of crocodiles and wolves.

---

5. Porphyry also notes that if we behave peacefully toward animals, that will increase the likelihood that we will behave peacefully toward other humans.

This strikes me as a powerful argument. Perhaps, though, we simply need to change the ways we treat animals before we slaughter them. But even if we then cause them no pain or fear (or at least very little) and we increase the amount of pleasure they feel, we are still unnecessarily shortening their lives and so causing them to forgo future pleasure.

The fly in the ointment for this reply is that many of these animals would never have existed at all had it not been for our desire to eat meat. Is it then unjust for us to have brought them into existence in the first place—if indeed we treat them well throughout their lives?

I am inclined to think that it isn't. Unfortunately, the reality is that many of the animals we eat are treated abominably, and, capitalism being what it is, this is not likely to change any time soon. So it is tempting to conclude that we should be vegetarians, at least until such time as our actual practices in raising, feeding, and slaughtering animals change, unless we can be assured that the particular animals we eat have been raised and lived in a very humane environment.

There is a further complication. In the case of some animals, most notably fish, it is hard to see how we can kill them for the purposes of eating without inflicting pain on them, for we seem to have two options: angling (undeniably painful if it is granted fish feel pain at all) and using nets to catch them (in which case the fish are left out of water in some holding area until they die—again unquestionably painful).

So pescatarians are perhaps in a more difficult place morally than those who eat beef, for cattle can be raised and slaughtered without their feeling pain, but fish can't. On the other hand, fish spend their lives in many cases in a natural setting, swimming free, without human interference. This is arguably a significant advantage.

Those who depend for their living upon factory farming or fishing will perhaps respond to the points made in this chapter by saying that it may well be rational to prefer the vegetarian position to that of meat eaters or pescatarians, but the question of whether it is rational to believe outright that we ought to be vegetarians remains open. This position might be supported by reflecting on the consequences of adopting the vegetarian view. Those who are in the meat or fish industry will lose their jobs, much human hardship will be created, and fish and livestock that would have existed will no more. Given these consequences, the standards for belief should be high. The level of confidence needed, it may be insisted, is higher here than it would be in other contexts in which less is at stake.

Consider, for example, my being locked in a room and being told that I must press one of two buttons, a red button and a green one. One button, when pressed, will cause me to explode instantaneously. The other, upon pressing, will result in my being given a million dollars. As I reflect upon my situation and I try to decide which button I should press, given various clues, it is surely true that the consequences of being wrong are such that the level of confidence I require in order to believe that *this* is the right button to press is much higher than it would be if, say, I were a judge in a cooking contest trying to come to a conclusion as to which of two cakes deserves first prize.

I have some sympathy with this response. Readers must judge whether the considerations adduced in this chapter provide them with the requisite degree of confidence to believe that they should become vegetarians rather than simply with grounds for rational preference in the vegetarian view. If the conclusion reached is that the latter is all that is really supported by my discussion, then no particular behavioral consequences need ensue, for, as I noted earlier in the book, the connection between rational preference and behavior is not straightforward. My earlier illustration was this: it's rational for me to prefer the hypothesis that you will throw an even number with the dice to the hypothesis that you will throw a 6.[6] But that, I said, doesn't make it rational for me to act as if you would throw an even number (e.g., by placing a large bet I can ill afford on that outcome).

At a more theoretical level, my most general point is that, while it is rational to prefer one's own species over others, and within a species it is rational to prefer those who are biologically closest (other things being equal), it doesn't follow from this that we shouldn't treat other species well. The simple fact is that we can't help but favor our own.

I want to close with a few remarks about whether medical research on animals is morally justified, given that it causes them pain and suffering.

---

6. It isn't rational for me to believe that you will throw an even number, however, since the odds are 50/50.

This is a difficult question. One way to think about it is by reference to a variant on the cliff case introduced at the beginning of this chapter. Suppose now that there is a man braced with a rope that extends over his shoulders. At one end of the rope is a dangling child, and at the other end is a dangling dog, both holding on for dear life (one with the use of arms and the other with the use of teeth). They are both hanging above a large fire at the base of the cliff that is beginning to warm them. You know that the man lacks the strength to pull them both up, and you also know that if you assist him, together you will be able to pull one up—but only if, in doing so, you let the rope lengthen on the other side so that the unlucky creature gets closer and closer to the fire. What should you do? Even though saving the child causes serious pain to the dog and perhaps ultimately death, the right thing to do, it seems to me, is to help pull up the child—provided that there really are no other options available to you.

Much the same is true when it comes to animal medical research. We must surely treat other animals with respect, but if the only way for us to make progress in preventing diseases that cause many human deaths is by experimenting on animals and thereby causing them pain, it is right to perform the experiments. But we must tread carefully, for the key word here is "only." Is there really *no* other way to make progress than by causing these animals to suffer? Will the experiments really make a decisive difference? Unless we are convinced that the experiments are required and that they will make a difference, we should desist. Too often in the past, experiments have been performed without sufficient cause, and nonhuman animals have been used in research as if they were brutes to be treated however we wish. The Cartesian view of animals has had few adherents in philosophy in the last fifty years, but too many scientists have behaved during that time period as if animals lack consciousness. It is ironic that these same scientists would be aghast at performing experiments on human babies that cause them pain, for animals *are* conscious, just as babies are, and they deserve not to be made to suffer needlessly. Of course, tight controls are now in place in scientific experiments to prevent needless suffering, so the ethical situation in scientific research has improved immensely. This is clearly a change for the good.

REFERENCES

Allen, C., and Bekoff, M. 1997. *Species of Mind: The Philosophy and Biology of Cognitive Ethology*. Cambridge, MA: MIT Press.

American Academy of Neurology. 1989. "Position of the American Academy of Neurology on Certain Aspects of the Care and Management of the Persistent Vegetative State Patient." *Neurology* 39: 125–126.

American Medical Association Council on Scientific Affairs and Council on Ethical and Judicial Affairs. 1990. "Persistent Vegetative State and the Decision to Withdraw or Withhold Life Support." *JAMA* 263: 426–430.

Appel, M., and Elwood, R. W. 2009a. "Gender Differences, Responsiveness and Memory of a Potentially Painful Event in Hermit Crabs." *Animal Behavior* 78: 1373–1379.

Appel, M., and Elwood, R. W. 2009b. "Motivational Trade-Offs and the Potential for Pain Experience in Hermit Crabs." *Applied Animal Behaviour Science* 119: 120–124.

Baars, B. J. 1988. *A Cognitive Theory of Consciousness*. New York: Cambridge University Press.

Balderrama, N., Díaz, H., Sequeda, A., Núñez, J., and Maldonado, H. 1987. "Behavioral and Pharmacological Analysis of the Stinging Response in Africanized and Italian Bees." In *Neurobiology and Behavior of Honeybees*, edited by R. Menzel and A. Mercer, 121–128. New York: Springer-Verlag.

Bateson, M., Desire, S., Gartside, S., and Wright, G. 2011. "Agitated Honeybees Exhibit Pessimistic Cognitive Biases." *Current Biology* 21.12: 1070–1073.

Bekoff, M. 2007. *The Emotional Lives of Animals*. Novato, CA: New World Library.

Bering, J., and Bjorklund, D. 2005. "The Serpent's Gift: Evolutionary Psychology and Consciousness." In *Cambridge Handbook of Consciousness*, edited by P. D.

Zelazo, M. Moscovitch, and E. Thompson, 597–603. New York: Cambridge University Press.

Bjursten, L. M., Norrsell, K., and Norrsell, U. 1976. "Behavioural Repertory of Cats without Cerebral Cortex from Infancy." *Experimental Brain Research* 25.2: 115–130.

Block, N. 1978. "Troubles with Functionalism." In *Readings in Philosophy of Psychology,* vol. 1, edited by N. Block, 268–305. Cambridge, MA: Harvard University Press.

Block, N. 1981. "Psychologism and Behaviorism." *Philosophical Review* 90: 5–43.

Block, N. 1997. "On a Confusion about a Function of Consciousness." In *The Nature of Consciousness,* edited by N. Block, O. Flanagan, and G. Guzeldere, 375–415. Cambridge, MA: MIT Press.

Block, N. 2002a. "Some Concepts of Consciousness." In *Philosophy of Mind: Classical and Contemporary Readings,* edited by D. Chalmers, 206–218. New York: Oxford University Press.

Block, N. 2002b. "The Harder Problem of Consciousness." *Journal of Philosophy* 99: 1–35.

Block, N. 2007. "Consciousness, Accessibility and the Mesh between Psychology and Neuroscience." *Behavioral and Brain Sciences* 30: 481–548.

Block, N. 2009. "Comparing the Major Theories of Consciousness." In *The Cognitive Neurosciences,* 4th ed., edited by M. Gazzaniga, 1111–1122. Cambridge, MA: MIT Press.

Block, N. 2013. "The Grain of Vision and the Grain of Attention." *Thought: A Journal of Philosophy* 1: 170–184.

Bradley, P., and Tye, M. 2001. "Of Colors, Kestrels, Caterpillars and Leaves." *Journal of Philosophy* 98: 469–487.

Brandt, R. 1963. "Toward a Credible Form of Utilitarianism." In *Morality and the Language of Conduct,* edited by H.-N. Castañeda and G. Nakhnikian, 107–143. Detroit: Wayne State University Press.

Brewer, W. 2005. "Do Sense Experiential States Have Conceptual Content?" In *Contemporary Debates in Epistemology,* edited by M. Steup and E. Sosa, 217–230. Malden, MA: Blackwell.

Britto, G., Subash, K., Rao, J., Varghese, B., and Kumar, S. 2012. "A Synergistic Approach to Evaluate the Anti-Nociceptive Activity of a GABA Agonist with Opioids in Albino Mice." *Journal of Clinical and Diagnostic Research* 6: 682–687.

Brodin, T., Fick, J., Jonsson, M., and Klaminder, J. 2013. "Dilute Concentrations of a Psychiatric Drug Alter Behavior of Fish from Natural Populations." *Science* 339.6121: 814–815.

Brown, C. 2015. "Fish Intelligence, Sentience and Ethics." *Animal Cognition* 18: 1–17.

Burge, T. 2010. *The Origins of Objectivity.* Oxford: Oxford University Press.

Burgess, J. W., Villablanca, J. R., and Levine, M. 1986. "Recovery of Function after Neonatal or Adult Hemispherectomy: Complex Functions." *Behavioral Brain Research* 20: 217–230.

Byrne, A. 2005. "Perception and Conceptual Content." In *Contemporary Debates in Epistemology*, ed. M. Steup and E. Sosa. Malden, MA: Blackwell.

Cabanac, M., Cabanac, A., and Parent, A. 2009. "The Emergence of Consciousness in Phylogeny." *Behavioral Brain Research* 198: 267–272.

Carruthers, P. 1989. "Brute Experience." *Journal of Philosophy* 86.5: 258–269.

Carruthers, P. 1992. *The Animals Issue.* Cambridge, UK: Cambridge University Press.

Carruthers, P. 1999. "Sympathy and Subjectivity." *Australasian Journal of Philosophy* 77: 465–482.

Carruthers, P. 2000. *Phenomenal Consciousness: A Naturalistic Theory.* Cambridge, UK: Cambridge University Press.

Cassam, Q., 2007. *The Possibility of Knowledge.* Oxford: Clarendon.

Chalmers, D. 1995. "Absent Qualia, Fading Qualia, Dancing Qualia." In *Conscious Experience*, edited by T. Metzinger, 309–327. Paderborn, Germany: F. Schöningh.

Clark, R. 1965. "The Learning Abilities of Nereid Polychaetes and the Role of the Supra-Oesophagenal Ganglion." *Animal Behavior* 13, Supplement 1: 89–100.

Cogan, T. 1802. *On the Passions.* First edition.

Cohen, J. 2009. *The Red and the Real.* Oxford: Oxford University Press.

Cooke, S., and Sneddon, L. 2007. "Animal Welfare Perspectives on Recreational Angling." *Applied Animal Behavior Science* 104: 176–198.

Cottingham, J. 1978. "A Brute to the Brutes? Descartes' Treatment of Animals." *Philosophy* 53: 551–559.

Cox, J. F. 2005. "In the Matter of Terri Schiavo: Some Science and Ethics." *Postcards from Winticomack*, http://www.winticomack.com/article.php?essay=a051231.

Danbury, T., Weeks, C., Chambers, J., Waterman-Pearson, A., and Kestin, S. 2000. "Self-Selection of the Analgesic Drug Carprofen by Lame Broiler Chickens." *Veterinary Record* 146: 307–311.

Darwin, C. 1871. *The Descent of Man in Relation to Sex.* Second edition.

Darwin, E. 1800. *Phytologia.* First edition.

Dawkins, M. S. 2012. *Why Animals Matter: Animal Consciousness, Animal Welfare, and Human Well-Being.* New York: Oxford University Press.

Dawkins, R. 2011. "But Can They Suffer?" *Boing Boing* (blog), http://boingboing .net/2011/06/30/richard-dawkins-on-v.html.

Dehaene, S., Kerszberg, M., and Changeux, J.-P. 1998. "A Neuronal Model of a Global Workspace in Effortful Cognitive Tasks." *Proceedings of the National Academy of Sciences USA* 95: 14529–14534.

Descartes, R. 1647. *Meditations on First Philosophy.*

Descartes, R. 1897. *Oeuvres de Descartes*, edited by C. Adam and P. Tannery. Paris: Ministère de l'instruction publique.

Descartes, R. 1991. *The Philosophical Writings of Descartes*, vol. 3. Translated by J. Cottingham, R. Stoothoff, and D. Murdoch. Cambridge, UK: Cambridge University Press.

Desjardins, J. K., and Fernald, R. D. 2010. "What Do Fish Make of Mirror Images?" *Biology Letters* 6: 744–747.

Devinsky, O., Morrell, M., and Vogt, B. 1995. "Contributions of Anterior Cingulate Cortex to Behavior." *Brain* 118: 279–306.

DeWaal, F. 1991. "Complementary Methods and Convergent Evidence in the Study of Primate Social Cognition." *Behavior* 118, 297–320.

Dimitrijevic, N., Dzitoyeva, S., Satta, R., Imbesi, M., Yildiz, S., and Manev, H. 2005. "Drosophila GABA(B) Receptors Are Involved in Behavioral Effects of Gamma-Hydroxybutyric Acid (GHB)." *European Journal of Pharmacology* 519.3: 246–252.

Dugas-Ford, J., Rowell, J., and Ragsdale, C. 2012. "Cell-Type Homologies and the Origins of the Neocortex." *Proceedings of the National Academy of Sciences* 109: 16974–16979.

Dunayer, J. 1991. "Fish: Sensitivity beyond the Captor's Grasp." *Animals' Agenda*, July/August, 12–18.

Dyer, C. 1992. "BMA Examines the Persistent Vegetative State." *British Medical Journal* 305: 853–854.

Edgar, J., Lowe, J., Paul, E., and Nicol, C. 2011. "Avian Maternal Response to Chick Distress." *Proceedings of Royal Society B* 278: 3129–3134.

Egan, A. 2012. "Comments on Jonathan Cohen, *The Red and the Real*." *Analytic Philosophy* 53: 306–312.

Ehrensing, R. H., Michell, G. F., and Kastin, A. J. 1982. "Similar Antagonism of Morphine Analgesia by MIF-1 and Naxolone in *Carassius auratus*." *Pharmacology Biochemistry and Behavior* 17: 757–761.

Eisemann, C. H., Jorgensen, W. K., Merritt, D. J., Rice, M. J., Cribb, B. W., Webb, P. D., and Zalucki, M. P. 1984. "Do Insects Feel Pain? A Biological View." *Experientia* 40: 164–167.

Eisner, T., and S. Camazine. 1983. "Spider Leg Autotomy Induced by Prey Venom Injection: An Adaptive Response to 'Pain'?" *Proceedings of the National Academy of Sciences USA* 80: 3382–3385.

Elwood, R. W., and Appel, M. 2009. "Pain Experience in Hermit Crabs?" *Animal Behaviour* 77: 1243–1246.

Endler, J., Endler, L., and Doerr, N. 2010. "Great Bowerbirds Create Theaters with Forced Perspective When Seen by Their Audience." *Current Biology* 20.18: 1679–1684.

Esteves, F., Dimberg, U., and Öhman, A. 1994. "Automatically Elicited Fear: Conditioned Skin Conductance Responses to Masked Facial Expressions." *Cognition and Emotion* 8: 393–413.

Evans, G. 1982. *The Varieties of Reference*. Oxford: Oxford University Press.

Farris, S. 2008. "Evolutionary Convergence of Higher Brain Centers Spanning the Protostome-Deuterostome Boundary." *Brain, Behavior and Evolution* 72: 106–122.

Ferrier, D. 1890. *The Croonian Lectures on Cerebral Localisation.* London: Smith, Elder.

Ffytche, D., and Zeki, S. 2011. "The Primary Visual Cortex, and Feedback to It, Are Not Necessary for Conscious Vision." *Brain* 134: 247–257.

Fields, H. 1999. "Pain: An Unpleasant Topic." *Pain*, Supplement 6: S61–S69.

Flanagan, O. 1992. *Consciousness Reconsidered.* Cambridge, MA: MIT Press.

Fleming, P. A., Muller, D., and Bateman, P. W. 2007. "Leave It All Behind: A Taxonomic Perspective of Autotomy in Invertebrates." *Biological Reviews* 82: 481–510.

Fodor, Jerry A. 1983. *Modularity of Mind: An Essay on Faculty Psychology.* Cambridge, MA: MIT Press.

Foley, R. 2009. "Belief, Degrees of Belief and the Lockean Thesis." In *Degrees of Belief*, edited by F. Huber and C. Schmidt-Petri, 37–47. Dordrecht, the Netherlands: Springer.

Foot, P. 1967. "The Problem of Abortion and the Doctrine of the Double Effect in Virtues and Vices." *Oxford Review* 5: 5–15.

Fossat, P., Bacque-Cazenave, J., De Deurwaerdere, P., Delbecque, J.-P., and Cattaert, D. 2014. "Anxiety-Like Behavior in Crayfish Is Controlled by Serotonin." *Science* 344: 1293–1297.

Fox, R. 2014. "Dissecting a Robot." *Reasonable Vegan* (blog), http://rvgn.org/2014/09/10/dissecting-a-robot/.

Gabriela de Brito Sanchez, M., Lorenzo, E., Su, S., Liu, F., Zhan, Y., and Giurfa, M. 2014. "The Tarsal Taste of Honey Bees: Behavioral and Electrophysiological Analyses." *Frontiers in Behavioral Neuroscience* 8: 1–16.

Gallup, G., Jr. 1970. "Chimpanzees: Self Recognition." *Science* 167: 86–87.

Gennaro, R. 2004. "Higher-Order Thoughts, Animal Consciousness, and Misrepresentation: A Reply to Carruthers and Levine." In *Higher-Order Theories of Consciousness: An Anthology*, edited by R. Gennaro, 45–66. Amsterdam: John Benjamins.

Gentle, M. J., and Hunter, L. N. 1991. "Physiological and Behavioural Responses Associated with Feather Removal in *Gallus gallus* var *domesticus*." *Research in Veterinary Science* 50: 95–101.

Giurfa, M., Zhang, S., Jenett, A., Menzel, R., and Srinivasan, M. V. 2001. "The Concepts of 'Sameness' and 'Difference' in an Insect." *Nature* 410.6831: 930–933.

Grahek, G. 2007. *Feeling Pain and Being in Pain.* Cambridge, MA: MIT Press.

Griffin, D. 1976. *The Question of Animal Awareness.* New York: Rockefeller University Press.

Griffin, D. 1984. *Animal Thinking.* Cambridge, MA: Harvard University Press.

Griffin, D. 1992. *Animal Minds*. Chicago: University of Chicago Press.

Grosenick, L., Clement, T., and Fernald, R. 2007. "Fish Can Infer Social Rank by Observation Alone." *Nature* 445: 429–432.

Halsey, R., and Chapanis, A. 1951. "Number of Absolutely Identifiable Hues." *Journal of the Optical Society of America* 41: 1057–1058.

Hare, R. M. 1981. *Moral Thinking: Its Levels, Method, and Point*. Oxford: Oxford University Press.

Harman, G. 1998. "The Intrinsic Qualities of Experience." In *The Nature of Consciousness*, edited by N. Block, O. Flanagan, and G. Guzeldere, 663–676. Cambridge, MA: MIT Press.

Heck, R. 2000. "Nonconceptual Content and the 'Space of Reasons.'" *Philosophical Review* 109: 483–523.

Heidelberger, M. 2004. *Nature from Within: Gustav Theodor Fechner and His Psychophysical Worldview*. Pittsburgh, PA: University of Pittsburgh Press.

Horowitz, K., Lewis, D., and Gasteiger, E. 1975. "Plant 'Primary Perception': Electrophysiological Unresponsiveness to Brine Shrimp Killing." *Science* 189: 478–480.

Huijbers, C., Nagelkerken, I., et al. 2012. "A Test of the Senses: Fish Select Novel Habitats by Responding to Multiple Cues." *Ecology* 93: 46–55.

Hurvich, L. 1981. *Color Vision*. Sunderland, MA: Sinauer Associates.

Huxley, T. 1866. *Lessons in Elementary Psychology*.

Ito, H., and Yamamoto, N. 2009. "Non-Laminar Cerebral Cortex in Teleost Fish?" *Biological Letters* 5: 117–121.

Jamieson, D. 1998. "Science, Knowledge, and Animal Minds." *Proceedings of the Aristotelian Society* 98: 79–102.

Jolley, N. 2000. "2 Malebranche on the Soul." In *The Cambridge Companion to Malebranche*, edited by S. Nadler, 31–58. Cambridge: Cambridge University Press.

Karpinski, S., Reynolds, H., Karpinska, B., Wingsle, G., Creissen, G., and Mullineaux, P. 1999. "Systemic Signaling and Acclimation in Response to Excess Excitation Energy in Arabidopsis." *Science* 284: 654–657.

Karten, K. 1997. "Evolutionary Developmental Biology Meets the Brain: The Origins of Mammalian Cortex." *Proceedings of the National Academy of Sciences* 94: 2800–2804.

Kazarian, R. 1983. "Some Evidence That Trees Communicate When in Trouble." *Environmental Conservation* 10: 173.

Key, B. 2015. "Why Fish (Likely) Don't Feel Pain." *Scientia Salon* (blog), scientiasalon.wordpress.com/2015/02/05/why-fish-likely-dont-feel-pain.

Koch, C. 2008. "Exploring Consciousness through the Study of Bees." *Scientific American*, December.

Laplace, P. 1814. *A Philosophical Essay on Probabilities*.

LeDoux, J. 1996. *The Emotional Brain: The Mysterious Underpinnings of Emotional Life*. New York: Touchstone.

Le Roith, D., Shiloach, J., Roth, J., and Lesniak, M. A. 1980. "Evolutionary Origins of Vertebrate Hormones: Substances Similar to Mammalian Insulins Are Native to Unicellular Eukaryotes." *Proceedings of the National Academy of Sciences USA* 77.10: 6184–6188.

Levine, J. 1983. "Materialism and Qualia: The Explanatory Gap." *Pacific Philosophical Quarterly* 64: 354–361.

Liang, Z., Nguyen, T., Mattila, H., Rodriguez-Zas, S., Seeley, T., and Robinson, G. "Molecular Determinants of Scouting Behavior in Honey Bees." *Science* 335.6073: 1225–1228.

Lipton, P. 1991. *Inference to the Best Explanation.* London: Routledge.

Lohman, A., and Smeets, W. 1991. "The Dorsal Ventricular Ridge and Cortex of Reptiles in Historical and Phylogenetic Perspective." *Neocortex* 200: 59–74.

Lozada, M., Romano, A., and Maldonado, H. 1988. "Effects of Morphine and Naloxone on a Defensive Response of the Crab *Chasmagnathus granulatus.*" *Pharmacology Biochemistry and Behavior* 30: 635–640.

Macphail, E. 1982. *Brain and Intelligence in Vertebrates.* Oxford: Clarendon.

Magee, M., and Elwood, R. 2013. "Shock Avoidance by Discrimination Learning in the Shore Crab (*Carcinus maenas*) Is Consistent with a Key Criterion for Pain." *Journal of Experimental Biology* 216: 353–358.

Malebranche, N. 1997. *The Search after Truth and Elucidations.* Translated and edited by T. M. Lennon and P. J. Olscamp. Cambridge: Cambridge University Press, 1997.

Manrod, J., Hartdegen, R., and Burghardt, G. 2008. "Rapid Solving of a Problem Apparatus by Juvenile Black-Throated Monitor Lizards." *Animal Cognition* 11: 267–273.

Marcel, A. 1986. "Consciousness and Processing: Choosing and Testing a Null Hypothesis." *Behavioral and Brain Sciences* 9: 40–41.

Masino, T. 1992. "Brainstem Control of Orienting Movements: Intrinsic Coordinate System and Underlying Circuitry." *Brain, Behavior and Evolution* 40: 98–111.

McDowell, J. 1994. *Mind and World.* Cambridge, MA: Harvard University Press.

McDowell, J. 1998. "Response to Peacocke." *Philosophy and Phenomenological Research* 58: 414–419.

McGinn, C. 1991. *The Problem of Consciousness.* Oxford: Blackwell.

McLaughlin, B. 2003. "A Naturalist Phenomenal Realist Response to Block's Harder Problem." *Philosophical Issues* 13: 163–204.

Medical Task Force on Anencephaly. 1990. "The Infant with Anencephaly." *New England Journal of Medicine* 3.2: 669–674.

Menzel, R., and Giurfa, M. "Cognitive Architecture of a Mini-Brain: The Honeybee." *Trends in Cognitive Sciences* 5: 62–71.

Merker, B. 2005. "The Liabilities of Mobility: A Selection Pressure for the Transition to Consciousness in Animal Evolution." *Conscious Cognition* 14: 89–114.

Merker, B. 2007. "Consciousness without a Cerebral Cortex: A Challenge for Neuroscience and Medicine." *Behavioral and Brain Sciences* 30: 63–134.

Mill, J. S. 1998. *Utilitarianism*. Edited by R. Crisp. Oxford: Oxford University Press.

Millsopp, S., and Laming, P. 2008. "Trade-Offs between Feeding and Shock Avoidance in Goldfish." *Applied Animal Behavior* 113: 247–254.

Morton, D. B., and, Griffiths. P. H. M. 1985. "Guidelines on the Recognition of Pain, Distress and Discomfort in Experimental Animals and an Hypothesis for Assessment." *Veterinary Record* 116: 431–436.

Multi-Society Task Force on PVS. 1994. "Medical Aspects of the Persistent Vegetative State." *New England Journal of Medicine* 330: 1499–1508.

Nagel, T. 1974. "What Is It Like to Be a Bat?" *Philosophical Review* 83: 435–450.

Neely, G., Hess, M. Costigan, M., et al. 2010. "A Genome-Wide Drosophila Screen for Heat Nociception Identifies $\alpha2\delta3$ as an Evolutionarily Conserved Pain Gene." *Cell* 143.4: 628–638.

Newby, N. C., and Stevens, E. D. 2008. "The Effects of the Acetic Acid 'Pain' Test on Feeding, Swimming and Respiratory Responses of Rainbow Trout (*Oncorhynchus mykiss*)." *Applied Animal Behavior Science* 114: 260–269.

Newton, I. 1687. *Principia Mathematica*.

Nicholls, J. G., and Baylor, D. A. 1968. "Specific Modalities and Receptive Fields of Sensory Neurons in CNS of the Leech." *Journal of Neurophysiology* 31: 740–756.

Nordgreen, J., Joseph, P., Garner, J. P., Janczak, A. M., Ranheim, B., Muir, W. M., and Horsberg, T. E. 2009. "Thermonociception in Fish: Effects of Two Different Doses of Morphine on Thermal Threshold and Post-Test Behaviour in Goldfish (*Carassius auratus*)." *Applied Animal Behaviour Science* 119.1–2: 101–107.

Núñez, J. A., Almeida, L., Balderrama, N., and Giurfa, M. 1997. "Alarm Pheromone Induces Stress Analgesia via an Opioid System in the Honeybee." *Physiology and Behaviour* 63.1: 75–80.

Palmer, S. E., and Schloss, K. B. 2010. "An Ecological Valence Theory of Color Preferences." *Proceedings of the National Academy of Sciences* 107: 8877–8882.

Panel on Animal Health and Welfare of the Norwegian Scientific Committee for Food Safety. 2010. *Risk Assessment of Catch and Release*. Norwegian Scientific Committee for Food Safety, http://english.vkm.no/dav/42f495efaf.pdf.

Panksepp, J. 1982. "Toward a General Psychobiological Theory of Emotions." *Brain and Behavioral Sciences* 5: 407–467.

Panksepp, J., Normansell, L., Cox, J. F., and Siviy, S. M. 1994. "Effects of Neonatal Decortication on the Social Play of Juvenile Rats." *Physiology and Behavior* 56: 429–443.

Papineau, D., and Selina, H. 2000. *Introducing Consciousness*. Cambridge, UK: Icon.

Pargetter, R. 1984. "The Scientific Inference to Other Minds." *Australasian Journal of Philosophy* 62: 158–163.

Peacocke, C. 1998. "Nonconceptual Content Defended." *Philosophy and Phenomenological Research* 58: 381–388.

Peacocke, C. 2000. "Does Perception Have a Nonconceptual Content?" *Journal of Philosophy* 98: 239–264.

Perry, J. 1977. "Frege on Demonstratives." *Philosophical Review* 86: 474–497.

Perry, J. 1979. "The Problem of the Essential Indexical." *Noûs* 13: 3–21.

Ploner, M., Freund, H.-J., and Schnitzler, A. 1999. "Pain Affect without Pain Sensation in a Patient with a Postcentral Lesion." *Pain* 81: 211–214.

Porphyry. 1977–1995. *De l'abstinence*. Translated by J. Bouffartigue and M. Patillon. Edited by J. Bouffartigue. 3 vols. Paris: Belles Lettres.

Pryor, J. 2000. "The Skeptic and the Dogmatist." *Noûs* 34: 517–549.

Raffmann, D. 1996. "On the Persistence of Phenomenology." In *Conscious Experience*, edited by T. Metzinger. Paderborn, Germany: Schöningh-Verlag.

Rainville, P., Feine, J., Bushnell, M., and Duncan, G. 1992. "A Psychophysical Comparison of Sensory and Affective Responses to Four Modalities of Experimental Pain." *Somatosensory Motor Research* 9: 265–277.

Rawls, J. 1971. *A Theory of Justice*. Cambridge, MA: Harvard University Press.

Reber, A. S. 1993. *Implicit Learning and Tacit Knowledge: An Essay on the Cognitive Unconscious*. New York: Oxford University Press.

Regan, T. 2004. *The Case for Animal Rights*. Berkeley: University of California Press.

Reid, T. 2002. *Essays on the Intellectual Powers of Man*. Edited by D. Brookes. University Park: Pennsylvania State University Press.

Robinson, G. 2006. "Insights into Social Insects from the Genome of the Honeybee *Apis mellifera*." *Nature* 443: 941–949.

Root, A. 1886. *Gleanings in Bee Culture* 14: 86.

Rose, J. D. 2002. "The Neurobehavioral Nature of Fishes and the Question of Awareness of Pain." *Reviews in Fisheries Sciences* 10.1: 1–38.

Rose, J. D., Arlinghaus, R., Cooke, S. J., Diggles, B. K., Sawynok, W., Stevens, E. D., and Wynne, C. D. L. 2014. "Can Fish Really Feel Pain?" *Fish and Fisheries* 15: 97–133.

Rosenthal, D. 1986. "Two Concepts of Consciousness." *Philosophical Studies* 49: 329–359.

Ruiz i Altaba, A., Palma, V., and Dahmane, N. 2002. "Hedgehog-Gli Signalling and the Growth of the Brain." *National Review of Neuroscience* 3: 24–33.

Ryder, R. 1970. *Speciesism*. Oxford: privately printed.

Sainsbury, M., and Tye, M. 2012. *Seven Puzzles of Thought (and How to Solve Them)*. Oxford: Oxford University Press.

Searle, J. 1992. *The Rediscovery of Mind*. Cambridge, MA: MIT Press, Bradford Books.

Shea, N., and Heyes, C. 2010. "Metamemory as Evidence of Animal Consciousness: The Type That Does the Trick." *Biology and Philosophy* 25: 95–110.

Shettleworth, S. 1998. *Cognition, Evolution, and Behavior.* New York: Oxford University Press.

Shewmon, A., Holmes, G., and Byrne, P. 1999. "Consciousness in Congenitally Decorticate Children: 'Developmental Vegetative State' as Self-Fulfilling Prophecy." *Developmental Medicine and Child Neurology* 41: 364–374.

Singer, P. 1979. *Practical Ethics.* Cambridge, UK: Cambridge University Press.

Singer, P. 2000. *Writings of an Ethical Life.* New York: Ecco.

Skelhorn, J., Rowland, H., Delf, J., Speed, M., and Ruxton, G. 2011. "Density-Dependent Predation Influences the Evolution and Behavior of Masquerading Prey." *Proceedings of the National Academy of Sciences* 108: 6532–6536.

Sneddon, L. U. 2003. "The Evidence for Pain in Fish: The Use of Morphine as an Analgesic." *Applied Animal Behaviour Science* 83.2: 153–162.

Sneddon, L. 2012. "Pain Perception in Fish: Evidence and Implications for the Use of Fish." *Journal of Consciousness Studies* 18: 209–229.

Sneddon, L. U., Braithwaite, V. A., and Gentle, M. J. 2003. "Do Fishes Have Nociceptors? Evidence for the Evolution of a Vertebrate Sensory System." *Proceedings of the Royal Society B* 270: 1115–1121.

Snodgrass, R. E. 1910. *Anatomy of the Honey Bee.* Washington, DC: Government Printing Office.

Sober, E. 2000. "Evolution and the Problem of Other Minds." *Journal of Philosophy* 97: 365–387.

Stefano, G. B., and Scharrer, B. 1981. "High Affinity Binding of an Enkephalin Analog in the Cerebral Ganglion of the Insect *Leucophaea maderae* (Blattaria)." *Brain Research* 225: 107–111.

Steup, M., and Sosa, E., eds. 2005. *Contemporary Debates in Epistemology.* Malden, MA: Blackwell.

Stich, S. 1978. "Beliefs and Sub-Doxastic States." *Philosophy of Science* 45: 499–518.

Swanson, L. 2000. "Cerebral Hemisphere Regulation of Motivated Behavior." *Brain Research* 886: 113–164.

Tan, K., Hu, Z., Chen, W., Wang, Z., Wang, Y., and Nieh, J. 2013. "Fearful Foragers: Honey Bees Tune Colony and Individual Foraging to Multi-Predator Presence and Food Quality." *PLOS ONE* 8.9: e75841.

Turing, A. 1950. "Computing Machinery and Intelligence." *Mind* 59: 433–460.

Tye, M. 1995. *Ten Problems of Consciousness.* Cambridge, MA: Bradford Books, MIT Press.

Tye, M. 1997. "The Problem of Simple Minds: Is There Anything It Is Like to Be a Honeybee?" *Philosophical Studies* 88: 289–317.

Tye, M. 2000. *Consciousness, Color, and Content*. Cambridge, MA: Bradford Books, MIT Press.

Tye, M. 2003. *Consciousness and Persons: Unity and Identity*. Cambridge, MA: Bradford Books, MIT Press.

Tye, M. 2009. *Consciousness Revisited*. Oxford: Oxford University Press.

Tye, M. 2010. "Attention, Seeing and Change Blindness." *Philosophical Issues* 20: 410–437.

Tye, M., and Wright, B. 2011. "Is There a Phenomenology of Thought?" In *Cognitive Phenomenology*, edited by T. Bayne and M. Montague, 326–344. Oxford: Oxford University Press.

Tye, M. Forthcoming. "Homunculi Heads and Silicon Chips: The Importance of History to Phenomenology." In *Themes from Block*, edited A. Pautz and D. Stoljar. Cambridge, MA: MIT Press.

Van Gulick, R. 1993. "Understanding the Phenomenal Mind: Are We Just All Armadillos?" In *Consciousness*, edited by M. Davies and G. Humphreys, 137–154. Oxford: Blackwell.

Viitala, J., Korpimaki, E., Palokangas, P., and Koivula, M. 1995. "Attraction of Kestrels to Vole Scent Marks in Visible and Ultraviolet Light." *Nature* 373.6513: 425–427.

Villablanca, J. R., Burgess, J. W, and Benedetti, F. 1986. "There Is Less Thalamic Degeneration in Neonatal-Lesioned Than in Adult-Lesioned Cats after Cerebral Hemispherectomy." *Brain Research* 368: 211–225.

Voltaire. 1764. "Beasts." *Dictionnaire philosophique portative*.

Watkins, S., and Rees, G. 2007. "The Human Superior Colliculus: Neither Necessary nor Sufficient for Consciousness?" *Behavioral and Brain Sciences* 30: 108.

Weiskrantz, L. 1990. "Outlooks for Blindsight: Explicit Methodologies for Internal Processes." *Proceedings of the Royal Society London* 239: 247–278.

White, G., and Brown, C. "Site Fidelity and Homing Behavior in Intertidal Fish." *Marine Biology* 160: 1365–1372.

Whitear, M. 1971. "The Free Nerve Endings in Fish Epidermis." *Journal of Zoology* 163: 231–236.

Wilkinson, A., Chan, H., and Hall, G. 2007. "Spatial Learning and Memory in the Tortoise." *Journal of Comparative Psychology* 121: 412–418.

Wilkinson, A., Coward, S., and Hall, G. 2009. "Visual and Response Navigation in the Tortoise." *Animal Cognition* 12: 779–787.

Wilkinson, A., and Huber, L. 2012. "Cold-Blooded Cognition: Reptilian Cognitive Abilities." *The Oxford Handbook of Comparative Evolutionary Psychology*, edited by J. Vonk and T. K. Shackelford, 129–143. Oxford: Oxford University Press.

Wittgenstein, L. 1953. *Philosophical Investigations*. Translated by G. E. M. Anscombe. Oxford: Blackwell.

Wright, Crispin. 2004. "Warrant for Nothing (and Foundations for Free)?" *Aristotelian Society Supplementary Volume* 78: 167–212.

Yarali, A., Niewalda, T., Chen, Y. C., Tanimoto H., and Duerrnagel, S. 2008. "'Pain Relief' Learning in Fruit Flies." *Animal Behavior* 76: 1173–1185.

Yoshida, M., and Hirano, R. 2010. "Effects of Local Anesthesia of the Cerebellum on Classical Fear Conditioning in Goldfish." *Behavioral and Brain Functions* 6: 20.

INDEX